LABOUR LAW AND ECONOMIC POLICY

This book studies labour institutions from an economic perspective to justify their existence and the advantages that they bring to innovation, efficiency, productivity and economic growth.

The philosophical foundations of labour law rely on the protection of the weaker party of the employment contract. However, after 40 years of political neoliberalism, these justifications seem insufficient for achieving progress in the area of labour and employment rights.

This book changes the narrative of why we need labour standards. It begins with a study of the reasons that gave rise to labour law in the context of the Industrial Revolution and its evolution, and moves on to analyse the current context dominated by globalisation and economic digitisation. It then proceeds to study the main justifications for intervention in the labour market in the current business-economic context on a global scale: economic growth; pre-distribution of wealth; a meritocratic allocation of working conditions and equality among workers.

Using case studies and examples from across the EU, the UK and the US, the book shows how the deregulation of labour markets harms innovation and the economy, especially when considering the challenges of platform work, algorithms and AI. It demonstrates that labour standards such as the minimum wage, sectoral collective bargaining and collective rights, protection against dismissal and discrimination, occupational risk prevention, and social security are necessary for the economy to function properly.

Labour Law and Economic Policy

How Employment Rights Improve the Economy

Adrián Todolí-Signes

•HART•
OXFORD • LONDON • NEW YORK • NEW DELHI • SYDNEY

HART PUBLISHING

Bloomsbury Publishing Plc

Kemp House, Chawley Park, Cumnor Hill, Oxford, OX2 9PH, UK

1385 Broadway, New York, NY 10018, USA

29 Earlsfort Terrace, Dublin 2, Ireland

HART PUBLISHING, the Hart/Stag logo, BLOOMSBURY and the Diana logo are trademarks of Bloomsbury Publishing Plc

First published in Great Britain 2024

A catalogue record for this book is available from the British Library.

A catalogue record for this book is available from the Library of Congress.

ISBN: HB: 978-1-50997-388-0
ePDF: 978-1-50997-390-3
ePub: 978-1-50997-389-7

Typeset by Compuscript Ltd, Shannon

GOBIERNO DE ESPAÑA MINISTERIO DE CIENCIA E INNOVACIÓN

This Research is part of the Ministry of Science and Innovation research project entitled 'Algoritmos extractivos y neuroderechos. Retos regulatorios de la digitalización del trabajo', ref. PID2022-139967NB-I00.

To all the masters of labour law who advocated and fought to build the foundations of this discipline.

It is only on the shoulders of giants that I have been able to write this story.

CONTENTS

PART III
THE CONCEPT OF 'GENUINE BUSINESS OWNER' AS A DETERMINANT OF LABOUR LAW

1

Introduction

We live in the age of 140 characters. The age of simple, short messages, repeated *ad nauseam*, which offer little room for debate, reflection and depth. This form of communication advocates catchy messages and creates prejudices and myths about anything and everything. In this scenario, preconceptions become entrenched while approaches become extreme as there is no time for reflection or thoughtful debate to reach a consensus. We live in an age where individual beliefs outweigh facts. Hard evidence is becoming less and less relevant when it comes to deciding a political or regulatory stance; instead, it is replaced with sensations, beliefs, assumptions and pre-conceived opinions. The consequences of privileging the latter over the former are well known: positions become more extreme.

In recent years, developed countries have seen an increase in political polarisation that many of us thought had been buried for good after the Second World War. Brexit, the Trump phenomenon in the USA, and events in Hungary, France and Italy all evidence a fragmentation of society that would have been unthinkable twenty years ago. Enthusiasts of *The West Wing* will know exactly what I mean. Today, a look back at the legendary series makes us realise just how strongly we believed in improving society through debate and reflection. Just two decades later, this way of envisioning politics seems not just overly optimistic, but utterly unrealistic. Unfortunately, series such as *The Loudest Voice*, in which television shows lazily shun debate and prefer instead to put a microphone in the hands of those who 'shout the loudest' over the voices of the rest, and deliberately only give the floor to those who repeat the mantras that the television station wants everybody to hear, are a much closer portrayal of the way society works today.

As social scientists our job is to do the opposite. Our aim is to analyse reality and offer interpretations about facts that help close the gap.[1] Our role is to build bridges so that each side understands what the other is putting forward. We refuse to label people, insisting instead on refuting arguments. It is our job to listen and talk, stepping away from pre-conceived ideas. Our job is to give arguments that destroy prejudice and myth. This is what this book (humbly) aims to do.

Labour law and economics are two disciplines that have historically looked in opposite directions. It is not just that they do not understand each another, but that they speak different languages. As a student of Economics and Law at university,

[1] A Banerjee and E Duflo, *Good Economics for Hard Times* (London, Allen Lane, 2019) 2.

I became aware very early on of the differing principles and rationales that drive each discipline. While Law is concerned with resolving conflict (if there are no disputes, there is no need for lawyers), Economics analyses how to optimise the use of resources, on the assumption that scarcity is always a source of conflict. While Law believes that individuals and their individual rights must be protected against the majority, Economics, or part of this discipline, argues that something which is useful for the majority can mathematically justify any damage inflicted on the remaining few. These and other disagreements have led to growing estrangement, resulting at best in mutual ignorance, and at worst in direct confrontation.

Reconciliation is not helped by the fact that those representing 'economists' on television and in the press are often corporate spokespersons, such as the Chief Economist of bank X or company Y, who are happy to ignore the evidence simply to feed their employer's interests into the public discourse. As a result, the social perception of 'economists' today is that they are all staunch believers in an omnipotent market that requires no regulation.[2] It is not surprising that this perception of what an 'economist' is, which is more misguided than accurate, makes jurists feel threatened and leads them to shun economic theories, if only because the legal profession would disappear in the absence of regulation.

This is particularly true for labour law. Since the 1980s, economic and labour policy has been dominated by the so-called 'Washington Consensus'.[3] Since then, both developed and developing countries have focused on liberalising the market and deregulating the labour market. Countries have adopted a free market and laissez-faire approach in their industrial and labour policies, increasing the unilateral power of the employer in making decisions. This has reduced the costs of hiring and firing workers (the misnamed external flexibility), has pushed down wages and has extended working hours (internal flexibility),[4] as the only way to achieve economic growth and efficiency. We should not forget that labour law has also been directly accused of undermining those it is meant to protect.[5]

This has led to a trade-off between economic growth and labour regulation.[6] Labour lawyers have mostly reacted to this trade-off in two different ways: (i) they have sought to minimise the effects of labour regulation on the economy, ie, by arguing that unemployment and economic growth depend on factors other

[2] Banerjee and Duflo, *Good Economics for Hard Times* (2019).

[3] This term was coined by the economist John Williamson. The aim was to describe a set of relatively specific formulas, which he regarded as representing the reform package for crisis-stricken developing countries, in agreement with US-based institutions such as the International Monetary Fund (IMF) and the World Bank. J Williamson, 'What Washington Means by Policy Reform', in J Frieden, M Pastor and M Tomz, *Modern Political Economy and Latin America* (Washington DC, Institute for International Economics, 1990).

[4] J Howe, 'The Broad Idea of Labour Law: Industrial Policy, Labour Market Regulation, and Decent Work', in G Davidov and B Languille, (eds), *The Idea of Labour Law* (Oxford, Oxford University Press, 2011) 309.

[5] D Card and A Krueger, *Myth and Measurement: The New Economics of the Minimum Wage* (New Jersey, Princeton University Press, 1995).

[6] AM Okun, *Equality and Efficiency: The Big Tradeoff*, (Washington DC, Brookings Institute, 1975).

than labour regulation; (ii) by arguing that, if there is a choice between economic growth and workers' rights, the latter should be chosen. In other words, they argue that labour rights respond to social values in a democracy that cannot be taken away by market-dictated conditions. They argue that when labour conditions are left to the market to decide, they become precarious and undesirable.

However, the reality is that 40 years down the line, neither of these two rationales seems to have succeeded in stopping the relentless onslaught on deregulation. Therefore, this study aims to add a different, complementary argument to justify the existence of labour law (while also seeking to bring positions closer together and initiate a thoughtful dialogue between economic policy and labour law) which opposes deregulation. This study contends that there is no trade-off between labour regulations and economic growth because employees' rights serve to foster economic efficiency and productivity in the workplace. Among other reasons, this is because workers' rights impose limits on firms who aim to compete solely on price by encouraging investment in technology, staff training and organisational innovation that ultimately lead to economic gains.

Current justifications of labour law, which refuse to recognise the effects they can have on the economy, have allowed deregulation to creep in. It must be acknowledged that regulation has a significant effect on individual behaviour (it is not neutral) and that it can be used to improve the economy.[7] The prevailing discourse that minimises the impact of labour regulation on the economy – 'labour reforms neither create nor destroy jobs' – hamper ambitious reforms to improve the economy and use regulation to redistribute wealth. Indeed, the anxiety generated by the fear that increasing labour rights could lead to market inefficiencies or unemployment often functions as a self-fulfilling prophecy mechanism. An example of this occurred in France with the introduction of the 35-hour working week.

The 35-hour working week was brought into force in France in 1998 by the socialist coalition government of Lionel Jospin. The new law, known as Aubry 1, established a maximum 35-hour working week in private companies. The reduced working week was to be implemented without wage cuts. The measure was phased in gradually depending on the size of the company, while tax incentives were given to companies that collectively negotiated the reduction, signing contracts with unions to ease the financial burden on businesses. Firms that increased employment by 10% by reducing working hours were offered rebates on their social security contributions.[8] The aim of the regulation was, firstly, to increase employment by sharing workloads and, secondly, to improve employees' welfare.

This 1998 regulation met with strong opposition from employers. It was argued that it would cut productivity and make companies less competitive. The outcome would lead to the closure of French firms, the decentralisation of production to

[7] M Mazzucato, *Mission Economy* (London, Penguin Books, 2021) 20.

[8] M Estevao, and F Sá, 'The 35-hour Workweek in France: Straightjacket or Welfare Improvement?' (2008) 23(55), *Economic Policy* 422.

countries with cheaper labour costs and, ultimately, to job losses. As a result of this confrontation, legislation was amended in 2001(Aubry 2). The 35-hour working week could now be calculated on an annual basis, and overtime was authorised, even though it exceeded 40 hours per week at certain times. Subsequently, the government made further adjustments, weakening the rules still further. In 2003, the Fillon Government increased the maximum limit on overtime thus effectively letting companies return to their previous working week. This meant that the 35-hour limit could be legally exceeded, even in terms of annual working hours, thanks to the overtime mechanism. In other words, the government gave in to pressure and 'abolished' the regulation before the real effects on employment and labour productivity could be ascertained. The fear of negative consequences outweighed the political will to implement changes that would improve the situation, or at least attempt to do so.

In fact, subsequent studies suggested that the policy had positive effects in terms of shorter working hours, job creation and productivity. Eurostat[9] figures revealed that average weekly working hours for full-time workers fell from 1998 to 2002 but started to rise again from 2003 onwards as a result of subsequent regulatory changes.[10] The study by Askenazy[11] suggests that the working hours of full-time employees fell by 10 per cent, resulting in the creation of 350,000 jobs.[12] In the same period, French ministry statistics revealed an increase in labour productivity.[13] Finally, French sociologist Dominique Méda, in a mass survey with over 1,000 respondents on the effects of the regulation in 2001, found positive results for the majority of workers and were particularly noticeable for women.[14] The study showed that many workers, predominantly women, were able to shift from part-time to full-time work, improving the economy from a gender perspective.[15] This proves that it was not the data, nor the 'economics' that made this a bad measure, but the fear of criticism and regulatory innovation in labour matters that made it disappear 'pre-emptively'.

This book aims to debunk the myths and prejudices surrounding workers' rights and to vindicate their role in improving economic efficiency.

The deregulation initiated in the Thatcher–Reagan era does not seem to be working well in the economies of developed countries. The response to the global

[9] EUROSTAT, 'Average number of usual weekly hours of work in main job, by sex, professional status, full-time/part-time and occupation (hours)' (2019). Available at: www.ec.europa.eu/eurostat/web/products-datasets/-/LFSA_EWHUIS.

[10] L Skidelsky, 'How to Achieve Shorter Working Hours', *PEF* 32. Available at: www.progressiveeconomyforum.com/wp-content/uploads/2019/08/PEF_Skidelsky_How_to_achieve_shorter_working_hours.pdf.

[11] P Askenazy, 'Working-time Regulation in France from 1996 to 2012' (2013) 37(2) *Journal of Economics* 335.

[12] Skidelsky, 'How to Achieve Shorter Working Hours'.

[13] Skidelsky (n 12).

[14] D Méda, 'The French Experience' in A Coote, and J Franklin, *Time on our Side: Why We All Need a Shorter Working Week* (London, New Economics Foundation, 2013).

[15] Askenazy, 'Working time regulation in France from 1996 to 2012', 336.

COVID-19 pandemic demonstrated the need for public intervention in the economy. As easy as it would be for us to blame echo chambers and social media for the rise of tension, frustration, anger and increased conflict in recent decades, the problem seems to run much deeper. The current radicalisation of society feels more like the outcome of growing inequality.

The 'losers' of globalisation – workers in the manufacturing industry – and of digital transformation – skilled and unskilled workers – feel both excluded from society and that their legitimate rights are being undermined.[16] Young people who have suffered two economic crises (the likes of which are supposed to happen only once in 100 years), before they have reached their thirties have less and less trust in the political class and the economic system. These groups' inability to improve their situation as they grow older is a breeding ground for radicalism, protest, violence and conflict. Even the International Monetary Fund (IMF) warned that the pandemic could be a catalyst for global social upheaval. In fact, the slowdown in economic growth and the rising inequality caused by COVID-19 has highlighted existing fractures in society, including a lack of social protection, the mistrust of institutions, perceived incompetence and government corruption.[17] In this context, it does not seem unreasonable to argue that history is repeating itself. We are returning to pre-Second World War levels of economic inequality, with its deregulated, precarious labour markets, and are experiencing the same consequences, namely division, conflict and violence.

In this sense, this book analyses how the governments in developed countries built the welfare state in response to this situation, to ensure that it would not happen again. This is where labour law flourished, becoming a cornerstone for safeguarding economic security and fair distribution of the profits generated in the economy. It also explains how the disappearance of these two elements as a consequence of deregulation and no intervention in the economy, has led inequality, frustration and conflict to rear their ugly heads once again.

However, relying on past justifications for the need for labour law is perhaps not sufficient. The current context, based on globalisation and digital transformation (especially fuelled by COVID-19), is very different from the years in which labour law flourished.

Accordingly, following an analysis of the current context, this book will present a clear, coherent, updated modern discourse on the functions of labour law and the reasons that justify its necessity, not as an academic discipline, but as a useful element for society in the twenty-first century. Liberal approaches question all labour conventions (minimum wage, severance pay, maximum working hours, collective bargaining). Therefore, it is essential to analyse them one by one to ensure that there are good grounds for upholding them or moving them forward.

[16] Banerjee and Duflo (n 1).

[17] T Saadi Sedik, and R Xu, 'A Vicious Cycle: How Pandemics Lead to Economic Despair and Social Unrest' (2020) *IMF Working Paper* 216.

This can only be done if there is an updated, coherent discourse on the need for labour law that answers questions firstly about its content, ie, what functions it needs to perform, and secondly, about its scope of application, ie, who needs labour regulation.

It is not feasible to dwell on old justifications (on 'past glories') in an ideological, business and technological context that is manifestly different, or at least not without a fresh analysis from today's perspective that validates or refutes these justifications and contrasts them with new ones.

This is not a straightforward task, given that laws are the result of history and of political engagements at any given moment in time.[18] Therefore, only justifications that are accepted by the entire ideological spectrum, within a current welfare state governed by the rule of law, can be considered valid. However, it is no less true that laws are also the result of a *narrative* that imposes its own ideas at a particular moment in time, which is why it will be difficult to reverse the so-called 'decline' of labour law without this modern discourse, which has been updated in line with today's values.

Thus, this book shall examine a series of justifications that endorse the validity of and need for labour law today, while assigning new functions, in addition to protecting the weaker party to the contract, in line with the current political, business and technological context.

This new context, involving very different forms of business organisation to those existing at the inception of labour law, also requires a new concept of the worker, which is less restrictive for the application of labour law than the current one. Today's labour regulation model revolves around the existence of legal dependence, ie, submission to instructions and supervision by the employer, in the provision of services as the main characteristic of the employment contract.[19]

However, if labour law is to be modernised, adapted to new forms of business organisation and serve as a useful instrument for economic policy, the first thing that must be done (this is something that is already underway[20]) is to remove the requirement of legal dependence on the employer as the gateway to labour

[18] H Collins, GL Lester, and V Mantouvalou, 'Introduction: Does Labour Law Need Philosophical Foundations?', in *Philosophical Foundations of Labour Law* (Oxford, Oxford University Press, 2018) 3.

[19] In Spain, Art 1 of the Statute of Workers' Rights includes dependency and also subordination but, over time, the first of the two has gained in importance, M Rodriguez Piñero, 'La dependencia y la extensión del ámbito del Derecho del Trabajo' (1996) 71 *Revista de Política Social* 147–68. In the USA, the courts mostly apply the 'right to control test' to discover whether subordination exists and to classify it as employment. R Sprage, 'Worker (Mis)Classification in the Sharing Economy: Square Pegs Trying to fit in Round Holes' (2015) 31 *ABA Journal of Labor & Employment Law*, University of Wyoming, 16. In Italy, art 2094 of the Civil Code regulating the standard employment contract refers to subordinate work. In the Netherlands, employment contracts are regulated in Art 7:610 para 1 of the Civil Code, where making oneself available to another person to provide services is the only qualifying element.

[20] A Todolí-Signes, 'The End of the Subordinate Worker? Collaborative Economy, On-Demand Economy, Gig Economy, and the Crowdworkers' Need for Protection' (2017) 33(2) *International Journal of Comparative Labour Law and Industrial Relations* 241–68 (IJCLLIR).

regulation. In fact, legal dependence as a defining criterion for the application of labour regulation needs to be abolished if labour law is to deliver in its promise of efficiency, wealth distribution and equality.

This book argues that the concept of legal dependence responded to the situation in which workers in large factories found themselves in the early days of labour law.[21] However, as a result of new ways of working, other actors, with much greater formal freedom to choose their working hours, decide where and how to perform their work, also need labour regulations. They are subjects that are part of the labour market since they sell their labour to a third party which then includes it in the products or services it offers the market. Therefore, they cannot be legally considered as employers. Thus, the last part of this book justifies the need for a new concept of employee that differentiates between an employee and a genuine employer in the service-provision context. Hence, only those who can be considered genuine employers in service-provision terms would be excluded from labour regulation.

[21] F Valdés Dal-Ré, 'Descentralización productiva y desorganización del derecho del trabajo' (2001) *Revista Universitaria de Ciencias del Trabajo* 45; F Pérez Amorós, 'El trabajador como sujeto del Derecho del Trabajo Español' (1982) 133 *Revista de Política Social* 87.

PART I

The Origins of the Need for Labour Law and Parallels with the Current Context

The need to 'modernise' labour regulations is an idea that has been repeated time and again. All political groups have advocated the need to change labour laws to adapt them to current times. However, this is where the consensus ends. There are different opinions when analysing what has really changed and why the regulation in force today is no longer useful in our current economic production model. Naturally, there is even less consensus when it comes to putting forward specific regulatory changes aimed at 'updating' labour regulations and their personal scope of application.

Thus, any self-respecting study that seeks to renew the justifications for the very existence of labour regulations must start with a study of the legal grounds that created them and the economic and manufacturing situation that gave rise to their inception. This will enable us to examine the current circumstances and to ascertain whether they have changed substantially, without disputing the fact that they have obviously moved on. This is essential to determine whether there is a real need for change, and in what direction and to what extent this should be undertaken.

The next chapter examines the causes that led to the need for regulatory intervention in the labour market. Firstly, the causes of the loss of workers' bargaining power over time are studied: (1) the separation between work and the attribution of the results of work; (2) the need for capital and technology to be able to produce efficiently; (3) the fungibility of workers vis-à-vis the technology-based market. Secondly, we will analyse how the loss of income of small landowners at the beginning of the twentieth century forced a large part of the petty bourgeoisie to live off their own labour. This increased the demands for labour market regulation.

We subsequently explore the changes that have taken place in the production model in recent decades. That is, the disappearance of vertically integrated companies and corporate hierarchies which have been superseded by employee self-management, the emergence of subcontracting and global production chains, and technological intensification as an essential production tool (digital transformation and automation).

It also examines the effects of these changes on the labour market: mainly its two-tiered system and the growing precariousness of work because of deregulation.

Thus, we will be in a position to broadly compare the situation that originally gave rise to the need for labour regulations and the current situation, and to conclude that, despite the need to modernise labour regulations, the reasons for their very existence (lack of bargaining power and the reasons behind it) do not seem to have disappeared, but instead have grown with the changes that have taken place in the production model over the last few decades (globalisation and digital transformation).

2

The Origins and Evolution of Labour Law

The Separation between Work and the Attribution of the Results of Work

The legal framework of labour relations has differed substantially throughout history. There are three main models for the attribution of the results of work.[1]

In Classical Greece and Rome, slave labour was the most common way of obtaining a workforce. At the time, people were regarded as things; they belonged to a slave-owner, who owned their labour power and received the fruits of their labour. To a lesser extent, this period also saw the existence of freedmen – labourers who worked in exchange for wages – and agricultural landlords.

Throughout the Middle Ages, labour relations were based on serfdom. In this feudal system, the lord of the land was entitled to benefit from the fruits obtained not only from the land but also from the labour of those who lived on it.

In addition, at this time, there were also guilds of artisans and other 'liberal' professions. Professions and services, which were strongly regulated by the guilds, provided services directly to the market. In turn, these professionals had wage earners and apprentices in their employ,[2] albeit on a small scale. The blue-nails of medieval Flandes and the Ciompi of medieval Florence are early examples of workers with nothing to sell but their labour.[3] Artisans were self-employed craftsmen who manufactured items to sell; artisans sold the products they produced; they did not sell their labour.[4]

In the Modern Age labour, through serfdom and strong guild regulation, diminished for the first time, giving way to other types of arrangements for the provision of services with relative autonomy. During this period, the number of liberal professionals, artisans and farmers who owned their own land and produced goods and services themselves, i.e., using their own tools and workshops, selling them directly

[1] E Borrajo Dacruz, *Introducción al Derecho del Trabajo*, 5th edn, (Madrid, Tecnos, 1988).

[2] R Steinfeld, *The Invention of Free Labor: The Employment Relation in English and American Culture* (Durham NC, University of North Carolina Press, 1991).

[3] DS Landes, *The Unbound Prometheus. Technological Change and Industrial Development in Western Europe from 1750 to the Present* (New York, Cambridge University Press, 1969) 7.

[4] K Stone, *From Widgets to Digits: Employment Regulation for the Changing Workplace* (Cambridge, Cambridge University Press, 2004).

to the end consumer, increased.[5] However, this set-up, in which workers owned the necessary means of production and, in addition, marketed their own products, was relatively inefficient.[6] Although the markets were local and close to production centres, going to the market to sell one's output, or simply one's agricultural surplus, meant losing working days on a farm or production days for the trades.

Gradually, as a result of economies of scale and the principle of specialisation, merchants or 'entrepreneurs' grew in importance during the Modern Age. These merchants placed orders with 'liberal' professionals, artisans and farmers and then traded these products on the market. This period saw a separation between production and distribution. Artisans no longer had direct contact with the end customers and, in many cases, no longer had sufficient power to negotiate the price of their goods, due to the lack of direct contact with the final consumer.[7] Over time, these merchants eventually built manufacturing and production into their business structure by setting up factories.

This does not mean that merchants always had the 'upper hand' when it came to setting the working conditions of artisans (prices, delivery times, way of working). The guilds managed to retain a kind of monopoly or oligopoly over production by determining how many artisans were 'allowed' to produce and by regulating how they were to produce.[8] This meant that artisans had relative bargaining power over the merchant thanks to the guild, which could impose 'penalties' of a social rather than administrative nature on artisans who engaged in unfair competition via prices on the products they sold. This meant that the guild could fix minimum conditions for merchants to buy the products it wanted to sell, as well as maintaining tight control over the number of merchants who had access to the necessary knowledge (training) to develop the products, which balanced power out between workers/producers and merchants.

Later, with the liberal revolution, the guilds were deregulated until they almost disappeared. The labour force was thus instrumentalised through the civil service-provision contract. Thus, the contractor's appropriation of the fruits of labour was legalised in accordance with liberal values. The impregnation of liberal values in this form of contracting was mainly manifested by deregulation and the primacy of the will of the parties.

Thus, the Industrial Revolution saw the transition from a system of labour based on the ownership of the individual, first through slavery and then through tying people to the land, to one in which labour power was chiefly for 'sale' under

[5] K Stone, 'The Origin of Job Structures in the Steel Industry', in D Gordon, M Reich. and R Edwards, *Labour Market Segmentation* (Lexington MA, DC Heath, 1975).

[6] DS Landes, *The Unbound Prometheus. Technological Change and Industrial Development in Western Europe from 1750 to the Present* (New York, Cambridge University Press, 1969).

[7] As Landes said "the artisan found himself bound to the merchant (…) who sold his finished work. This subordination of the producer to the intermediary was consequence of the growth of the market", *The Unbound Prometheus. Technological Change and Industrial Development in Western Europe from 1750 to the Present*, (New York, Cambridge University Press, 1969) 43.

[8] K Stone, *From Widgets to Digits: Employment Regulation for the Changing Workplace* (Cambridge, Cambridge University Press, 2004).

market conditions. Labour could be freely bought and sold by the parties, supplied and demanded like any other product without differentiating its legal status from that of other goods or things.

Thus, during the second half of the eighteenth century and throughout the nineteenth century, labour was considered as simply another commodity to be traded. Economists of the time, such as Thomas Malthus (1766–1834), went so far as to point out the direct connection between people's lives and the labour market. In this sense, he argued that the 'natural' level of wages was subsistence, since if real wages were above subsistence level, this would increase the population, increasing the demand for food and causing prices to rise which, in turn, would bring *real* wages back to subsistence level.[9] David Ricardo (1772–1823) also considered that wages should be equal to what was necessary for the worker to 'exist', that is, to 'subsist and perpetuate their race'.[10] Given the prevailing ideas of the time, regulation of any kind made no sense: the market solved 'everything', even at the cost of starvation and death.

In short, this period created the social, ideological, political and economic conditions that resulted in a favourable context for the inception of labour law in its initial stages.

The Separation of Capital and Labour: Technology

Labour law can only be regarded as a specific branch of law after workers' acceptance of working for others, in a relationship of legal dependence, became widespread at a specific time in history, namely during the Industrial Revolution. In the common law system, the juridical form of this idea can be found in the 'master-servant' model and then on to the traditional concept of contract of hire.[11]

This separation from other branches of law took place historically through the convergence of a series of factors:[12]

(i) Firstly, a sociological factor emerging from the economic consequences of the Industrial Revolution.
(ii) Secondly, a legal factor involving shortcomings in regulation.
(iii) Thirdly, workers' reactions to the situation of social inequality and lack of bargaining power.
(iv) Finally, state interventionism aimed at regulating social conflict.

[9] TR Malthus, *An Essay on the Principle of Population* (1798), critical edition by P James, (Cambridge, Cambridge University Press, 1989).

[10] D Ricardo, *On the Principles of Political Economy and Taxation* (1817) (Cambridge, Cambridge University Press, 1951).

[11] B Veneziani, 'The evolution of employment relationship', in B Hepple (ed) *The Making of Labour Law in Europe* (Mansell, 1986).

[12] T Sala Franco and J López Gandía, 'El Derecho del Trabajo', in I Montesinos Albiol et al *Derecho del Trabajo. Tomo I. Fuentes y relaciones colectivas*, 3rd edn (Valencia, Tirant lo Blanch, 2001).

During the Industrial Revolution, in addition to changes in production technologies and organisation, there were also shifts in ideological tenets, ie, the Enlightenment, and in political and economic constraints that gave rise to what is known as the 'class society'.[13]

Nevertheless, the many industrial and technical advances were one of the essential factors in the transition to this new era. The mechanisation of manufacturing processes and the appearance of new inventions such as James Watt's steam engine in 1765 and John Key's flying shuttle for fabric manufacture in 1733 increased labour productivity, reducing production costs per piece, and creating fresh demand for consumer goods, especially in the textile, and iron and steel sectors.

In addition, the modernisation of techniques in the countryside, as well as the liberalisation of the labour market with the disappearance of serfdom, produced a rural population surplus that moved to the cities to cater for the growing demand for labour in the new production centres. This was accompanied by a significant drop in mortality, which led to a demographic increase throughout the world from 1750 onwards. This, in turn, brought an increase in the demand for consumer goods.

The modernisation of industry and mass production had another effect: the separation of capital and labour.[14] In the Modern Age, labour had already been disconnected from the sale of products, thus diminishing the bargaining power of the service provider (artisan). Later, with industrialisation, the service provider was not only cut off from the market, but also from the very means of production required for manufacture. Previously, artisans owned the workshop where they worked, but during industrialisation, a workshop was no longer sufficient: technology in the shape of machinery was needed to produce goods efficiently. In addition, mass production brought economies of scale that reduced prices, implying that small workshops could not produce efficiently, even if they had the technology. Instead, large facilities were needed to achieve economies of scale.

Finally, workers, including artisans and peasants, were unable to accumulate the capital required to produce competitively, and were thus forced to sell their labour power in exchange for a wage to those who did have the capital (machinery and infrastructure). This effectively meant they were forced to become wage labourers.

This shows that the original difference between a self-employed worker (a former artisan) and a salaried worker was not that the latter undertook to carry out the orders of the employer, but that they did not have the manufacturing resources required to be productive, and therefore needed to sell their labour power. Nor did they have direct access to the market, and so became economically dependent on those who did.

[13] T Dos Santos, 'The concept of social classes' (1970) 34(2) *Science & Society* 166.

[14] DS Landes, *The Unbound Prometheus. Technological Change and Industrial Development in Western Europe from 1750 to the Present* (New York, Cambridge University Press, 1969) 43.

Industrial modernisation and the advent of production machinery had another effect: the fungibility of labour. While artisans needed years of training to be able to produce parts and products, the learning curve became much faster when factory workers appeared on the scene.[15] Once again, this implied a reduction in the worker's bargaining power given that one worker could easily be replaced with another. Thus, the fact that costly training was not required greatly increased the number of potential job seekers for each available job. Therefore, as the worker was now 'hidden' from the final customer, given that merchants performed this function, and did not own the production resources, which were in the hands of the capital owner, and no specific training was required to perform this type of work, the worker had no bargaining power whatsoever to dictate, or at least to negotiate, the conditions of work.

In addition to these sociological and economic factors, the inception of labour law coincided with a political context which, though fostering the accumulation of capital and investment in industrialisation, eventually revealed its socially dysfunctional nature and the impossibility of sustaining it over time.

The consolidation of the bourgeoisie as the dominant class and its manifest opposition to the absolutist, oppressive state from which it had emerged, caused the theories of political and economic liberalism to gain traction. The clearest manifestation of the liberal ideological foundations was the defence of state abstentionism in regulating the relations between labour and capital. In fact, the only state intervention at this time was limited to guaranteeing freedom of choice in setting the conditions under which the provision of services was to be carried out. In fact, Liberalism argued that any interference or limitation of the exercise of parties' free will would have undesirable effects on the labour market. Laissez-faire economics and Social Darwinism – the survival of the fittest, as propounded by Charles Darwin, applied to the development of human societies – together represented the dominant 'orthodox' school of thought during the nineteenth century at the beginning of the twentieth century. Both doctrines share four basic assumptions.[16]

(1) The presence of irrefutable law of nature, as competition and survival of the fittest, and inalienable natural rights – private property and individual freedom.
(2) The efficiency of self-interest as explained by Adam Smith. The people pursuit if their self-interest is the most efficient way to produce and promote good for society.
(3) The benefits of free competition as a way to obtain a better society thought personal initiative. It was believed that 'free competition' made the success of individuals a function of ability and effort, not status or privilege.

[15] Stone, *From Widgets to Digits: Employment Regulation for the Changing Workplace* (2004).
[16] S Fine, *Laissez Faire and the General Welfare State: A Study of Conflict in American Thought, 1865–1901* (Ann Arbor, University of Michigan Press, 1956).

(4) Avoid government intervention. Escaping from absolute monarchies and authoritarian forms of government, public intervention was seen as corrupt and self-serving.

This era enshrined what Piketty[17] called 'proprietarianism', an ideology in which the right to private property was privileged above all other rights, including life. Thus, the owner of capital was protected by the state and the law, ensuring inheritance, the free disposal of property and buying and selling. In addition (these rights are still guaranteed today), the parliaments of the time actively safeguarded private property and the rights of the owner over and above other rights. As a result, the creation of a progressive tax on wealth and income generated by capital was blocked on many occasions. Similarly, associations of workers were prohibited on the grounds that they interfered with an owner's freedom. This repressed any trade-union initiatives. These theories posited that the aim of these unions was none other than to promote wage bargaining and improve labour conditions for the working class, against which the capitalists deserved protection. In this context, it is not surprising that national parliaments actively criminalised the various expressions of workers' unions.

There are examples of employment laws that have been declared unconstitutional. One illustrative example of the power of ideology of laissez faire is the decision of the Pennsylvania Supreme court in a case involving a state law requiring that wages be paid in cash rather than tokens. The court, in 1886, said:[18]

> 'The act is an infringement alike of the right of the employer and the employee; more that this it is an insulting attempt to put the laborer under a legislative tutelage which is not only degrading to his manhood, but subversive of his rights as citizen of the U.S. He nay sell his labor for what he thinks best, whether money or goods, just as his employer may sell his iron or coal, and any or every law that proposes to prevent him from so doing is an infringement of his constitutional privileges, and consequently vicious and void.'

Under this liberal conception, labour relations began to be regulated in civil law based on principles derived from the free will of the parties and free agreement to determine the scope and obligations of these relations. In this sense, the civil service- provision contract fulfilled its dual foundational and regulatory functions, i.e., first, free choice, embodied in the fact that any workers could contractually bind themselves to cede their labour power in exchange for remuneration, freely stipulated in the contract with any employer who owned an industry and, second, its regulatory function, consisting of the fact that the contract was the only source of the obligations between the parties in the absence of state intervention or any kind of collective agreement.[19]

[17] T Piketty, *Capital and Ideology* (Cambridge MA, Belknap Press, 2020).

[18] S Lehrer, *Origins of Protective Labor Legislation for Women, 1905–1925* (New York: University of NY Press, 1987).

[19] D Montgomery, *The Fall of the House of Labour: The Workplace, the State and the American Labor Activism, 1865–1925* (New York, Cambridge University Press, 1987).

However, this supposed freedom was merely a reflection of the society in which the capital-owning party was able to impose its will and its interests on non-owners. Hence, workers had no choice but to accept the conditions offered, or not to work. Similarly, this lack of bargaining power was not only manifested by the fact that workers had to accept the conditions offered by the employer, but also that, during the term of the employment contract, the owner could give instructions and check and supervise the provision of the service. In other words, what we today call legal dependence as a prerequisite for the existence of an employment contract was originally a consequence of the industrial service provision (and the socio-economic conditions of the workers), not a prerequisite.

This is one of the major contradictions of liberal societies. As Boltanski and Chiapello have pointed out,[20] the service-provision contract for industrial labour was seen as a step forward in liberal societies, i.e., it abolished serfdom (where a person belonged to a landowner or local nobleman) which implied the liberation of the individual. However, these people, who had no property, no capital and no other way of earning a living, had to work to live, so had no choice but to submit 'voluntarily' to the regime imposed by the master. Thus, the service provision contract, which was established as a form of liberation for the individual (an ideal of liberal societies) ended up becoming a new form of slavery.

However, for the purposes of this book, the lack of bargaining power and liberal regulation ended up having a damaging effect on the working class: long hours, industrial accidents, poverty incomes, excessive work speed, irregular work, workplace autocracy and conflict.[21]

This gave birth to the industrial proletariat and the workers' movement which challenged these ideologies to eradicate the exploitation and misery that workers, who were helpless to fight the impositions of the ruling capitalist system, were forced to endure.[22]

As the prevailing ideologies of the time continued to put property rights above all other interests, the idea of a collective conscience made up of a disadvantaged working class began to take root in society through various union-based proposals which put forward alternatives to the capitalist system through several revolutionary ideas.

Although the first reactions were to ban and persecute these movements, the relentless force of the workers' collective and, above all, its success in Russia and the fear of the model's expansion to other territories, forced a change in mentality to calm the revolutionary movements and preserve the existence and stability of the system.

[20] L Boltanski, and E Chiapello, *The New Spirit of Capitalism*, (Cambridge, Verso, 2005) 39, 536, 538.

[21] To see the data for the USA, see BE Kaufman, 'The Old Institutionalists', in Kaufman (ed), *Government Regulation of the Employment Relationship* (Madison WN, Industrial Relations Research Association, 1997) 16.

[22] S Webb and B Webb, *The History of Trade Unionism (revised edition extended to 1920)* (London, Longmans, Green and Co, 1894), reprinted 2021).

The incipient threat of the so-called 'social problem' and the imminence of a possible working-class revolution forced both the state and the bourgeois ruling classes to change tack.[23]

Following this period of confrontation and prohibition, a period of tolerance towards these working-class movements ensued before conclusive recognition was finally reached through the first legislative initiatives aimed at protecting the working conditions of the proletariat.[24]

This is how the provision of services between employer and employee began to move away from the provision of services in the Civil Code. Labour law began to emerge as an independent legal discipline thanks to the emergence of the 'employment contract' as the focal point of a whole new body of law and as a legal instrument for regulating working conditions.

Thus, labour law became an independent legal discipline. In a 1910 article, Sinzheimer (the founding father of German labour law[25]) justified labour law as a legal discipline that was distinct from civil law for a variety of reasons, including the importance of the subject matter, the special nature of the subject matter of the discipline including public law and private law, the special treatment of labour law at an interpretative level, the legal construct and the social and labour policies involved, the need for an interdisciplinary approach involving sociology, social policy and business organisation, and the inherent purpose of labour law, which sets it apart from other legal disciplines.[26] According to Sinzheimer, labour law has four specific characteristics: (1) it is not only created by the state but also by social agents; (2) the labour contract is distinct from civil law; (3) the labour contract is based on the individual subordination of labour; (4) the source of worker subordination comes from the employer's ownership of the means of production, i.e., the worker needs the employer as the owner of the means of production in order to be able to live and work.[27]

Particularly, in Britain, this process was completed very late. It was only with the National Insurance Act of 1946 that the single status of the 'employee' subsumed the older categories of wage-dependent worders; as a result, the moder concept of employment was born.[28]

[23] A Montoya Melgar, *Ideología y lenguaje en las leyes laborales de España (1873–1978)*, 1st edn (Madrid, Civitas, 1992).

[24] Hence, the English Trade Union Act of 1871 and the French Waldeck-Rousseau Act of 1884. For collective bargaining and strike action see the German Weimar Constitution of 1919.

[25] See, O Kahn-Freund, *Labour Law and Politics in the Weimar Republic* (Oxford, Blackwell, 1981) 75.

[26] Thus, Sinzheimer saw labour law as being the guardian of human beings in the age of almost uncontrolled materialism.

[27] On this see B Hepple, (ed), *The Making of Labour Law in Europe: A Comparison of Nine Countries up to 1945* (Oxford, Hart Publishing, 2010) 32 and R Dukes, 'Hugo Sinzheimer and the Constitutional Function of Labour Law' in G Davidov and B Languille (eds), *The Idea of Labour Law* (Oxford, Oxford University Press, 2011) 59.

[28] S Deakin, 'The Evolution of the Contract of Employment 1900–1950: The Influence of the Welfare State', in N Whiteside and R Salais (eds), *Governance, Industry and Labour Markets in Britain and France, The Modernising State in the Mid-Twentieth Century* (London, Routledge, 1998) 212–30.

Evolution of Labour Law

The existence of labour law as a discipline can be divided into three main periods. The first period consists of the beginnings or origins of labour law in which its foundations were laid and its roots as an independent legal discipline were established as we have just seen. This period lasted approximately until the Second World War. After this turbulent period, which has been called the Golden Age of Labour Law (at least in Europe, the USA and Canada)[29] where, together with the construction of the welfare state and strong trade unions, individual and collective protection against capital ownership expanded. The length of this period varied from country to country, but the end came in the 1970s at the time of the oil crisis. From this period onwards, labour law went into a period of decline, coinciding with the rise of neo-classical economic policies and political neo-liberalism, which advocated downsizing the welfare state.

Expansion of Labour Law

The expansion of labour law mainly took place in the years following the Second World War. A series of economic and political conditions were conducive to this expansion: i) the development of a strong state responsible for the protection of its citizens, including workers; ii) the construction of vertically integrated companies and the development of hierarchies; (iii) workers' search for security; (iv) the gendered relationship between the male worker and the female 'housewife', (v) the strength of industrial trade unions, many of them partly responsible for the victory against Nazi Germany in Europe; and (vi) social democratic parties and their alliances with trade unions.

Although the end of the Second World War marked the start of the expansion of labour law in European and Anglo-Saxon countries, much of the groundwork had been laid before then. As Boltanski and Chiapello pointed out,[30] currency devaluations during the inter-war period and the subsequent 1930s crisis led to a decline in purchasing power and incomes that pushed members of the bourgeoisie, who lived off the rents from small properties that had now beocme worthless, into paid labour. This meant that it was no longer just uneducated factory workers who became paid workers. Now, a large part of the petty bourgeoisie sought to earn a living through labour, since they too had lost the ability to live off their property and rental income. These educated people (engineers, professionals, managers and middle managers) saw a significant drop in their standard of

[29] B Hepple, and B Veneziani, 'Introduction' in B Hepple, B Veneziani (eds), *The Transformation of Labour Law in Europe* (Oxford, Hart Publishing, 2009); B Laskin, *A Selection of Cases and Materials on Labour Law* (Toronto, University of Toronto Press, 1947).

[30] Boltanski, and Chiapello, *The New Spirit of Capitalism*, (2005).

living in the inter-war period, especially as a result of the widespread destruction of property during the Second World War bombings, until the post-war years saw the beginning of a fresh distribution of economic resources through paid labour.

These collectives demanded a new social contract, through trade unions and political parties, whereby they could 'live like the bourgeoisie' in a social position as a salaried employee. Thus, safeguards such as retirement, unemployment benefits, the opportunity to pursue a career in a vertically integrated company, salary reviews in line with inflation, and job security through severance pay were put in place. All these were measures and instruments that sought to give security to those who lived off their labour – not off income – which helped those who never had capital or assets to live off, i.e., the working class, but also those who had previously owned assets that provided them with that financial security (the petty bourgeoisie), but who subsequently lost them and sought refuge and security in a set of protective laws and collective agreements that gave them economic stability from living off their labour power. In short, the petty bourgeoisie became the working class and, from that moment on, the interests of the 'former' petty middle class and the working class converged.

One of the most widely accepted narratives about the achievements of the welfare state, and of labour law as an inherent part of it, was the emergence of the great middle class. Though true, this heroic narrative probably conceals the fact that initially these regulations did not seek to benefit the lower class, but rather the petty bourgeoisie that already existed at the beginning of the twentieth century. It was this middle class which, as a result of the economic crisis and the devastation caused by the war, was forced to live entirely off their labour. The small petty bourgeoisie which was not used to economic hardship (thanks to the income they earned from rents), and which had sufficient political contacts to influence the regulation of their new way of life as salaried employees.

Thus, a much more cynical account would say that, at least partially, the improvement in lower-class social conditions, which ended up becoming truly middle class (thanks to the welfare state and labour law), was only a side-effect of regulations that sought to protect a bourgeoisie fallen from grace.

There is little doubt that, although there may have been diverse interests within the working class in this period of labour law expansion, the fact that regulation did not distinguish between these interests, and that there was true working-class solidarity encouraged and facilitated the construction and evolution of protective regulations. In other words, this cynicism ceased to be cynical, as soon as regulation (whatever its aim) did not seek to provide economic security only for skilled jobs performed by qualified members of the petty bourgeoisie, but for all those who made a living from their labour, including unskilled workers. Thus, it was the solidarity of the working class, as a single class made up of all those who lived off their labour, because they had no wealth or capital to maintain them, regardless of their origins or other considerations, which gave sufficient political clout to the regulatory changes that took place.

In short, it was not only the fact that the middle and lower class had joined forces in seeking economic security through wage labour but that, in these early moments of expansion, both groups sought to defend what they had in common in their demands against capital instead of focusing on their differences.

This homogeneity of class, and of demands to benefit the entire collective without distinction, culminated in the golden years of labour law. The principles of social justice, equality and human rights aimed to restrict the freedom of contract and the unilateral powers of the employer. The main objective of labour law in these years was to contain the inequality of bargaining power between employer and employee and to implicitly improve the redistribution of income earned in the enterprise. This was done in two ways: firstly, by introducing procedures that allowed collective bargaining, including the recognition of the right to strike and industrial democracy techniques and, secondly, by defining essential working conditions (maximum number of working hours, minimum wage, severance pay, safety at work, etc.).[31]

Of course, labour law, even in its golden age, was concerned with productivity and not just with protection. Thus, labour law guaranteed managerial powers and prerogatives so that employees were legally, not just economically, subordinate to the employer.[32] All this coincided with the type of organisation that existed at the time: a highly hierarchical, vertically integrated company.

The Demise of Labour Law

Ideological and Regulatory Changes ...

As soon as labour law became an independent discipline with well-established boundaries and a specific objective, i.e., redistribution and rebalancing wealth, it began to be called into question.[33] Thus, after the oil crisis, neo-liberal positions began to ignore the need to distribute income fairly and to rebalance bargaining positions between capital and labour.[34] The argument was that the distribution of income channelled through labour law (but also through taxes) hampered capital returns and, as a result, reduced investment.[35] Today, globalisation has led states

[31] P Davies and M Freedland, *Kahn-Freund's Labour and the Law* (London, Stevens, 1983) 6.

[32] J Fudge, 'Labour as a "Fictive Commodity"', in G Davidov and B Langille (eds), *The Idea of Labour Law* (Oxford, Oxford University Press, 2011) 123.

[33] B Hepple, (ed), *The Making of Labour Law in Europe: A Comparison of Nine Countries up to 1945* (2010) 32.

[34] It is important to differentiate between conservatives and neo-liberals in 1970. While the former gave an important role to the state, trade unions and the protection of workers, neoliberalism held that the state should not interfere in the economy and argued that the power of markets and the maximisation of profits should be the main guide to its functioning. A position held by FA Hayek, *Law, Legislation and Liberty* (London, Routledge, 1980) 89–90 who saw labour law as a special privilege that offered protection from operating according to market laws.

[35] B Jobert and B Théret, 'France: la consécration républicaine du néo-libéralisme', in B Jobert (ed), *Le tournant néo-liberal en Europe* (Paris, Le Harmattan, 1994).

to compete to attract increasingly mobile international funding. As a result, labour law, which sought to ensure fairer distribution of the wealth generated between capital and labour, was rapidly seen as an impediment to attracting international investment.[36] Of course, the fall of the USSR and with it the disappearance of the 'fear' of revolution also gave the economic elites the opportunity to re-impose their vision of the free market.

In addition, the depoliticisation of trade unions and the weakening of their links with communist, socialist and conservative parties reduced the direct influence they had hitherto wielded over labour legislation (links that had previously been a crucial factor).[37] In fact, this now global phenomenon has occurred at different times in history, depending on the social and political context in the different countries. Thus, while the loss of trade union influence over labour and economic policy in many countries began in the 1970s, in countries such as Spain, Portugal and Greece, the contribution of trade unions to the fight against dictators and for democracy was rewarded with comprehensive, modern legislation supporting trade unions, collective bargaining and the right to strike.[38]

Another cause behind the demise of labour regulations was that some well-intentioned reforms brought unforeseen consequences that undermined the rebalancing role of labour law. Thus, the purported strengthening of trade unions through the introduction of trade unions and workers' representatives at company level, which was initially viewed with dread by employers, turned out to be an excellent opportunity to boost company-level bargaining. This had the unexpected effect of breaking with the hitherto centralised industrial relations system.[39] Thus, first, companies were able to put more effective pressure on trade unions to make workers shoulder some of the inherent business risk by threatening workplace closures due to losses, etc. At the same time, some companies began to take advantage of competitive advantages based, not on productivity improvements, but on reductions in labour rights that they had managed to obtain in company-level negotiations, which ended up triggering a downward spiral in workers' rights. This was accompanied by a change of emphasis in the role of unions, from co-regulators of terms and conditions of employment, to monitors and enforcers of employees' legal rights.[40]

Thus, during this period, government supervision of employment, dismissals, etc. was reduced, minimum standards were lowered, leaving more room for negotiation in the field of employment contracts (especially in terms of working

[36] S Deakin, *Renewing Labour Market Institutions* (Budapest, Central European University, 2004) 59–76.

[37] Hepple, and Veneziana, 'Introduction'.

[38] Hepple (ed), *The Making of Labour Law in Europe* (2010).

[39] On this see Boltanski, and Chiapello, The New Spirit of Capitalism, (2005) 288; E López Terrada and T Sala Franco (dir. tes.), La descentralización de la estructura de la negociación colectiva y sus posibilidades de articulación (1999).

[40] W Brown, S Deakin, D Nash and S Oxenbridge, 'The Employment Contract: From Collective Procedures to Individual Rights' (2000) 38 *British Journal of Industrial Relations* 611.

hours), individual and collective rights were downgraded, dismissals were facilitated, temporary and part-time work was encouraged, and many workers were excluded from labour law through 'new forms' of organisation.[41]

Led to a Two-Tiered Labour Market

In the mid-1970s, *directly* dismantling the employment contract rights achieved in the preceding decades would have been highly contentious, despite the new 'prevailing' free market ideology. For this reason, a two-pronged strategy was adopted. Firstly, there was an increase in the number of types of contracts (temporary, part-time) which had fewer employment rights than the standard employment contract (permanent, full-time).[42] Secondly, the ways companies interacted with each other to manage the labour force changed. Thus, recruitment agencies, temping agencies, subcontractors, multi-service providers, company groups and subsequently digital platforms emerged.[43] Their main aim was to circumvent labour regulation and to be able to pass on to the worker the risks inherent to a business.

At the same time, individual bargaining was strengthened, recovering the central role of the employment contract to govern working conditions, and essentially moving back to the end of the nineteenth century.[44] This also promoted the disappearance of career paths shaped by collective bargaining (promotions, seniority bonuses, etc.), giving way to a system of individual rewards based on the employer's discretion and on a system based on performance appraisals and on reaching individual objectives set by the company in the best scenario.[45]

A second consequence was the juridification of disputes. As regulation reduced the role of collective bargaining as a way of governing industrial relations and increased the rights-based perspective of individual workers, human resource managers and trade unions increasingly turned to the courts.[46]

In the end, the rise of flexibility as a paradigm, new methods of business management, the prevailing political ideology and legislative changes in the field of company reorganisation finally led to dismissals becoming 'normal'[47] acts of business management, reducing the financial security for the working class achieved during the golden age of labour law.

[41] Boltanski and Chiapello, *The New Spirit of Capitalism.*

[42] Stone, *From Widgets to Digits.*

[43] A Todolí-Signes, 'The "Gig Economy": Employee, Self-Employed or the Need for a Special Employment Regulation?' (2017) 23(2) *Transfer: European Review of Labour and Research* 193–205.

[44] Even in the field of safeguards, the role of collective bargaining was reduced to give greater emphasis to individual rights: image rights, privacy rights, data protection, work-life balance, the principle of equality, and the right to a fair trial, etc. (J Fudge, 'Labour as a "Fictive Commodity"', in G Davidov and B Langille (eds), *The Idea of Labour Law* (Oxford, Oxford University Press, 2011) 124).

[45] A Todoli-Signes, *El bonus salarial* (Tirant lo Blanch, 2017).

[46] B Hepple, 'Factors Influencing the Making and Transformation of Labour Law in Europe', in Davidov and Languille (eds), *The Idea of Labour Law* 39.

[47] Boltanski Chiapello, *The New Spirit of Capitalism.*

However, the decline of labour law in the 1980s and 1990s did not affect everyone equally. This was precisely because of the strategy pursued, i.e. the creation of new types of employment contracts and the individualisation of working conditions. This meant that initially the changes did not significantly affect skilled workers and those already on the labour ladder. Instead, only the 'weaker' members of the working class (women, immigrants, young people and unskilled workers) were affected. Thus, those who were excluded from the labour market or had been pushed out no longer enjoyed the same protection that they or their parents had previously experienced when they entered or re-entered the labour market. This two-tier market, caused by the system itself, has subsequently been used on countless occasions to push for a reduction in the labour rights of the 'insiders'.[48]

This issue was certainly part of the intellectual acquis of the time advocated by the strongest neo-liberal movements. The maxim of 'there is only the individual' not only helped to destroy collective and class interests in favour of the individualisation of working conditions, but also shattered all class solidarity. The myth of the 'man' who can do anything if he works hard was created,[49] and with it came individual responsibility for failure. Under this way of thinking, those who do not succeed in life, or those who are unable to hold down a job, are the only ones responsible for this failure, deserving neither 'pity' for their situation, solidarity from their better-off comrades[50] nor any help from the state.

This leads us to draw two conclusions. First, it is clear that the demise of labour law has been linked to the division into subgroups of what has been called the working class (understood as all those who live off their labour because they have no capital from which to earn income). In the same way that the golden age of labour protection came from the union of skilled (petty bourgeoisie) and unskilled workers with the same demands that gave rise to a single labour law that protected both groups, its demise came from dividing this group. Thus, the fact that skilled workers, graduates, engineers, and middle managers did not rally because they were not affected by the shifts in labour law made it easier for these changes to take place. This brings us to the second issue, which will be developed in the following section, i.e., contemporary labour law, and how these changes, which initially did not affect this group, have also had a negative impact on the protection of everyone who makes a living from their labour.

[48] That is, those protected by labour law.

[49] A Rand, *Atlas Shrugged*, (New York, Random House, 1957).

[50] We shall not say 'comrades who were luckier' since, according to these tenets, nothing depends on luck but on individual ability. This succeeded in breaking down class solidarity, at least for the purposes of discourse.

3

Changes in the World of Work: Contemporary Labour Law

The Ideological–Political Context

The factors that drove labour law into a period of decline are the same elements shaping it today, but in a more extreme form.

Thus, whereas global production chains led to downward competition between countries' labour regulations caused by the fear of deindustrialisation, today technology (digital platforms, teleworking) has globalised not only industry, but also the service sector, in general. Nowadays, it is relatively easy to place an order for a translation, a website, the design of a logo or the creation of a computer programme anywhere in the world via the internet and, in fact, there are now companies whose business model is based on hiring workers anywhere in the world. Companies such as Freelancer and Amazon Mechanical Turk have millions of workers from all over the world 'signed up' on the platform, waiting for a client, wherever they are, to entrust them with a job. These companies facilitate this provision of services by dividing workers into different categories based on professions, languages, skills and, above all, by ranking the 'quality' of the services they provide.

The globalisation of labour, in the absence of a globalised political and regulatory framework, results in two issues: firstly, it is very easy for companies to circumvent laws (labour, tax, regulatory, etc.) by seeking out countries with less protective legislation; and secondly, ever-increasing competition, which means companies have no choice but to lower their costs even at the risk of non-compliance with legislation. If they don't, another company will step in (increased price competition and reduced effectiveness of labour regulations).

In addition, countries not only have to compete with each other to attract investment to manufacturing, but they also need to compete with the appeal of financial markets, which have become a source of high returns on capital.[1] These

[1] This issue is not a coincidence. It is closely related to the prevailing ideology and politics of the last few decades. The deregulation of financial markets in the 1990s (unparalleled since the crisis of 1929, when financial markets were regulated to prevent a similar crisis in the future), their liberalisation, disintermediation and the creation of new financial products have multiplied the scope for purely speculative profits through which capital is increased without the need for investment in productive activities. L Boltanski and E Chiapello, *The New Spirit of Capitalism* (London, Verso, 2005) 20. Thus, a

markets currently monopolise the lion's share of money moving it away from industrial and productive investment, often without adding any value to society in the shape of goods and services.[2]

Whereas temporary and part-time contracts were the first escape routes from job security, today subcontracting, employment agencies, temping agencies and direct hiring of the self-employed afford a greater variety of loopholes which are increasingly used to compete and to circumvent labour safeguards.

The decline in trade union membership has also been exacerbated in recent decades. According to the OECD (Organisation for Economic Co-operation and Development),[3] in 2015 only 17 per cent of workers were members of a trade union compared to over 30 per cent in 1985. This has direct consequences for collective bargaining representation. In 1985, 45 per cent of workers in OECD member states were covered by a collective bargaining agreement whereas in 2015, this figure was only 33 per cent.[4]

Effectively, the end of Fordist and Taylorist manufacturing systems has undermined the collective bargaining model. This model was based on physical proximity as a way of generating solidarity, of selecting trusted leaders, of reflecting their common interests over and above their differences and, finally, of responding collectively to shared injustices.[5] Thus, new network companies, business groups and subcontracting have alienated workers not only physically but also in the imaginary, creating a perception that they do not share the same interests or purpose.[6]

The growing influence of employers in economic policy, the almost uncritical acceptance of the market as the perfect self-regulator with no need for public intervention, and the shift from Keynesian to openly neo-liberal policies has led to the disappearance of the State and of public administration as the guardians of justice, equity and redistribution. Thus, the role of the State has become secondary. It is now merely a facilitator of market transactions or, at best, an agency that must ensure that the cogs of the market's wheels are *well-oiled*. In the labour market, this has come to mean that, in many cases, the State shoulders business costs. Thus, the State has become responsible for training employees. This is becoming increasingly specialised and is a far cry from the ideal in which the State educates *citizens*. Now, the State must also take care of workers when they are no longer needed (unemployment, retirement), but not to the extent of discouraging them from

large part of the economic crises and the 'necessary' corporate restructurings are nothing more than the effect of the disinvestment of capital in the industrial sector to invest it in the financial sector where profitability is more secure, regardless of the effects on workers or affected regions.

[2] M Mazzucato, *The Value of Everything: Making and Taking in the Global Economy*, (Public Affairs, 2018).

[3] OECD, 'Collective Bargaining in a Changing World of Work' in *OECD Employment Outlook 2017* (Paris, OECD Publishing, 2017).

[4] OECD, 'Collective Bargaining in a Changing World of Work'.

[5] H Arthurs, 'Labour Law After Labour', in G Davidov and B Langille, (eds), *The Idea of Labour Law* (Oxford, Oxford University Press, 2011) 22.

[6] On this, see, K Stone, 'The Legacy of Industrial Pluralism: The Tension Between Individual Employment Rights and the New Deal Collective Bargaining System' (1992) 59 *The University of Chicago Law Review* 575.

working (active ageing, low unemployment benefits), or when they are supposed to be less productive (subsidies for hiring young workers or early retirement for workers over 55). The State even pays to support workers when demand decreases during a short period of time, without these contractual commitments having to be covered by the company (furloughing during COVID-19).

Finally, while in the early years of the demise of labour law, the division between the working class and weaker labour protection centred on the skilled (and highly educated) and the unskilled, its effects now include the skilled.

In addition, other working-class subgroups have gained relevance as identifiers or mobilisers of votes or of grievance, such as issues with race, gender, religion, home region or nationality.[7] Thus, whereas in the 1980s the disengagement of trade unions from politics caused them to lose influence on labour issues, in recent years it is the very concept of labour itself that has lost all political clout. As Trottman stated,[8] workers vote for conservative parties not because they are unaware that these parties weaken labour safeguards which will ultimately undermine their rights, but because these conservative parties serve other interests that are higher priority for them.

Hence, political parties, including the social democrats, have little incentive to use their political capital on social and labour market measures, instead preferring to use it on other measures that will secure them votes. However, despite this apparently straightforward conclusion, it is not clear what is the cause and what is the effect. That is, while improving labour rights may not bring votes today, it could also be that progressive political parties are not providing effective alternatives to the prevailing discourse which are sufficiently appealing to mobilise votes along these lines.[9]

Nevertheless, the existence of other less political and more technical issues (economic and business organisation) defining the world of work today which pose a threat to contemporary labour law should not be overlooked.

The Business Context

The Reduction of Hierarchy and of Control Over Workers

It is well known that Fordism and Taylorism were based on vertically integrated, extremely hierarchical companies, with a host of middle managers charged with

[7] H Arthurs, 'What Immortal Hand or Eye? Who will Redraw the Boundaries?', in G Davidov and B Languille (eds), *Boundaries and Frontiers of Labour Law* (Oxford, Hart Publishing, 2006) 376.

[8] M Trottman, 'AFL-CIO Poll Shows Union Households Boosted Brown' *The Wall Street Journal* (22 January 2010).

[9] Thus, as Boltanski and Chiapello pointed out, the left-wing experts who are close to the political power included employers' demands and, in particular, the demands for flexibility into their culture very quickly (*The New Spirit of Capitalism* 290). Thus, the lack of ambitious alternatives can easily lead voters to give their vote to those who respond to their 'second agenda'.

monitoring employees, and thus the quality and standardisation of the product or service produced for the market. This was done for three reasons: (i) the cultural and educational level of the workers was low and they required precise instructions on how to carry out their work and ensure compliance; (ii) the costs of transmitting information were high, so a large hierarchical middle-management structure was essential to ensure orders and instructions were issued; (iii) there was a great deal of social and labour unrest, i.e., workers' stoppages, strikes, etc, which was countered by business owners with more managers and executives to keep an eye on their employees.

This way of running industrial and service companies was a highly inefficient way of doing business for the companies themselves and it was also strongly criticised by the trade unions. The large workforce supervision structures entailed huge operating costs that contributed little to productivity. Moreover, the lack of worker autonomy led to disaffection with the company, lack of motivation and worker alienation. In fact, it was a vicious circle: the greater the company's control, the greater the workers' discontent, to which employers responded by increasing the number of middle managers which, in turn, generated more conflict.[10]

As a consequence, business management literature began a struggle to largely eliminate this company model. First, this implied the delegitimisation of vertically integrated companies and, on the other, the delegitimisation of hierarchy, planning, authority, supervision and quality control.[11] Two other factors have also influenced the reduction of hierarchy: firstly, the general increase in worker training and culture (paid for by public funds) means that fewer instructions and quality control are required to do a job, with workers' expertise even exceeding that of the employer in many cases. The second factor is information and communication technology. New technologies have reduced transaction costs in a way that was unimaginable until a few decades ago. Nowadays, no large intermediate structures are required to transmit information inside or outside the organisation.

Thus, in response to criticism of company hierarchies and demands for autonomy made by the now better-trained staff, companies did not respond with a greater number of middle managers, but with the search for greater worker autonomy, for engagement through job satisfaction, and the development of concepts such as mutual trust, self-monitoring and control by colleagues and by the market.

In practice, physical, immediate and strict supervision by hierarchical superiors has been reduced, but this does not mean that the company's control over work has disappeared. On the contrary, some monitoring techniques have been replaced with others that are deemed to be more modern and better suited to the new circumstances (employees' new cultural and training skills and the new technologies available).

[10] K Stone, *From Widgets to Digits: Employment Regulation for the Changing Workplace* (Cambridge, Cambridge University Press, 2004) 86.

[11] Boltanski and Chiapello (n 1) 114.

The increase of individualised labour relations and the ability to dismiss has coincided with the appearance of performance appraisals (bonus or dismissal), annual reviews, 360°, etc. The aim is to get workers to do what they have to do without having to instruct them to do so. External and corporate control is replaced with self-control. Thus, workers become their own exploiters, knowing that if they do not do what they are supposed to do, they will be dismissed.

The concepts of individual responsibility and trust become key. Thus, in this new era of business management driven by easy hiring and firing, companies move away from controlling how work is performed by the worker to looking for people who are "trustworthy" and driving betrayers out of the business. In fact, in such a complex and specialised world, with such high levels of training, companies often lack sufficient technical knowledge to give precise instructions. Thus, a company that lacks the know-how to check the work performed, has to rely on monitoring the attitude, rather than the skills, of the employee towards the job.

Group-based bonuses for reaching targets and the ease with which regulations now permit the inherent risks of the business to be passed on to workers in the shape of wage reductions and dismissals (and the fear of unemployment) also lead to control by colleagues and staff. Worker solidarity is broken from the moment that any setbacks suffered by the company are swiftly passed on to the workers, which makes workmates the first ones interested in checking work and reporting unproductive colleagues.[12]

New technologies have also made it easier for customers to monitor the service provided by specific employees. Traditional forms of monitoring and controlling the quality-of-service delivery by workers consisted of company-specific on-the-job training and precise instructions on how to perform a task, coupled with a monitoring system that ensured compliance with instructions. With the advent of digital reputation systems, companies rely on customer reviews made via mobile apps and email to ensure high standards of service delivery. Thus, instead of giving instructions and monitoring performance to ensure quality, companies delegate these functions to customers, and then use this information to make decisions about dismissal.[13]

In general, all these techniques replace hierarchical control with market or market-type control in which legal subordination is no longer necessary since there is economic subordination that performs the same function. Thus, companies nowadays treat their workers as if each one was a company. Workers who are at the mercy of market supply and demand and live with insufficient protection (as well as the threat of unemployment) have no choice but to exercise self-control and to understand what the company and its customers expect of them in advance so

[12] JR Barker, 'Tightening the Iron Cage: Concretive Control in Self-managing Teams' (1993) 38 *Administrative Science Quarterly* 408.

[13] A Todolí-Signes, 'The Evaluation of Workers by Customers as a Method of Control and Monitoring in Firms: Digital Reputation and the European Union's General Data Protection Regulation' (2020) 160(1) *International Labour Review* 65.

that they can tailor their behaviour to these clients' wishes, all without the need for complex, lengthy instructions.

In other words, the dismantling of labour law, and the safeguards from dismissal, increases workers' *economic subordination*. The original premise of the employment contract was to isolate employees from the risks inherent to a business. That is, in exchange for a fixed salary and a promise of continued employment, the worker relinquished any claim to corporate profits. Thus, since employers took the business risk, they were encouraged to train workers to do a good job, to plan the best way to produce, to give the right instructions and to check the quality of service. However, in the absence of job security, the risk and responsibility for business failure and fluctuating economic cycles fall on the worker.

This brings about a number of effects. Firstly, flexibility or freedom to choose working hours and timetables, which can be viewed as a source of freedom and autonomy (in some cases, this is the case) usually implies that the worker is responsible for completing the tasks assigned to them regardless of the time it takes to do so. Again, if a worker does not deliver on this, they will be dismissed. The same applies to the freedom to choose the place of work and teleworking. The company has no interest in checking where or how the work is done, but simply that it is completed to the expected quality standards. Thus, any time or place becomes suitable for work, putting an end to the separation between work and personal life – one of the original principles of labour law.

Secondly, these new organisational methods and ways of working have led to an increase in the intensity of work.[14] Peer control, self-control and fear of unemployment have proved highly effective in increasing the volume of work produced in the same amount of time. It is also common to blame customers for the frenetic pace of work needed to meet demand, thus eliminating worker complaints to the Company.[15] These methods (and threats) force workers to use all their intelligence, observation, strength, speed and endurance for the benefit of the company, simply to keep their job, even at the expense of their emotional and/or physical health (stress, anxiety, depression, burnout).[16] Thus, those who fall sick or simply cannot cope with the new pace of work are pushed out of the company and, ultimately, out of the labour market.

[14] Work intensification refers to an increase in the intensity of effort, and therefore of work effort, related to the 'pace' of work, irrespective of its duration. Pérez Zapata et al, 'Digitalización, intensificación del trabajo y salud de los trabajadores españoles', (2019) 5. Available at: www.ccoo.es/24c0e370fa4b4d1f3682b1780854af9c000001.pdf; Boltanski and Chiapello (n 1) 346.

[15] It is not just a reference to holding a particular customer accountable but, in general, to the market and the way demand works. Thus, a company can easily suggest that if work is not conducted at a particular pace or in a particular way, it will lose customers and have to lay off workers, because other companies will work at that pace or in that way.

[16] The European Occupational Safety and Health Administration stated in its survey on emerging risks that the main source of stress reported by employees is working hours and workload (EU-OSHA, 'Second European Survey of Enterprises on New and Emerging Risks (ESENER-2). Overview Report: Managing Safety and Health at Work' (2013). Available at: www.osha.europa.eu/en/tools-and-publications/publications/second-european-survey-enterprises-new-and-emerging-risks-esener, accessed 29 August 2019).

Thirdly, company-specific training is no longer the responsibility of the firm. Employees must be fully trained if they wish to find a job and cannot expect the company to train them in-house in specific skills, as has occurred in the past. This, in turn, leads citizens/workers to call on the State to pay for and provide more and more specialised training geared to the demands of the labour market. This kind of training is different from the education required as citizens.

In short, the demise of labour law has taken the labour market back to its original starting point, a time when the employer did not need to explicitly state the legal dependence (instructions, supervision and checks ...) granted by the employment contract to obtain the desired performance from their employees, given that the economic subordination of the worker already fulfils this function.

Thus, the company only exerts strict control over its employees (legal dependence) when there is job security. Take, for example, public employment. Given that civil servants benefit from extensive protection against dismissal, the administration must issue instructions and check the work of its employees to ensure the provision of public services. Failure to comply with these instructions justifies dismissal under civil service rules. However, where these safeguards are absent or ineffective, the company has no need to train its employees, issue instructions or check their work, and employees can be given all these responsibilities or risk losing their job. The ease of dismissal enables the company to transfer business risks to employees, while at the same time obliging them to exercise self-control to hold down their jobs.

This is why the meaning of the employment contract, as a trade-off between legal dependence in exchange for job security, can only be sustained if substantial safeguards against dismissal have been implemented. When these are removed, the employer does not need to exercise any direct control over the worker, barring a few exceptions.

Finally, if firms can treat workers as if they were a business thanks to higher levels of training, lower transaction costs and reduced safeguards against dismissal, why not directly hire businesses? Indeed, as we shall now see, outsourcing and subcontracting between firms, including hiring self-employed workers without dependent employees, is one of the main features of the way firms operate today.[17]

Production Outsourcing and Subcontracting

From an economic perspective, the outsourcing of processes in a company aims to bring in knowledge or skills that the company does not have, or that external organisations can provide more efficiently than if the company were to do it in-house.[18] Therefore, outsourcing was originally inextricably linked to sporadic,

[17] D Weil, *The Fissured Workplace, Why Work Became So Bad for So Many and What Can Be Done to Improve It* (Cambridge MA, Harvard University Press, 2014).

[18] RL Click and TN Duening, *Business Process Outsourcing: The Competitive Advantage* (Hoboken, NJ, Wiley, 2004).

non-permanent tasks within the company. In other words, it only made sense to outsource something that had to be done by the firm on a one-off basis, as it was more efficient to internalise something that was ongoing. However, due to changes in mentality and business management techniques, including the desire to downsize companies, reduce middle management, respond quickly to market needs, transfer business risks to a third party and reduce costs, companies began to outsource everything that was not part of the company's core business. Thus, today, an external contractor does not provide efficiency or knowledge that the main company does not have. Instead, in most cases, the original company deliberately decides to stop doing certain tasks and to lay off the permanent workers who performed them in order to hire an external company to carry them out on a contract basis.

The pandemic has provided revealing insights into this way of working and its consequences: let's take the case of Airbnb as an example. Through its website, this organisation acts as a middleman providing access to tourist accommodation. Its brand and its website are the cornerstones of its business. Therefore, if a user/customer (owner or tourist) does not know how to use its website or encounters problems in using it or is unsure about how it works, Airbnb may lose revenue. The importance of customer service for the growth of any company is fundamental. However, this key factor did not stop Airbnb from outsourcing this role to another company (Call Centre) to provide customer services on behalf of Airbnb. When the pandemic hit and sales fell drastically, Airbnb simply had to terminate its contract with the company that provided the call centre services. Thus, it was the subcontracted company that had to make the workers redundant, at its own expense,[19] irrespective of Airbnb's profits or its real need for workers.

The main pretext or justification for this was yet again 'market forces' as fixed laws of nature. The argument is that outsourcing makes the company more flexible and versatile when it comes to discontinuing a line of business, since terminating a contract with another company when part of the production process is no longer required is much cheaper than breaking up or closing down part of the company's own business. However, there is another factor and, at the same time, another consequence: growing inequality between companies themselves.

The accumulation of capital and authorised mergers between companies has led to oligopolies in most sectors. These are dominated by a few companies that control their market through a vast network of subcontractors that are economically subordinate to them. Thus, companies that provide high added value (and have strong bargaining power) no longer wish to keep all the elements of their production process in their parent company, preferring instead to solely hold onto the core of the business to decentralise and subcontract the rest of their processes

[19] In Spain, 1,000 workers were dismissed from the call centre, e.g., Supreme Court of Catalonia 11/12/2020 (No 66/2020). On subcontracting and employment stability see Weil, *The Fissured Workplace* (2014).

to other organisations. This enables them to adapt their cost structure to the needs of the market very easily.

In this way, the existing inequality between organisations has encouraged a process of decentralisation, the upshot of which is that there are 'first-class' companies, i.e., those that retain their productive value, and 'second-class' companies, i.e., ancillary services or those that add little or no value. In short, outsourcing enables better-positioned companies to wield their superior bargaining power over weaker second-class companies which, given their manifest economic subordination, have no choice but to submit to the will of the former. Thus, the first-class companies divest themselves of everything that adds little value or requires greater risk-taking, while the second-class companies must shoulder this burden.

This widespread outsourcing movement partially explains the growth of small establishments and micro-enterprises, including the sharp increase in the number of companies with no employees (they are simply self-employed sole traders) made up exclusively of the 'owner' who is also the one who does the work, thus transforming employees into subcontractors.[20]

An emblematic case of this is the company CEPSA, which sells fuel through its network of petrol stations. At some point in time, not related to a particular economic crisis, the company decided that its less-profitable petrol stations should be managed by self-employed workers. Thus, it told its employees at these petrol stations that if they became self-employed, they could keep their jobs and work in exchange for a commission on the sales of the petrol station they managed, belonging to CEPSA.[21] This example, which is by no means just an anecdote from Spain, represents a way of doing business all over the world. In the US state of California, the Court of Appeal decision of 26 April 2018 ruled on an identical case involving Shell, which owned and operated a petrol station under its company brand managed by a *self-employed* individual.

Of course, on this point, mention must also be made of digital platforms, i.e., the so-called *gig economy*, in which companies offer their services directly to the market, but these services are performed entirely by workers who are not employed by the company. Thus, the platform company sells a product or service which is provided by an independent third party (without employees) with whom it has a formal commercial contract.[22]

[20] Weil, *The Fissured Workplace* (2014).

[21] A Todolí-Signes, 'Falsos autónomos en contrato de Agencia: Análisis a el acta de la Inspección de Trabajo de CEPSA (I)' (2020) *Argumentos en Derecho Laboral*. Available at: www.adriantodoli.com/2020/03/11/falsos-autonomos-en-contrato-de-agencia-analisis-a-el-acta-de-la-inspeccion-de-trabajo-de-cepsa-i/.

[22] On this, see M Cherry, 'Working for (Virtually) Minimum Wage: Applying the Fair Labors Standards Act in cyberspace' (2009) 60(5) *Alabama Law Review* 1077–110; V De Stefano, 'The Rise of the "Just-in-Time Workforce", On-demand Work, Crowdwork and Labour Protection in the Gig Economy' (2016) 37(3) *Comparative Labour Law and Policy Journal* 471; A Aloisi, 'Commoditized Workers. The Rising of On-Demand Work, Case Study Research on a Set of Online Platforms and Apps' (2016) 37(3) *Comparative Labor Law & Policy Journal* 653; EUROFOUND 'Self-employed or not self-employed? Working conditions of economically dependent workers' (Dublin, 2013) Background

However, even in those cases where the subcontractor is a real organisation with workers in its employ, the economic subordination of these firms makes the working conditions of their workers extremely complicated, as they are subject to market constraints as if labour law barely existed.

Thus, if labour law is intended to provide employees with security, the reality is that, when outsourcing takes place, workers are doomed to temporary employment, which is terminated (justified dismissal on objective grounds) as soon as the main company tears up its commercial contract with the outsourced firm, and it is the State that pays workers' income through unemployment benefit. If collective bargaining seeks to prevent workers from competing with each other on low wages, the reality is that with outsourcing, companies compete head-to-head on costs in the free market. This means that the company that manages to pay the lowest wages (through the necessary legal manoeuvring) will be awarded the commercial contract with the main company. Finally, if the employment contract is based on the premise of isolating the worker from the risks inherent to the business, outsourcing and economic subordination between companies will transfer the economic risks of the main company to the contractors and, by extension, to the workers. In essence, outsourcing means excluding these workers from the principles of labour law and subjecting them to market laws.

Outsourcing also means less kinship between workers. The disappearance of large vertically integrated companies makes it difficult to create bonds of solidarity between employees, even when they work in the same physical space, as they have different employers as the focus of conflict.[23]

The outsourcing of production also undermines the scope for negotiating improvements in working conditions with the employer.[24] In fact, a small employer may find himself economically incapable of improving the conditions of their workers, as their finances are also constrained by the economic subordination to which they are subjected by the main employer. Thus, in the absence of head-to-head confrontation with the main company which, when it occurs, can be quickly resolved by the termination of the commercial contract,[25] there is no real way for employees to better their conditions.

paper; JJ Horton and LB Chilton, 'The Labor Economics of Paid Crowdsourcing' (2010) *Proceedings of the 11th ACM conference on Electronic Commerce*; A Todolí-Signes 'The "Gig Economy": Employee, Self-Employed or the Need for a Special Employment Regulation?' (2017) 23(2) *Transfer: European Review of Labour and Research* 193–205.

[23] On this, see R Teodoro et al, 'The Motivations and Experiences of the On-Demand Mobile Workforce' (New York, 2014), *Conference on Computer Supported Cooperative Work and Social Computing (CSCW 2014)* 5.

[24] Weil, *The Fissured Workplace*.

[25] This has happened when strikes by the subcontractor's workforce have been settled by the main company terminating the contract and finding another company to provide the services without any conflict, see W Sanguineti Raymond, 'La tutela sustancial del derecho de huelga en las estructuras empresariales complejas' (2016) 74 *Revista de Derecho Social* 11.

The Technological Context

Automation and Robots

The origin of labour law is inherently linked to technological change. The increments in productivity brought about by technology in the first industrial revolution meant that artisans and small farmers without capital were no longer competitive and had to close their cottage industries. Instead, they had to offer their labour force to companies that did have the capital to invest in the necessary technology. Once they were employed and providing services in industry, the second industrial revolution arrived amid fears that productivity gains would lead to mass layoffs and unemployment. This fear of unemployment was one of the reasons why trade unions demanded job security and stable employment contracts at the time. In turn, employers also agreed to provide stability to curb social conflict and to ensure that workers accepted the introduction of new technologies.

Thus, the importance of the technological context can never be underestimated when talking about the labour market and labour regulations, especially at a time like the present, in the midst of the fourth industrial revolution.[26] Indeed, it is difficult to analyse the labour market and its context without mentioning the relentless process of automation and robotisation in industry and services.[27]

Once again, there is concern that as artificial intelligence and robots take hold, workers will be replaced by new machines that are more efficient in performing tasks or jobs previously carried out by humans. If this is true, technological progress could make millions of people redundant, mainly those performing manual or repetitive jobs.[28]

We are certainly living in a time of technological upheaval.[29] According to the European Centre for the Development of Vocational Training (CEDEFOP), 43 per

[26] K Schwab, *The Fourth Industrial Revolution* (Geneva, World Economic Forum, 2016).

[27] C Frey and M Osborne, 'The Future of Employment: How Susceptible are Jobs to Computerisation?' (2017) 114 *Technological Forecasting and Social Change* 254; D Autor, 'Work of the Past, Work of the Future' (2019) 25588 *NBER Working Paper*.

[28] M Ford, *The Rise of the Robots* (New York, Basic Books, 2016); W Dauth, S Findeisen, J Südekum and N Wössner, 'German Robots – The Impact of Industrial Robots on Workers' (2017) 30 *IAB Discussion Paper* 5.

[29] There is an interesting debate in the literature as to whether technological change is continuous and permanent or, instead, occurs in waves. In this respect, although in the eyes of the average user or citizen it may seem that change is continuous, the specialised theory posits that significant technological change comes in waves, hence the term first, second, third, fourth revolution, etc. The main explanation is that capital investment in technology needs to be amortised before the technology is changed. In fact, from the perspective of the employer (the owner of the capital) each wave of automation reduces the effective cost of labour, which discourages further automation, at least for a while (D Acemoglu and P Restrepo, 'Artificial Intelligence, Automation and Work' (2018) 24196 *NEBER Working Paper* 1491). Indeed, empirical evidence supports this hypothesis. When examining the level of investment in technology in the Netherlands, J Bessen ('How computer automation affects occupations: technology, jobs and skills' (2016) *Boston University School of Law, Law and Economics Working Paper* 15) concluded that there is a high level of investment in some periods and a low level of investment in others.

cent of EU workers have seen a change in the technologies used in their jobs in the last five years.[30] At the same time, predictions suggest that half of all jobs in the developed economy are likely to be automated with robots and new technologies in the light of current technological progress.[31]

However, this is nothing new. These kinds of statements and predictions have been made in the past, but they have never come true. Keynes (1930)[32] predicted that productivity increases would create mass unemployment as humans were replaced by machines,[33] but this did not happen.

Thus, the debate is currently being re-run. First, part of the economic literature argues that this time, technology is different from before, which means that it will not generate increases in employment, as has occurred on other occasions, and will simply push people into unemployment. These arguments are based on the fact that the rapid advance of technologies associated with machine learning, artificial intelligence, language processing by machines, and visual and special perception, among others, will make human replacement feasible at a rate that will make it difficult for the economy to adapt.[34]

Second, some believe that technical progress comes with improvements in the level of employment.[35] The main argument of those who argue that robots will not destroy employment is based on the fact that new occupations and professions are expected to appear. That is, these authors do not argue that robots will not destroy jobs, but rather that these jobs will be replaced by new professions that emerge, either based on this technology (new technological professions) or on new types of services and consumption that are created. Indeed, as Acemoglu and Restrepo argued,[36] the advent of industrial robots, digital technology, computer-controlled machines and AI is destroying jobs, but new occupations such as audiovisual specialists, data managers, analysts and others not related to technology, such as social workers, are also appearing.

[30] CEDEFOP, 'People, Machines, Robots and Skills' (2017) 9121 *Briefing note*; CEDEFOP, *Insights into skill shortages and skill mismatch: learning from CEDEFOP's European skills and jobs survey* (Luxembourg, 2018).

[31] Frey and Osborne, 'The Future of Employment' (2017).

[32] JM Keynes, 'Economic Possibilities for our Grandchildren' in *Essays in Persuasion* (New York, Harcourt Brace, 1932) 358–73. Available at: www.aspeninstitute.org/wp-content/uploads/files/content/upload/Intro_and_Section_I.pdf.

[33] These predictions were repeated in 1965 and 1983, see Acemoglu and Restrepo, 'Artificial Intelligence, Automation and Work'.

[34] E Brynjolfsson and A McAfee, *The Second Machine Age: Work, Progress, and Prosperity in a Time of Brilliant Technologies* (New York, WW Norton & Company, 2014).

[35] M Vivarelli, 'Innovation, Employment and Skills in Advanced and Developing Countries: A Survey of Economic Literature' (2014) 48(1) *Journal of Economic Issues* 123; Bessen 'How Computer Automation Affects Occupations: Technology, Jobs and Skills'; DH Autor, 'Why Are There Still So Many Jobs? The History and Future of Workplace Automation' (2015) 29(3) *Journal of Economic Perspectives* 3.

[36] D Acemoglu and P Restrepo, 'The Race Between Man and Machine: Implications of Technology for Growth, Factor Shares, and Employment' (2018) 208(6) *American Economic Review* 1489.

Thus, what does seem clear is that, regardless of a positive or negative net employment result, the workers affected by the automation of their tasks will be adversely affected (either by losing their jobs and having to look for another type of job, or by wage reductions).[37] Along these lines, the OECD (2019)[38] pointed out that technological change will cause 14 per cent of jobs in the EU to disappear and 32 per cent will probably change completely as a result of the automation of the majority of the tasks inherent to these jobs. Finally, this OECD report joins the so-called 'techno-optimists' and suggests that the disappearance of these jobs will be offset by new jobs stemming from fresh demand. However, it points out that this process may be traumatic for the employees affected and states that many do not have the necessary skills to re-join the subsequent labour market, leading to a poorer quality of life for many workers.

Studies indicate that low-skilled workers with no digital or soft skills will be worst off.[39] The effects analysed so far are listed below.

In the USA, Acemoglu and Restrepo[40] concluded that, for each additional industrial robot, total employment fell by three to six jobs. Similarly, the wages of workers who were not laid off also fell. The same correlation was found in Germany[41] where researchers concluded that 23 per cent of the reduction in industrial employment was caused by robots. Specifically, the introduction of one additional robot resulted in the elimination of two jobs. This study also concluded that the introduction of technology was linked to an increase in capital gains and labour productivity, but a decrease in wages. These authors suggested that the weaker job destruction figures compared to the USA probably stemmed from higher levels of unionisation in the industrial sector in Germany. The argument goes that unions prefer to accept collective wage reductions, rather than allowing any layoffs.[42] In short, the new technology mainly benefits the owners of capital, but not the workers involved.[43]

[37] Dauth, Findeisen, Südekum and Wössner, 'German Robots – The Impact of Industrial Robots on Workers' (2017).

[38] OECD, *Employment* (Paris, 2019).

[39] Acemoglu and Restrepo (n 29); F Pérez García et al, *Cambios tecnológicos, trabajo y actividad empresarial: el impacto socioeconómico de la economía digital* (XXI Premio de Investigación del CES, 2019).

[40] D Acemoglu and P Restrepo, 'Robots and Jobs: Evidence from US Labour Markets' (2017), *NBER Working Paper* 23285; D Acemoglu and P Restrepo 'Secular Stagnation? The Effect of Aging on Economic Growth in the Age of Automation, American Economic Growth in the Age of Automation' (2017) 107(5) *American Economic Review Papers and Proceedings* 174.

[41] Dauth, Findeisen, Südekum and Wössner (n 28).

[42] At the same time, these authors point to another interesting issue. According to the data, the reduction in employment in the German industrial sector resulting from robotisation came not so much from direct redundancies, but from the fact that robotised firms created fewer job opportunities for young people than industrial firms with fewer robots.

[43] D Autor et al, 'The Skill Content of Recent Technological Change: An Empirical Exploration' (2017) 118 (4) *Quarterly Journal of Economics* 1279; M Kehrig and N Vincent, 'Growing Productivity without Growing Wages: The Micro-Level Anatomy of the Aggregate Labor Share Decline' (2017) 244 *Economic Research Initiatives at Duke (ERID)*, Working Paper. Available at SSRN: www.ssrn.com/abstract=2943059.

This outcome should come as no surprise, given that it is consistent with what we have seen so far in the history of the labour market. Technology increases the value of capital and reduces that of workers. As technology becomes more and more relevant to production (once it was the steam engine, now it is robots), those who have no capital, and who live only by selling their labour, have less bargaining power. In a market without labour regulation to rebalance this situation, wages will tend to zero.[44]

In fact, a report by the BBVA Foundation[45] warned of a sharp drop in the share of labour income in the economy and an increase in capital income. This translates into a lower wage bill paid to workers. One of the main factors explaining this decline is digital transformation. This theory argues that new digital firms are less labour-intensive than traditional firms and generate higher profits with a smaller number of workers. Indeed, some authors have highlighted that the sum of the income obtained by GM, Ford and Chrysler in the 1990s is practically identical to that reported by Google, Apple and Facebook, the latter three requiring nine times fewer workers than the former.[46] This means there is little doubt about the importance of technology in replacing labour and as a way of capturing the lion's share of revenue.

Digital Platforms

However, this situation not only occurs as a result of industrial robots, i.e., job cuts. It also happens whenever an element of capital (technological or otherwise) becomes more necessary or essential to be competitive in the marketplace.

This is the case with digital platforms. As illustrated elsewhere,[47] digital platforms do not create new productive sectors or new professions, but essentially change the way services are offered in the market and the way pre-existing professions organise their work.

Thus, the platform becomes an essential element for contacting clients and distributing (using algorithms) tasks among service providers,[48] without there being any reduction in employment in this scenario, as occurs with the use of robots. In any case, the consequences of implementing new technology for workers

[44] JS Coon, 'Collective Bargaining and Productivity' (1929) 19(3), *The American Economic Review* 419–27.

[45] BBVA, 'La participación del trabajo en la renta nacional'. Available at: www.bbva.com/es/la-participacion-del-trabajo-en-la-renta-nacional/.

[46] M Tegmark, *Life 3.0: Being Human in the Age of Artificial Intelligence* (London, Allen Lane, 2017) 121.

[47] A Todolí-Signes, 'Judgment Designating Deliveroo "Rider" an Employee and Analysis of Its Impact on the "Gig Economy"' (2018) 24(4) *Transfer* 487.

[48] A Todolí-Signes, 'The End of the Subordinate Worker? Collaborative Economy, On-Demand Economy, Gig Economy, and the Crowdworkers' Need for Protection' (2017) 33(2) *International Journal of Comparative Labour Law and Industrial Relations (IJCLLIR)* 241–68.

in the sector are the same as those seen in the introduction of robots: reduced wages and poorer working conditions.

In this sense, a report by the JP Morgan Chase Institute[49] based on a study which looked at the salaries of Uber drivers and other digital platforms in the transport sector in 2018 and what these same workers earned in other jobs in 2013, concluded that they earned significantly less in Uber than in their previous jobs. On average, they earned 53 per cent less per month than in their former jobs outside the platform economy. Therefore, in the absence of further research, it would appear that heavily tech-enabled work has a negative impact on workers' total job earnings.

It should be noted, then, that the inclusion of technology, and the need for it to be able to access the market, diminishes the bargaining power of those who make a living from their work without owning it, which is exactly what happened with the first industrial looms. This reduction in bargaining power increases workers' *economic subordination* (they must adapt their behaviour for the benefit of the enterprise or forgo the opportunity to work) and reduces the share of total income that goes on paying wages.

This is not only true for unskilled work, but also extends to skilled work and the liberal professions. According to the COLLEM survey[50] carried out by the European Commission, the majority of jobs carried out on platforms correspond to technical, professional jobs, such as IT and translation, and the liberal professions. The conclusions are that, firstly, the sectors affected by platform jobs are all based on the provision of a service (regardless of whether this requires high or low-level qualifications), and secondly that the platform economy does not in itself create a new productive sector, but instead modifies or transforms pre-existing sectors; it does so by increasing the power of the platform owner over the worker who does not have this platform.

In this context, liberal professions, which have traditionally been independent and have been able to protect themselves without the need for the intervention of labour law, may now be subject to the same risks and the same (or similar) subordination with regard to the owner of the technology (and the brand[51]) as factory workers. Let's take the case of a lawyer who has their own individual practice and who has traditionally reached their clients directly through the market, using and advertising their own brand, and setting their own fees by negotiating with the end client, ie, what is commonly known as a 'liberal' profession. However, if consumers get used to finding their lawyers through digital platforms, these lawyers would

[49] JP Morgan Chase Institute, *Uber drivers are earning 53% less than they did in 2013* (2018). Available at: www.bigthink.com/technology-innovation/uber-drivers-earning-less.

[50] A Pesole et al, 'Platform Workers in Europe Evidence from the COLLEEM Survey' (Brussels, Publications Office of the European Union, 2018).

[51] A platform, in addition to being a technological environment consisting of web portals, mobile applications, algorithms and data collection to 'feed the algorithms', it is also a 'brand' in that it is a distinctive element known and recognised by consumers that is necessary to be able to access the market and provide services.

lose their ability to find clients without registering on a digital platform. This implies that, if they wish to continue to practice, they would either need to have their own digital platform or be included on a third-party platform that provides them with clients (markets their services). Thus, as soon as they depend on a third party to market their services, which provides them with a well-known brand, the process of economic subordination begins, especially if there are few alternative platforms to choose from. Additionally, the digital platform has reasons to control the quality of the lawyer's service provision to protect its brand and reputation, which also reduces the liberal professional's freedom.

Finally, if predictions come true, and consumers increase their demand for services (including those offered by the liberal professions) through digital platforms, these liberal professionals will no longer be able to provide services in their private practices, as they have traditionally done, without registering on a platform. These platforms, which tend to be monopolies or oligopolies,[52] will exert their bargaining power over the workers who provide services using their technology and brand, just as factory owners exerted their power over the workers who needed their machinery to produce goods. In short, this may make these liberal professionals, who traditionally provided totally independent services, become economically or legally dependent on the owner of the platform, in one way or another.[53]

Digital Transformation and Lifelong Training

As well as the challenge we have just described, i.e., the reduction in bargaining power as an outcome of technology, there is another issue on the table: the amount of training required to keep pace with change. Technological change brings two main consequences: first, bargaining power is reduced as workers are replaced by machines and technology becomes an essential element in the provision of services; and, secondly, the necessary changes in skills and abilities required to redeploy workers affected by technology.

Indeed, while some workers may be positively affected by technological change (i.e., those performing skilled jobs such as engineers) given that they are engaged in new jobs with a limited supply of skilled workers, many others (i.e., those doing manual and routine jobs) may be adversely affected. This has been called 'the Digital Divide',[54] and is a phenomenon whereby digital transformation

[52] On this issue, see the conclusions of the report drawn up by IVIE, Pérez García et al, *Cambios tecnológicos, trabajo y actividad empresarial: el impacto socioeconómico de la economía digital*.

[53] Todolí-Signes, 'The End of the Subordinate Worker? Collaborative Economy, On-Demand Economy, Gig Economy, and the Crowdworkers' Need for Protection' (2017).

[54] CW Smith, *Digital Corporate Citizenship: The Business Response to the Digital Divide* (Indianapolis, The Center on Philanthropy at Indiana University, 2002); M Hilbert, 'The End Justifies the Definition: The Manifold Outlooks on the Digital Divide and Their Practical Usefulness for Policy-making' (2011) 35(8) *Telecommunications Policy* 715.

is especially detrimental to workers with little training in digital skills, but also in cross-cutting skills such as speed of learning and adaptability.[55] At the same time, it improves the situation of the skilled, thereby increasing inequality among employees.

It should be noted that not all jobs that *can* be automated will actually *be* automated. The low wages paid to some groups of workers deter automation. Thus, what is likely to happen is that routine jobs with salaries closer to the average will be automated. This leads to an even greater increase in wage polarisation, ie, the disappearance of jobs with average wages, increasing the number of low-wage jobs (where there is no incentive to automate) and high-wage jobs (those that cannot be automated).[56]

Nevertheless, it is important not to fall into 'technological determinism', since these effects, ie, wage reductions and polarisation, do not depend on technology, but on the rules and regulations in force in the society in which they are implemented. Thus, empirical studies show that wage reductions in jobs that can be automated do not occur to the same extent in companies with collective bargaining.[57] They also demonstrate the positive effects of this in terms of wage polarisation and inequality among employees. In fact, there is a large body of empirical research that supports the ability of collective bargaining to reduce wage polarisation and improve worker equality.[58] In general, the studies carried out provide significant empirical support for the ability of collective bargaining to strike a better balance in the distribution of income generated between capital and labour.[59]

[55] Thus, the OECD *Employment Outlook 2019* claims that with the advance of new digital technologies "Not everyone has been able to benefit from the better jobs that have emerged, and many are stuck in precarious working arrangements with little pay and limited or no access to social protection, lifelong learning and collective bargaining".

[56] MJ Böhm, 'The Price of Polarization: Estimating Task Prices under Routine-Biased Technical Change' (2017) 11220 *IZA (Institute for the Study of Labor) Discussion Paper Series*; D Acemoglu and D Autor, 'Skills, Tasks and Technologies: Implications for Employment & Earnings' (2011) in *Handbook of Labor Economics* 1043–171; S Firpo, NM Fortin and T Lemieux, 'Occupational Tasks and Changes in the Wage Structure' (2011) 5542 *IZA (Institute for the Study of Labor) Discussion Paper Series.*

[57] P Denice and J Rosenfeld, 'Unions and Non-union Pay in the United States, 1977–2015' (2018) 5 *Sociological Science* 541.

[58] OECD, *Employment Outlook* (Paris, 2018); J Visser and D Checchi, 'Inequality and the Labour Market: Unions' in Wiemer Salverda, Brian Nolan and Timothy M Smeeding (eds) *The Oxford Handbook of Economic Inequality* (Oxford, Oxford University Press, 2011); B Western and J Rosenfeld, 'Unions, Norms, and the Rise in US Wage Inequality (2011) 76(4) *American Sociological Review* 513.

[59] BT Hirsch, 'What Do Unions Do for Economic Performance?' (2004) 25 *Journal of Labor Research*; SJ Nickell and M Andrews, 'Unions, Real Wages and Employment in Britain 1951–79' (1983) 35 *Oxford Economic Papers* 183; Western and Rosenfeld, 'Unions, Norms, and the Rise in U.S. Wage Inequality; F Jaumotte and C Osorio Buitron, 'Inequality and Labor Market Institutions' (July 2015) *IMF Staff Discussion Note*; Y Abdih and S Danninger, 'What Explains the Decline of the U.S. Labor Share of Income? An Analysis of State and Industry Level Data' (Washington DC, 2017) *IMF Working Paper* (WP/17/167); I Álvarez et al, 'Missing Links in the Inclusive Growth Debate: Functional Income Distribution and Labor Market Institutions' (2011) *International Labour Review*, C Bull, 'Business Cycle and Wage Determination in the United States' in HR Nalbatian (ed), *Incentives, Cooperation, and Risk Sharing: Economic and Psychological Perspectives on Employment Contracts* (Totowa, New Jersey, Roman & Littlefield, 1987).

Finally, before work disappears completely, which is currently no more than science fiction, it is worth asking about the role of labour regulations in the progressive decline of the usefulness of work (the more things machines can do, the less useful the owner of the work becomes). Historical and empirical studies tell us that progressive automation and digital transformation is causing (and will cause) a correlative decline in the bargaining power of those who make a living from their work, making the role of labour regulations even more relevant, if at all possible, as an economic policy instrument.

PART II

The Narrative in Labour Law: Justifications for and Objectives of Labour Regulations

The traditional, broadly accepted narrative justifying the need for labour law is unequal bargaining power. As such, this legal discipline counterbalances the power wielded by business owners. This imbalance stems from civil law and the strict protection of property rights over other rights, and from the weak economic situation of those who have no other way to make a living than to sell their labour power.[1]

In this context, liberal market theories based on free will cannot be applied. It is understood that, given the lack of real choices for workers, there is no freedom to contract and no freedom to bargain, i.e., workers have no real autonomy when it comes to accepting the terms and conditions of employment. This imbalance seems to be the cause of all the misfortunes workers suffer: low wages, excessive working hours, uncertain timetables, transfer of business risks to the worker, health hazards, etc.

Thus, civil law, based on free will, cannot justifiably be applied if this will is not real. Hence the need for: (i) the introduction of state regulations establishing minimum rights; (ii) the promotion of trade union membership to enable real bargaining on equal terms; (iii) or both at the same time to complement each other. This approach has traditionally argued that public regulation, in the shape of labour law, is necessary.

However, political and ideological changes in recent decades have challenged this justification. Liberal and neo-liberal theories believe that the protection of private property is the only state intervention required. Beyond that, the market should be left to function, without public interference, as it always ends up finding a balance.[2]

Specifically, the argument contests the claim that asymmetric bargaining power is sufficient justification for public intervention on two grounds. First, it is argued that unequal bargaining power is a vague concept that does not actually identify which individuals should come under the scope of labour law protection, nor does it justify which exact labour regulations are acceptable to redress the balance.[3]

[1] P Davies and M Freedland (eds), *Kahn-Freund's Labour and the Law* (London, Stevens, 1983).

[2] F Hayek, *Law, Legislation and Liberty* (London, Routledge, 1980).

[3] B Langille, 'Labour Law's Theory of Justice', in G Davidov and B Languille, (eds), *The Idea of Labour Law* (Oxford, Oxford University Press) 105–110.

Second, it is argued that this inequality does not prevent free bargaining,[4] i.e., although the imbalance in bargaining power may make it difficult for the less fortunate party to obtain the desired conditions, this is not the same as claiming there is no free will or real consent.

In any case, and irrespective of the validity of these arguments (which will be discussed below), the reality is that labour law is going through an identity crisis, as a result of a lack of political support, the demise of trade unions, organisational changes at business level, and the globalisation of work brought about by technological change.[5] Hence, international labour theory has begun an intense debate to redefine the purpose and boundaries of labour law.[6]

Thus, this section of the book analyses a series of justifications that support the validity and need for labour law today, whilst also ascribing new functions to labour law in the current political, business and technological context, over and above protecting the weaker party to the contract.[7]

For this purpose, the functions of labour law have been divided into three main groups: (i) efficiency/productivity; (ii) redistribution between capital and labour; and (iii) equality/redistribution among the workers themselves.

[4] H Spector, 'Philosophical Foundations of Labour Law' (2006) 33 *Florida State University Law Review* 1133.

[5] H Arthurs, 'Labour Law after Labour', in G Davidov and B Languille, (eds), *The Idea of Labour Law* (Oxford, Oxford University Press, 2011).

[6] Spector, 'Philosophical Foundations of Labour Law'.

[7] S Sciarra, 'National and European Public Policy: The Goals of Labour Law', in G Davidov and B Languille, (eds), *Boundaries and Frontiers of Labour Law* (Oxford, Hart Publishing, 2006) 258 calls the 'split between old loyalties and new demands'.

4

The Quest for Efficiency

Efficiency, Economic Growth and Productivity

Since its inception, labour law has been concerned with production. Though it is argued that the purpose of labour regulations is to protect workers, the reality is that employment contracts have always been concerned with satisfying business interests. Thus, the granting of managerial power to the company, the possibility of issuing instructions to fulfil the purpose of the contract and legal authorisation for supervision and checking employees' work are provisions far removed from a strictly civil law view of contract theory, but which have been deemed necessary to achieve legitimate ends such as economic growth, competitiveness and efficiency.

In recent years, this version of the discipline has gained traction by conceptualising labour law as the 'law of the labour market'.[1] The forerunners of this school of thought argued that the discipline aims to regulate the labour market so that it works properly for the common good. From this theoretical perspective, labour law promotes economic growth by supporting and facilitating labour market operations. The justification for the discipline, therefore, stems from the need to regulate the labour market, admitting that it has market failures, in order to become efficient.[2]

While these authors' tenets embrace a market ideology,[3] the fact is that they all diverge from the concepts of the neoclassical labour market model. Thus, while neoclassical arguments advocate the innate capacity of the labour market to self-regulate, and to find a balance without the need for public intervention, generally tending towards deregulation, authors who advocate a 'law of the labour market' reject these 'magical' capacities attributed to the market.[4] From this perspective,

[1] S Deakin and F Wilkinson, 'Justifications and Techniques of Legal Regulation of the Employment Relation', in H Collins, P Davies and R Rideout (eds), *Legal Regulation of the Employment Relation*, (London, Kluwer, 2001); H Collins, 'Regulating the Employment Relationship for Competitiveness' (2001) 30 *Industrial Law Journal* 17; C Arup, P Gahan, JB Howe, RS Johnstone, R Mitchell and A O'Donnell, *Labour Law and Labour Market Regulation: Essays on the Construction, Constitution and Regulation of Labour Markets and Work Relationships* (New South Wales, Federation Press, 2006); A Hyde, 'What Is Labour Law?' in G Davidov and B Langille (eds), *Boundaries and Frontiers of Labour Law* (Oxford, Hart Publishing, 2006); P Davies and M Freedland, *Towards a Flexible Labour Market: Labour Legislation and Regulation since the 1990s* (Oxford, Oxford University Press, 2007).

[2] Davies and Freedland, *Towards a Flexible Labour Market* (2007).

[3] D Cabrelli and R Zahn, 'Civil Republican Political Theory and Labour Law', in *Philosophical Foundations of Labour Law* (Oxford, Oxford University Press, 2018) 107.

[4] Hyde, 'What is Labour Law?' (2006) 54.

labour law serves a purpose precisely because the labour market is flawed and is incapable of achieving the desired economic and social objectives on its own.

As Solow suggested,[5] the neoclassical theory that the labour market can be flexible in terms of price (wages) and quantity (level of employment) until there are no more efficient operations that can take place (employed staff) does not stand up to empirical scrutiny. Reality shows that low wages and a persistent level of involuntary unemployment could be the outcome of a 'deregulated' market. Therefore, there is no natural trend towards full employment in the free market. Thus, given that unemployment is an inefficient choice and a waste of 'resources', from the market ideology's own perspective, there is an opportunity for economic policy to improve the state of the economy, through labour law.

The assumption that if everyone acts selfishly, the maximum benefit is obtained for society thanks to the 'invisible hand of the market'[6] was refuted by the Nobel Laureate in Economics John Nash, who demonstrated, in his famous 'Nash equilibrium', that, in many cases, if stakeholders managed to cooperate instead of acting selfishly, they would all end up better off.[7] However, as this author also suggested, economic agents do not normally have enough incentives to cooperate and work together, making external intervention (which may well be public) advisable to obtain the maximum benefit (maximum utility) for all those involved.

To explain this problem, Nash used the well-known 'prisoner's dilemma'. A game theory problem in which two convicts, who have committed a crime together, are separately given the chance to confess, with the first one to do so being given a reduced sentence and the other one being convicted. The problem also states that if neither of them confesses, the police would have no evidence to convict either of them, so both would go free. In this scenario, the best approach for the two prisoners is to cooperate with each other and not to confess. However, their selfish actions and not knowing what the other is going to do, brings an irresistible incentive to confess which will leave them both worse off than if they had cooperated with each other by keeping their mouths shut. Thus, by acting rationally and selfishly, they are both worse off than if they had cooperated. This scenario in which stakeholders acting egotistically end up worse off than if they had cooperated occurs on many occasions in the economy and is known as 'market failure'.[8]

Thus, labour regulations would be justified by identifying these market problems (market failures or situations in which freely acting parties fail to achieve the greatest possible social welfare) and intervening through regulations that would bring about optimum efficiency or would at least improve on the previous unregulated situation.

[5] R Solow, *The Labour Market as a Social Institution* (Oxford, Blackwell, 1990) 50, 76.

[6] A Smith, *La riqueza de las naciones* (1776).

[7] On this, see G Hardin, 'The Tragedy of the Commons' (1968) 162 (3859) *New Series* 1243.

[8] This analysis has been applied to workers participation by DI Lavine and L Tyson, 'Participation, Productivity, and the Firm's Environment', in AS Blinder (ed), *Paying for Productivity: A Look at the Evidence* (Washington DC, The Brookings Institution, 1991) 183–237; RB Freeman, and EP Lazear, 'An Economic Analysis of Work Councils' in J Rogers, and W Streeck (eds), *Works Councils: Consultation,*

Before analysing the justification of these assumptions, it is important to specify the objective of this proposed 'law of the labour market'. The aims of this law are economic growth, competitiveness and efficiency, as mentioned above. Although these three concepts are potentially confusing, they respond to very different realities. Indeed, although the three concepts may seem similar in terms of the values pursued by society, the reality is that they are sufficiently different for this book to choose to concentrate on efficiency over the other two.

Firstly, 'economic growth' is based on increasing the output generated by an economy without considering the price of this growth in terms of labour, social, environmental and other costs. Secondly, competitiveness refers to the return obtained by the company (shareholders) for each monetary unit invested in obtaining that return, so when we talk about competitiveness, we are referring to the interest of one part of society, not society as a whole, in obtaining a return on its investment. Thus, for example, competitiveness can be increased by simply reducing wages without creating social welfare (e.g., the reduction in wages could lead to a drop in demand and thus to lower economic growth and inequality).

Finally, productivity/efficiency (in this book they are treated as interchangeable concepts, although this is not the case in all circumstances as we had the opportunity to demonstrate in the book *Salario y productividad*[9]) refers to the quantities of product obtained taking into consideration the costs required to make them. Thus, productivity increases if a society produces more with the same resources, and if the same quantities are produced with fewer resources. So, while economic growth does not take costs or cost savings into account, efficiency does.[10]

Market Failures

As Deakin states 'the blind spot of neoliberalism, in its turn, is its inability to analyse the necessary role of regulation in a market context. (…) The goal of a perfectly competitive market order necessitates the intervention of ever more forms of state intervention into market processes'.[11] In this sense, the literature[12] has pinpointed

Representation, and Cooperation in Industrial Relations (Chicago IL, University of Chicago Press, 1995) 27–50.

[9] A Todolí-Signes, *Salario y productividad* (Tirant lo Blanch, 2017).

[10] Thus, establishing efficiency as an objective of labour law makes it compatible with theories such as 'degrowth', which undoubtedly aim to reduce the social and environmental costs of certain forms of production.

[11] S Deakin, *Renewing Labour Market Institutions* (Budapest, Central European University, 2004).

[12] Hyde, (n 1); GK Dow, 'The New Institutional Economics and Employment Regulation', in BE Kaufman (ed), *Government Regulation of the Employment Relationship* (Madison WN, Industrial Relations Research Association, 1997) 64. Although others can be added as 'Public Goods' in the sense that the shortage of skilled labour is a problem for the whole industry but individual employers do not want to invest in training, see D Belman, and M Belzer, 'The Regulation of Labor Markets: Balancing the Benefits and Costs of Competition' in Kaufman (ed), *Government Regulation of the Employment Relationship* (1997) 188.

a series of market failures that would warrant legislative intervention to justify labour regulations. These are: (a) information asymmetries; (b) inelasticity of supply; (c) collective action problems; (d) low level of trust and cooperation; (e) transaction costs; and (f) negative externalities.

Information Asymmetries

One of the basic premises that must be met for markets to function properly is that all the agents involved must have perfect information. This means that they must be aware of all the available options, the short and long-term effects of each interaction, and so on. Obviously, this requirement does not occur in the labour market. On the contrary, a firm does not know how productive a particular worker will be and whether there are other workers on the market who would be a better fit. In turn, workers are also unaware of whether there are better opportunities in the market for them or what added value the company obtains from their labour. If there is a need to obtain this unknown information, this entails greater costs (e.g., think of the cost of a worker looking for several jobs, or an employer looking for several workers for one job) and mistrust between the parties.

Thus, in order to reduce information asymmetries, the imposition of transparency obligations on companies, such as those arising from Directive (EU) 2019/1152 of the European Parliament and of the Council of 20 June 2019 on transparent and predictable working conditions in the European Union, are justified, as are the obligations to inform and consult works councils and trade unions in collective bargaining processes, collective dismissals, etc.

For the company, the comprehensive options provided by the legal system for the supervision and checking of workers would be justified to solve the problems arising from information asymmetries.

One of the major issues caused by not having perfect information is the mistakes people make when calculating the risks of a specific harmful event happening to them. In an environment of uncertainty, workers are likely to under-insure against income-damaging contingencies in the event of illness, unemployment or retirement because they underestimate their risks and consequences (so-called economic myopia). Sufficient insurance cover would be purchased by a rationally acting agent with perfect information. The solution to this comes from social security rules, which force individuals to behave rationally and insure themselves against loss of income in certain circumstances.[13]

In fact, these risk coverage systems are vital for those who do not have alternative sources of income, such as capital, shares, movable property or real estate

[13] In addition to solving market failures, social protection also improves economic growth by stabilising consumption in times of economic crisis, providing training for the unemployed, etc. see CSI, *Invertir en protección social y su impacto en el crecimiento económico* (CSI, 2021).

income, and are precisely those who acquire the lowest level of coverage when they are not obliged to do so, mainly because they need their scarce income to survive.

However, the way the market works means that all agents must have the same obligations to acquire coverage, including them in the social security system at the same level, preventing exclusion from coverage from becoming an element of competition between workers. Indeed, if workers could choose not to have social security cover at the cost of being exposed to risk, employers would hire these people, because of the lower cost, leaving the others unemployed. This would lead to a 'race to the bottom' in which all workers would have to accept not being covered to have access to a job. This is an anti-efficiency outcome.

Other economic reasons justify making the social security system public and universal. An unregulated private system would only insure those workers with a low risk of losing their jobs against unemployment, leaving the most vulnerable workers without protection. Instead, these workers would have to resort to public social security coverage: which would be much more costly as the system would not be able to diversify the risk to less vulnerable workers.[14] Thus, there is also an efficiency rationale for social security to be public (or at least regulated) and universal.

Transaction Costs and Collective Action Problems

Individual negotiation of new contracts is costly. If each new labour market transaction had to come with an individual schedule of the specific duties to be performed (tasks, specifications, qualifications, etc.), the salary to be paid and all other contingencies that may occur during the contract period (which is expected to be long or permanent), companies would waste huge amounts of resources. In turn, workers would also have to engage in an arduous process of information gathering, about the market value of their job, what the competition is offering, etc., which would also be costly and inefficient. This is the reason why collective bargaining and the standardisation of job categories, with their assigned tasks, qualifications, salaries and benefits, are justified.[15]

Transaction costs have fallen dramatically in recent years, thanks to technology. An example of this is the platform economy companies who use applications to interact with their employees. However, even these organisations have not relinquished the standardisation of employment contracts, i.e., all riders in a company have the same working conditions. Therefore, it seems that collective bargaining

[14] S Deakin, 'The Contribution of Labour Law to Economic and Human Development', in G Davidov and B Languille, (eds), *The Idea of Labour Law* (Oxford, Oxford University Press, 2011) 165.

[15] Hyde (n 1) 57; J Albrecht, 'Search Theory: The 2010 Nobel Memorial Prize in Economic Sciences' (2011) 113(2) *The Scandinavian Journal of Economics* 237.

and representation can still be justified to reduce transaction costs for companies and workers.[16]

In fact, as Davidov pointed out,[17] civil law is not prepared for, nor does it efficiently regulate, collective action problems. Entering into individual, worker-by-worker negotiations is not the only problem with a labour contract.[18] Imagine renegotiating contracts one by one in case of a collective transfer or a production change that involved modifying employees' tasks. Obviously, this does not seem complicated in a world where the bargaining power of workers is zero and they are only contract-acceptors or simply adhere to the wishes of the employer. However, in a situation where workers possess a modicum of power, bargaining can be arduous and complex.

Therefore, we could actually call collective bargaining and bargaining power '*Schrödinger's bargaining power*'. That is, either workers have absolutely no bargaining power and, in this scenario, collective bargaining is justified by the lack of individual free will; or workers have some bargaining power and collective bargaining is justified by the high transaction costs (and inefficiency) that one-to-one negotiations involve. However, it does not seem plausible to argue that collective bargaining is irrelevant on the grounds that both arguments (workers have/do not have bargaining power) are valid at the same time.

Civil law is equally inefficient when it comes to handling conflicts with employees. Thus, bringing individual lawsuits for a collective legal problem, e.g., closing the company canteen, makes no sense from many perspectives, including that of efficiency. Thus, the legal system needs to provide special collective solutions to problems of this kind.

Low Level of Trust, Cooperation and Conflict

One of the main problems highlighted by economists about the neoclassical labour market model is that it treats the labour market as if it were a trading market (e.g., a market to buy and sell melons).[19] The criticism made by these economists does not stem from the fact that the neoclassical model treats workers as a commodity from a moral or ethical perspective, but because a 'melon' and a job are substantially different 'commodities'. In this sense, the argument states that while a melon

[16] A Todolí-Signes, 'The End of the Subordinate Worker? Collaborative Economy, On-Demand Economy, Gig Economy, and the Crowdworkers' Need for Protection' (2017) 33(2) *International Journal of Comparative Labour Law and Industrial Relations* 241–68 (IJCLLIR).

[17] G Davidov, *A Purposive Approach to Labour Law* (Oxford, Oxford Monographs on Labour Law, 2016).

[18] O Williamson, M Wachter and J Harris, 'Understanding the Employment Relation. The Economics of Idiosyncratic Exchange' (1967) 6 *Bell Journal of Economics and Management Science* 250; O Williamson, *The Economic Institutions of Capitalism* (New York, Free Press, 1985).

[19] JT Addison and BT Hirsch, 'The Economic Effects of Employment Regulation: What are the Limits?', in Kaufman (n 12) 127.

is bought to be consumed on the spot and has no opinions or preferences about what will happen to it, a worker is usually hired for a long period of time and has his or her own independence.

This difference is pointed out mainly because, while the melon purchaser does not need the melon's cooperation (the property rights over the melon can be fully exercised), the same is not true for an employee.[20] Thus, for a company to function, the worker's collaboration and cooperation are necessary, even beyond the provisions of the contract,[21] and, I would add, beyond contractual good faith.

Thus, it has been contended that an employer's opportunistic (or simply unilateral) behaviour can lead to worker discontent at a macroeconomic level (voluntary unemployment) and at a microeconomic level (non-cooperation with the employer), both resulting in inefficiencies.

Thus, this occurs in cases where employers can push wages below the market rate due to monopolistic (monopsonistic) or strategic behaviour, for example. In such cases, 'artificially low' wages may lead to low incentives for workers to offer their labour to firms, thus creating unemployment, which is the same effect as when firms use their monopolistic power not to remove dangerous or unhealthy working conditions due to a lack of compulsory regulation. In these scenarios, minimum wages or collective bargaining can bring wages back to their market 'optimum' while simultaneously raising wages and employment. In this way, the excess profits that employers make through their market power are absorbed by the costs of employing additional workers, making society generally better off through more efficient allocation of resources.[22]

Nobel Laureate in economics David Card and Alan Kreuger conducted an empirical study of fast-food industry workers and found that increases in the minimum wage do not necessary lead to a decline in employment opportunities. The study concluded that small increases in the minimum wage could lead to expanded employment opportunities and thus to increased efficiency.[23]

In fact, a report published by the OECD[24] found that monopsony or oligopsony in the labour market, understood as the power of the employer to fix wages, can harm the economy in much the same way as a monopoly. In this sense, it is argued that the firm with this bargaining power has every reason to keep wages below their competitive level by reducing the number of employees below the optimum number, since hiring more employees would force it to increase the wages

[20] P Marginson, 'Power and Efficiency in the Firm: Understanding the Employment Relationship in C Pitelis (ed), *Transaction Costs, Markets and Hierarchies* (Oxford, Blackwell, 1993).

[21] A Fox, *Beyond Contract: Trust, Power, and Work Relations*, (London, Allen & Unwin, 1974).

[22] A Manning, *Monopsony in Motion: Imperfect competition in Labor Markets* (New Jersey, Princeton University Press, 2003) 15–16; FD Blau and LM Kahn, 'Institutions and Laws in the Labor Market', in O Ashenfelter and D Card (eds), *Handbook of Labour Economics* (North-Holland, Elsevier, 1999); Addison and Hirsch (n 19) 131.

[23] D Card and A Kreuger, *Myth and Measurement: The New Economics of the Minimum Wage* (New Jersey, Princeton University Press, 1995) 20–69.

[24] OECD, *Competition in Labour Markets* (Paris, OECD, 2020).

of the existing workforce, and reduce its output, thereby increasing the prices of the products it puts on the market. Thus, the bargaining power of employers over workers secured either through company mergers, or through *de-unionisation*,[25] or through labour market 'frictions' (fear of unemployment, workers' mobility costs, job search costs) damages the economy.

Monopsony is a situation that is anything but theoretical. In fact, a study carried out in the USA to analyse the concentration index of firms in the labour market[26] found a high level of market concentration. It concluded that between 17 and 33 per cent of jobs were in highly concentrated markets. In turn, other empirical studies analysing the effects of concentration on wages found that it reduced overall wage levels in these firms.[27] Indeed, as Philippon pointed out,[28] there is a consensus that corporate mergers are harming workers.[29]

This is also true for digital platform employment. Online platforms operate in a system in which, due to high entry costs and network economies, the more users a platform has, the more attractive it becomes to other users in comparison to its competitors, and there is a tendency towards concentration (*winner takes all* model[30]). This, in turn, leaves workers with little real choice to seek work on alternative platforms. Dube et al.[31] analysed the market power of one of the largest global digital labour platforms, *Amazon Mechanical Turk*, and concluded that the company held a monopsonistic position over workers that was exploited to capture the lion's share of income.

All in all, regardless of whether a monopsony exists, the reality is that low wages are detrimental to efficiency and innovation. When companies are in a position to push workers' wages down, they can afford to forgo other measures required to be competitive, such as reorganising production, training company managers, upgrading technology to become more productive, etc and there are few incentives to do so.[32] Thus, inefficient firms can survive in the market on the back of low wages. In turn, this reduces the incentives for other firms to invest in innovation.

[25] E Benmelch, NK Bergman and H Kim, 'Strong Employers and Weak Employees: How does Employer Concentration Affect Wages?' (2018) 24307 *NBER Working Paper*. RB Freeman and JL Medoff, *What Do Unions Do?* (New York, Basic Books, 1984).

[26] JA Azar, M Marinescu, M Steinbaum and B Taska, 'Concentration in US Labor Markets: Evidence from Online Vacancy Data' (2018) 24396 *NBER Working Paper*.

[27] E Benmelch, NK Bergman and H Kim, 'Strong Employers and Weak Employees: How Does Employer Concentration Affect Wages?' (2018) 24307 *NBER Working Paper*; D Berger, K Herkenhoff and S Mongey, 'Labour Market Power' (2019) 25719 *NEBER Working Paper*.

[28] T Philippon, *The Great Reversal* (Cambridge MA, The Belknap Press of Harvard University Press, 2019) 281.

[29] N Countouris, V De Stefano and I Lianos, 'The EU, Competition and Workers' Rights' (2021) 2 *Center for Law, Economics and Society. Research Paper Series*.

[30] A Todolí-Signes, 'The "Gig Economy": Employee, Self-Employed or the Need for a Special Employment Regulation?' (2017) 23(2), *Transfer: European Review of Labour and Research* 193–205.

[31] A Dube, J Jacobs, S Naidu and S Suri, 'Monopsony in Online Labour Markets' (2018) 24416 *NBER Working Paper*.

[32] Deakin and Wilkinson, 'Justifications and Techniques of Legal Regulation of the Employment Relation', in Collins, Davies and Rideout (eds), *Legal Regulation of the Employment Relation*, (2001) 55.

Basically, they will not be able to earn what they deserve as they have to contend with firms who sell their products at lower prices, not because they are efficient, but because they pay their labour force low wages.

In the long run, the success of an economy depends on productivity based on innovation, development, design and product quality. All these strategies are incompatible with underpaid workers.[33] This highlights the importance of labour regulations (minimum wage, collective bargaining at industry level) applying to all firms equally in a sector, since a firm's ability to pursue high productivity strategies to improve its competitiveness is limited if its rivals compete on the basis of low costs and job precarity (hence the need for collective bargaining at industry level to prevent competition based on poorer working conditions). As Commons – Father of the institutionalism in USA[34] – said: 'It is an application of well-recognized principle of political economy that the competition of the worst employers tend to drag down the best employers to their level.'[35]

Again, minimum wages and collective bargaining help to boost efficiency, thus encouraging firms to invest in innovation to remain competitive.

Digital platforms are a prime example of what under-innovation in technology can do. Many people are surprised to see hundreds of people on bicycles making deliveries in cities in the 'developed' world. The platforms use arguments related to environmental welfare and delivery drivers' hobbies to justify the use of bicycles instead of other motor vehicles. However, there is a more prosaic, economic reason behind it.

Since the company pays the riders per delivery and not per hour of work, there is no incentive to upgrade the digital platform delivery industry. However, if the company had to pay per hour of work, and according to a minimum wage, it would have every incentive to ensure high worker productivity in the shape of the maximum possible number of deliveries per hour to maximise the return on the employee's wages. In turn, this would give the firm an incentive to purchase motor vehicles for its delivery drivers so that they could deliver as many orders as possible during the working day. However, with no minimum wage and an infinite supply of workers (unemployment), the firm has no incentive to invest in technology to make the worker more productive. It is enough to use more workers to achieve the delivery output level required by its customers. This is a highly inefficient solution for the economy as a whole and severely damages a country's productivity.[36]

Moreover, low wages for workers mean that society lacks purchasing power, perpetuating a downward spiral of decline and unemployment.[37] Thus, the minimum

[33] Deakin and Wilkinson (n 1) 60.

[34] Kaufman, 'The Old Institutionalists', in Kaufman (n 12) 24.

[35] JR Commons, *Labor and Administration* (New York, McGraw-Hill, 1923) 411.

[36] A Todolí-Signes, *El trabajo en plataformas digitales en la Comunidad Valenciana* (Cátedra de Economía Colaborativa, Universitat de Valencia, 2019).

[37] R Edsforth, *The New Deal: America's Response to the Great Depression* (Oxford, Blackwell Publishers, 2000); A Banerjee and E Duflo, *Good Economics for Hard Times* (New York, Hachette, 2019) 82.

wage and collective bargaining are seen as the legislative response to halt this downward slide.[38]

In addition, opportunistic behaviour by employers can also lead to a lack of cooperation on the part of workers and, by extension, to inefficiencies.[39] In general terms, it is argued that although managerial control and supervision over workers is essential for efficient production, excessive use of this control prevents the development of more efficient working relationships based on cooperation and information sharing.[40]

Investment in human capital and training is key to improving business productivity and efficiency.[41] To do so, workers need to invest time and effort in gaining company-specific skills and knowledge. Workers will only have an incentive to do so if they can expect a long contractual relationship with the employer in exchange for acquiring this knowledge. However, the employee does not know whether the employer really intends to keep them on the payroll for a long or a short period of time, so the fear of opportunistic behaviour by the employer may discourage employee training, making both parties worse off.[42]

As empirical studies have shown, high staff turnover in a company can lead to poor productivity. In fact, economic theory argues that workers on temporary contracts are less productive due to the very nature of temporary work.[43] According to an observational experiment carried out by Autor,[44] it was found that higher dismissal costs were positively linked to job productivity gains. The training invested in temporary and high-turnover employees, their on-the-job experience, as well as any incentive to work hard is lower than that of permanent employees (who are effectively protected against dismissal). Thus, a temporary worker's commitment to the tasks assigned to him can only be as great as the commitment the employer makes to them by giving them a temporary contract.

This justifies the legal preference for permanent contracts over temporary contracts, as well as severance pay in the face of arbitrary dismissals that effectively protect stable employment. Therefore, today's 'new forms of business organisation'

[38] M Cherry, 'Working for (Virtually) Minimum Wage: Applying the Fair Labor Standards Act in Cyberspace' (2009) 60(5) *Alabama Law Review*.

[39] On the productivity benefits of worker cooperation in companies see J Able and FR Fitzroy, 'Cooperation and Productivity: Some Evidence from West German Experience' (1980) 14(2) *Economic Analysis and Workers Management* 163.

[40] H Collins, 'Justification and Techniques of Legal Regulation of the Employment Relations', in Collins, Davies and Rideout (n 1) 7–11.

[41] A Alba Ramírez, 'Capital humano y competitividad en la economía española: una perspectiva internacional' (1993) 56 *Papeles de economía española* 131. There has been historic criticism that technology-driven productivity gains generally led to a reduction in employment, E Huertas Arriba and MC Larraza Kintana, 'Tecnologías de la información e innovación organizativa en la empresa española' (2010) 340 *Economía industrial* 57.

[42] Deakin 'The Contribution of Labour Law to Economic and Human Development' 160.

[43] S Ruesga Benito, 'Reforma laboral, salarios y productividad en España' (2005) 55(2) *Comercio Exterior*, 174, 176 and 178.

[44] DH Autor, et al, 'Does Employment Protection Reduce Productivity? Evidence from US States' (2007) 117(521) *The Economic Journal* F189.

(subcontracting) should be rejected if they allow the company to pass on business and economic cycle risks to the worker. The same goes for reductions in dismissal protection given that they produce socially inefficient results from an economic point of view.

In this sense, if workers are to contribute to productivity improvements, they need to be given job security.[45] No worker will be willing to show a cooperative spirit in the search for greater productivity if they have no stability in the company and if there are insufficient guarantees against dismissal. Workers need to believe that the productivity improvements they bring through hard work will not lead to their own dismissal. Note that the reference here is to job security, not to employment security. The European 'flexicurity' strategy seeks, in theory, to exchange job security for employment security, which can indirectly discourage employees from improving productivity in a company. Indeed, as mentioned above, some studies have confirmed that an increase in dismissal costs is positively linked to gains in labour productivity.[46] Consequently, as posited above, this would justify labour regulations that protect employees from arbitrary dismissals to promote business efficiency.

In general, preventing opportunism and 'abuse' enhances employee cooperation, but above all it reduces social conflict such as strikes and work stoppages. One of the major problems in increasing productivity and efficiency in the past was precisely the high degree of conflict between employers and workers. This complex situation not only caused social conflict, violence and deaths, but also reduced efficiency and production, in terms of the number of working hours lost to strikes, arguments, confrontations, etc. Thus, once again, as a guarantor of social welfare, the State must intervene by curbing abusive practices for the sake of efficiency and growth, among other reasons.

As we have seen so far, there are good reasons to restrict corporate power for the benefit not only of workers, but also of the employer himself and the economy in general in terms of productivity, national competitiveness and economic growth. Thus, given these economic justifications, labour reforms that promote freedom of enterprise, unilateral business power and free will as the best way to improve the economy must be rejected. In fact, unilateral business power can end up damaging the country's economy and taking the employer's own company down with it. It is difficult to accept that the private property rights of a business owner can be used to undermine economic growth and the common good. Therefore, legislative intervention is necessary and justified to curb inefficient employer behaviour and to promote business productivity for the benefit of society.

History proves that the private sector has often lagged in implementation of efficient labour practices. Legislation has been indispensable to the propagation of efficient labour practices. Before the First World War, when 12-hour shifts

[45] Kelley and Harrison, 'Unions, Technology and Labor Management Cooperation', in Lawrence Mishel and Paula Voos (eds), *Unions and Economic Competitiveness* (New York, ME Sharpe, 1991).

[46] Autor et al, 'Does Employment Protection Reduce Productivity? Evidence from US States' F212.

were common, scientific managers and industrial psychologists established that productivity at work declined sharply after eight hours. Empirical studies found that conversion to an eight-hour work day was inexpensive because the increase in sustained work effort balanced the decline in working time. Despite such evidence, few employers shifted to eight-hours shift voluntary until it became law.[47]

Today, one of the most notable examples centres on the issue of sharing profits with employees. Although economists agree on its benefits for the companies and the economy, very few countries have actually regulated this.[48] Dozens of theoretical[49] and empirical studies[50] argue that employee profit-sharing improves a company's productivity, as it brings greater cooperation between the company and its employees. In addition, it mitigates the severity of economic downturns and reduces unemployment and the number of companies that go out of business when there is an economic crisis. In fact, employee profit-sharing schemes have been advocated by the European Commission for decades, which has encouraged Member States to adopt them, but without success.[51] Thus, there is sound economic justification for countries to introduce or promote this type of remuneration scheme, though this has not led to the implementation of the corresponding labour regulations.[52]

[47] Belman, and Belzer, 'The Regulation of Labor Markets: Balancing the Benefits and Costs of Competition'.

[48] A Todolí-Signes, *Salarios y productividad* (Tirant lo Blanch, 2017).

[49] M Weitzman and F Kruse, 'Profit Sharing and Productivity' in *Paying for Productivity: A Look at the Evidence* (ed AS Blinder) (Washington, DC, The Brookings Institute, 1990); R Drago and GK Turnbull, 'On the Incidence of Profit Sharing' (1996) 31 *Journal of Economic Behavior & Organization*; S Estrin and S Wadhwani, 'Profit-sharing' in D Sapford and T Zafiris, (eds), *Current Issues In Labor Economics* (New York, Macmillan, 1990).

[50] ML Weitzman, 'Some Macroeconomic Implications of Alternative Compensation Systems' (1983) 93 *Economic Journal* 763; ML Weitzman, *The Share Economy* (Cambridge MA, Harvard University Press, 1984); ML Weitzman, 'Profit Sharing as Macroeconomic Policy' (1985) 75 *American Economic Review* 41. In general, profit sharing improves productivity and other types of wages as well. EP Laezar, ('Performance Pay and Productivity' (2000) 90(5) *American Economic Review* 1346) found that piecework led to a 40 per cent increase in productivity. In an earlier study, the same author found an increase of 36 per cent. In turn, HJ Paarsch and B Shearer, ('Piece Rates, Fixed Wages and Incentive Effects: Statistical Evidence from Payroll Records' (2000) 41 (1) *International Economic Review* 59) found an increase of 23 per cent after the implementation of a performance-based system. However, it is true that these studies have been criticised as they refer to a single company and are therefore not representative, see AC Guielen, MJ Kerkhofs and JC Van Outs, 'How Performance-related Pay Affects Productivity and Employment' (2010) 23 *Journal of Population Economics* 293. In any case, other studies in the manufacturing sector have also provided positive productivity results after the implementation of performance systems but with much lower intensity (productivity gains between 2.8% and 3.5%), DL Kruse, 'Profit Sharing and Productivity: Microeconomic Evidence from the United States' (1992) 102 *Economic Journal* 24. This author found an increase in productivity of between 2.5 and 4.2 per cent for non-manufacturing firms.

[51] European Commission, *Promotion of Participation by Employed Persons in Profits and Enterprise Results II*, 1996; European Commission, *PEPPER II Report – Promotion of Employee Participation in Profits and Enterprise Results in the Member States of the European Community*, 1997.

[52] Profit-sharing is only compulsory in a few countries, such as France, the Dominican Republic and Chile. For more information on these systems and the reasons for their rejection see Todolí-Signes, *Salario y productividad* (2017).

Inelasticity of Labour Supply

The neoclassical equilibrium theory centres on the ability to increase or decrease supply and demand in line with needs and the equilibrium price. However, people cannot decrease or increase their numbers in line with market needs, i.e., while a factory can stop producing to reduce the supply of goods and adapt to the market, people cannot 'switch off' to wait for better times. This is an issue that has concerned economists since the beginning of capitalism, though their views differed from those of today.

Thus, Thomas Malthus (1766–1834)[53] and David Ricardo (1772–1823)[54] observed that 'adjustments' in the labour force were made through famine and death. That is, when the birth rate increased and with it the demand for wheat, real wages decreased. This, in turn, led to the inability of many families to feed themselves, leading to disease and death, thus balancing out the cycle.

Obviously in a social, constitutional state, people's deaths should be ruled out as a way of adjusting the labour market. However, the reality is that whereas a wheat producer can store wheat to be sold at a later date, or a manufacturer can reduce their output to adapt to market demand, labour power cannot be stored, and people's need for subsistence (when they have no other form of income) prevents them from putting their labour supply on hold. The labour market cannot 'self-regulate' as the neoclassical model suggests. The consequence is that wages will always fall resulting in unemployment.[55]

Thus, deregulation of the labour market can never reach its 'optimal equilibrium'. Instead, the unregulated free market will inevitably lead either to subsistence wages, starvation or death (developing country model) or to social conflict and violence due to resistance to this situation (developed country model).[56]

Negative Externalities

A negative externality occurs when the costs of producing goods or services are not reflected in their market price.[57] In other words, negative externalities are

[53] TR Malthus, *An Essay on the Principle of Population* (1798), critical edition by P James, (Cambridge University Press, 1989).

[54] D Ricardo, *On the Principles of Political Economy and Taxation* (1817) (Cambridge University Press, 1951).

[55] Hyde (n 1) 55.

[56] It is a different matter if labour law is not the only solution to prevent any of the above-mentioned undesirable and inefficient solutions from occurring. Collins, 'Justification and Techniques of Legal Regulation of the Employment Relations' 22. In other words, it is suggested that people should be guaranteed a minimum subsistence income by the State so that they are not forced to enter the labour market. Thus, with a guaranteed minimum income, workers would be able to restrict their labour supply until wages have reached equilibrium. However, this option undoubtedly also has its efficiency drawbacks, since the universal basic income could be (depending on how it is configured) a subsidy for inefficient firms, which could hire more cheaply because the rest of the income comes from the State, paid by the most efficient firms.

[57] Kaufman (n 12) 24; D Weil, 'Implementing Employment Regulation: Insights on the Determinants of Regulatory Performance', in Kaufman (n 12) 430.

activities that adversely affect a third party but are not paid for by those who profit from these activities. Negative externalities occur when private costs are lower than social costs.

A typical example in the product market is that of a factory which discharges polluting waste into a river in its manufacturing process. Here, the factory sells its product at a lower price because it does not assume the costs of cleaning up or disposing of the waste generated, and instead outsources these costs. Of course, if a good environmental protection system is in place, the company's actions will not go unnoticed and the State will claim the cost of cleaning up the river – as well as imposing a penalty to discourage the company from doing it again. However, this requires effective environmental regulation, not environmental deregulation.

A very similar situation exists in the labour market in the area of occupational health and safety. Imagine an employer seeks to profit by shirking their responsibilities in the event of an accident by referring cases to the social security system or by making the workers suffer the consequences themselves. This would be inefficient for two reasons. Firstly, if the social security system must shoulder the costs of work-related accidents and illnesses, this is tantamount to externalising (and socialising) a production cost. Secondly, if the employer does not pay any accident-related costs, they have little incentive to reduce them, thereby increasing the number of work-related accidents and illnesses.[58]

However, the private tort system proved to be incapable of reducing accidents;[59] with the cost of bringing claims and the fear of reprisal discouraging workers who had been involved in accidents from pursuing legal claims. The pre-accident situation was exactly the same. Workers had to accept unsafe working conditions as the only alternative to unemployment, which led to social conflict and accidents. This was a very inefficient social formula but did not harm employers because it was easy to replace workers.

In general, as firms do not own labour but rent labour by hours, weeks or years, the employer has no incentives to bear the costs of maintenance and training. The optimal labour policy is to get the maximum work effort from the employee each and every hour and, when the employee's health or physical stamina cracks, replace them with a new worker. The economic problems from this policy are threefold: some of the nation's labour input is wasted; the cost of the damaged/injured worker is transferred to a third party/society and not incorporated into the cost of production of the goods or services; feelings of rancor and bitterness/lack of cooperation with the company develop in the work force over policy employees see as exploitative.[60]

[58] In fact, according to the European Commission's Community strategy on occupational health and safety (2007–2012). Available at: www.eur-lex.europa.eu/LexUriServ/LexUriServ.do?uri=COM:2007:0062:FIN:en:PDF, 'occupational health and safety plays a vital role in increasing the competitiveness and productivity of enterprises'.

[59] Collins (n 40) 19; Addison and Hirsch (n 19) 129.

[60] Kaufman (n 12) 26.

Thus, legislation was introduced to safeguard national productivity and to prevent the imposition of private costs on society to protect workers' health and safety.[61] To be effective, these regulations should include not only quasi-objective responsibilities in the event of an accident in the workplace and during working hours, but also sanctions to discourage non-compliance.

In fact, although there is broad political consensus on the need for specific legislation to safeguard health and safety at work this is not as far-reaching as it should be. I am referring to work-related psychological illnesses. Thus, although occupational health and safety systems and a relatively successful monitoring and accountability system exist for physical risks, there are more and more work-related psychological illnesses such as anxiety, depression and burnout which are going unnoticed.[62] Therefore, there is something wrong with the current legislation.

Unjustified dismissal is another of the regulations justified by the existence of negative externalities. The premise that defends freedom of dismissal is based on the right of private property whereby 'the company belongs to the employer, and they can do whatever they wish with it'. However, the reality is that redundancies and high unemployment are detrimental to society as a whole. First, unemployed people are a waste of resources, and second, the income of the unemployed is paid by the state. Thus, in general terms, it is better for the economy to have people in employment than workers who are unemployed, thus justifying regulations that discourage arbitrary or unjustified dismissals.

The fact is that it is also better to keep the worker employed from a business perspective. Once again, we are faced with the 'prisoner's dilemma'. Thus, if all companies start laying off workers at the beginning of a mild economic downturn, this will eventually reduce the demand for products and services even further. The unemployed will consume less which, in turn, will lead to a deeper recession and the need to lay off more workers.[63] It is therefore in the interest of each individual employer to ensure that other employers do not lay off workers so that people can consume their products.

However, a company will only maintain employment if it knows that other businesses are going to do the same. Hence, the need for legislation that makes it equally difficult for all companies to make people redundant. Conversely, legislation that permits dismissals in some companies and not in others, without sufficient justification, could upset the equilibrium and, once again, lead to a 'race to the bottom' across the business spectrum.

[61] Weil, 'Implementing Employment Regulation: Insights on the Determinants of Regulatory Performance' 430.

[62] JA Fernandez Avilés, 'NTIC y riesgos psicosociales en el trabajo: estado de situación y propuestas de mejora' (2017) 2 *Diritto della Sicurezza sul Lavoro* 69.

[63] DI Levine and JP Richard, 'Work Organization, Employment Security and Macroeconomic Stability' (1995) 24(3) *Journal of Economic Behavior and Organization* 251; Banerjee and Duflo, *Good Economics for Hard Times* (2019) 82.

The same conclusion can be reached from a training perspective. Companies operating in a sector whose technology has changed need workers who are trained in these new working tools. Firms can use at least two ways to acquire these skills: they can either train their existing workforce, or they can lay off untrained workers and hire new staff who already have these skills.

Imagine the case of marketing companies. Before social media, marketers had perfect control over their advertising channels (TV, radio, newspapers, etc.). However, advertising on social media (X, Facebook, Instagram) is a different story. Thus, marketing agencies have had to decide how to acquire the skills needed to continue to provide their services to their clients.

In this case, if there is no regulation, the company will decide to lay off (usually older) workers and hire already trained (usually young) employees, since this ensures that training costs will be passed on to society or to the workers, but in neither case will the company have to shoulder them. However, this is inefficient from a social perspective as it leads to negative outsourcing. That is, the company manages to externalise a production cost: training. In addition, from a social perspective, the dismissal of middle-aged people who have difficulties in returning to the job market is more damaging.

In fact, many studies have shown that middle-aged workers who are made redundant for economic, technical or productive reasons do not fully recover in economic terms. In other words, many do not find work again and those who do, on average, find lower-paid, less-stable jobs or jobs with weaker social security protection (e.g., self-employment).[64] In short, we are not only talking about a worse economic situation but also about a poorer state of health. One study found that when an older, long-serving worker was included in a mass redundancy programme, their probability of dying in the years immediately following redundancy increased, as did the likelihood of having other health problems such as alcoholism, depression, pain and addiction. Overall, the study concluded that middle-aged workers who were made redundant lost between 12 and 18 months of their life expectancy.[65]

Again, one of the ways to ensure this does not happen, and for the company to internalise the social cost of its actions, is to penalise arbitrary or unjustified dismissal to prevent this type of situation.

Finally, parental leave has been advocated on externality (and efficiency) grounds too. It being argued that the care of children of working parents leads to healthier and more productive adults, thereby placing lesser strain on government support systems[66] and providing future workers.

[64] On all, see S Davis and T Von Wachter, 'Recession and the Costs of Job Loss' (2011) *Brooking Papers on Economic Activity* 1–72.

[65] D Sullivan and T Wachter, 'Job Displacement and Mortality: An Analysis Using Administrative Data' (2009) 124 (3) *Quarterly Journal of Economics* 1265.

[66] Addison and Hirsch (n 19) 129.

5

Economic Policy

The acceptance of labour law, social security and regulations in occupational health and safety to improve efficiency in the labour market and to facilitate economic growth, helps to overcome the artificial divide between 'economic' and 'social' aspects. The neo-classical and neo-liberal model's preference for deregulation has led labour theory to understandably reject anything that comes from the economic world. However, in the current ideological context (pro-market), burying one's head in the sand to continue defending positions that are alien to the prevailing economic rationale may actually have been one of the reasons behind the demise of labour law.

In addition, accepting certain economic justifications for the existence of labour law, in addition to putting labour law back at the heart of the debate (and perhaps increasing intellectual and citizen mobilisation) may provide new areas of interest in the discipline, as well as the creation of new labour regulations that are suited to achieving these objectives.

Recently, labour law has turned its attention to the legal and political role of social security, employment policies, training and education, wage and income policies, unemployment and immigration in labour terms. However, economic policy is much broader than this and how it develops has direct effects on the labour market.

New Content for Economic Policy

'Industrial policy', defined as a set of measures to boost specific economic activities and promote structural change,[1] is a clear example. In fact, the recent ideological shift towards greater market 'freedom' and restraint in the public sector has not prevented hundreds of measures and millions of euros being invested in addressing market failures and promoting market behaviour that is understood to be beneficial (public loans to companies, subsidies, tax exemptions, etc …).

The main issue with these policies has probably been the assumption that economic growth will automatically improve people's lives in real terms. This is

[1] D Roderik, 'Normalizing Industrial Policy' (2008) Working paper 3 *World Bank Commission on Growth and Development*. Available at: www.openknowledge.worldbank.org/handle/10986/28009.

all the more serious when it is expected to also improve the situation of the most disadvantaged. This has not been the case.

This opens up an area for mobilisation and new labour law instruments to ensure that the benefits of economic policy are well distributed between capital and labour and between different types of workers.

There is increasing support for public investment in the capital of private companies, public loans to companies, public non-repayable subsidies, etc.,[2] with a view to improving the situation of companies and the country's economy. However, many of these public policies (which are otherwise highly desirable) are often granted on the assumption that the benefits obtained will be shared equally among all citizens. However, more often than not, public-private partnerships do not distribute wealth fairly between the company and the workers, but lead instead to precarity and polarisation among the workforce. It would therefore seem more reasonable for this public investment to be legally linked to labour-related obligations, such as commitments to maintaining jobs, wage improvements, and reductions in working hours to share out employment.

In fact, public resources should not be used in the 'hope' that the company will subsequently 'do the right thing' by distributing profits fairly and improving the situation of workers. Many studies have shown that economic policies, which bring about economic growth, do not automatically improve the situation of the most disadvantaged or of workers in general.[3] Thus, growth-enhancing economic policy must include labour obligations that improve market efficiency and ensure proper distribution.

In Europe, progress is already being made in this direction, albeit slowly. Firstly, during the COVID-19 pandemic, several European countries (Germany, Portugal, Spain) tied social security rebates to maintaining jobs. That is, the aim was not simply to offer subsidies to keep companies in business, but to ensure that the success of these companies also contributed to maintaining quality employment.

Secondly, a much clearer case in point comes from the new European regulation on public procurement. Traditionally, public procurement only took into account the price quoted to provide the service. Thus, government had to contract the company that provided the service at the lowest price. This prevented any kind of control over the employment situation of workers who provided public services through private companies. In fact, the reality was that this arrangement rewarded precarity. The companies that offered the cheapest services (including paying lower wages or making their employees work longer hours) were awarded the contracts. This provided companies with an incentive to squeeze workers as much as possible, otherwise they would not win the contract.

[2] M Mazzucato, *The Entrepreneurial State: Debunking Public vs. Private Sector* (London, Penguin Books, 2017).

[3] A Banerjee and E Duflo, *Good Economics for Hard Times* (New York, Random House, 2019) 204.

This legal situation left government hamstrung, as it could do nothing to use public procurement as a way to improve the situation of workers. This is no trivial matter given that, in Europe, 19 per cent of GDP comes from public procurement.[4] This legislation has recently been modified to enable public administrations to introduce social clauses (labour and environmental clauses) where aspects other than the price of the contract are taken into account. This will help government to ensure that the money spent on the contract is distributed equally between capital and labour or even among the workers themselves, as these clauses promote the hiring of young people, women, people with functional diversity, etc.

This will not only have a positive effect on the workers involved in the tender,[5] but can also be used as a powerful weapon to send messages to the market about working conditions. Just as government procurement has traditionally been used as a way to create competition in the labour market (better conditions in the public sector will push up demands for better conditions in the private sector) so social clauses in public procurement will drive efficiency and redistribution in the private sector.

New Objectives for Labour Law in the Framework of Economic Policy

Globalisation, company mergers, de-industrialisation, the liberalisation of capital markets and the average size of companies are central economic policy issues that reduce the effectiveness of labour law. They should therefore also represent areas of interest for the discipline.

Free Trade Agreements

Thus, in recent years (and as much as it is probably 'thanks' to Trump who brought the issue to the forefront of public debate), the positive effects of free trade agreements for certain sectors of the population have been called into question. Since the times of David Ricardo, economists have venerated free trade as a sacrosanct, inviolable dogma which improves the situation of all the countries which deal in it. Thus, its main objective was to reduce tariffs and barriers to trade. However, in recent years, economists have begun to realise that, while the premise of economic growth remains true, free trade agreements do not benefit everyone equally.[6] Quite

[4] Data from European Commission, European Commission, *European Semester Thematic Factsheets on Public Procurement* (Brussels, European Commission, 2017).

[5] This also leads to better quality public services by reducing the level of conflict and increasing employee cooperation based on better working conditions.

[6] Banerjee and Duflo, *Good Economics for Hard Times.*

the contrary, it seems to cause (just as technology does) increasing polarisation among workers, i.e., an increase in wages for better-educated employees and a reduction in conditions for less-educated workers.

The premise is relatively straightforward. Free trade benefits all countries involved because it ensures that each country focuses on its comparative advantage.[7] Basically, countries specialise in what they do best. Obviously, this means that they will stop doing what they do less well. Thus, free trade causes some sectors in each country to benefit from trade and other industries to be disadvantaged. Thus, even if the positive outcomes outweigh the negative ones and the net result is economic growth for the country's economy, the reality is that this situation will have increased inequality.

In labour terms, developed countries are unlikely to specialise in labour-intensive tasks, since developing countries have a comparative advantage in this area (poorer working conditions). Instead, developed countries are likely to specialise in capital-intensive industries and sectors, which are more widely available and therefore cheaper.

In short, in developed countries, this means that the owner of capital will generally benefit from free trade and the owner of labour will generally be disadvantaged. There will also be discrepancies within the labour force that will generally be adversely affected: better-educated workers will be less disadvantaged (as they will be called upon to use the technology in capital-intensive industries) than less-educated workers (polarisation).

Telecommuting and online digital platforms cause similar effects. The spread of telecommuting for jobs that can be done over the internet, driven by the pandemic, means that companies can find cheaper sources of labour, especially skilled labour, in countries where there are fewer labour rights, thereby cutting employment and putting downward pressure on working conditions in developed countries. This, in turn, will benefit companies and capital owners who will be able to run their businesses at a lower cost and have the whole world at their fingertips as a potential labour market. Again, workers in developed countries will not be equally affected. Thus, although highly educated workers will be hit (India is known for its highly skilled, native English-speaking IT workers), this impact will be less severe as their chances of finding a job without having to relocate will increase. Second, less skilled and less specialised workers will have to compete directly with the entire world.

Therefore, free trade and telecommuting have a direct, two-fold effect on the labour market in developed countries: firstly, the number of labour-intensive industries declines, and secondly, polarisation and inequality among workers increases. This is why labour law should seek to engage in this type of free trade agreements. There are many ways of involvement, for example, social clauses that

[7] D Ricardo, *On the Principles of Political Economy and Taxation (1817)* (Cambridge, Cambridge University Press, 1951).

limit competition in terms of labour costs and force the countries with the worst labour conditions to improve them; agreements for the redistribution of the wealth generated, and contingency plans that limit polarisation.

In any case, for the purposes of our discussion here, the powerful impact of such agreements on employment justifies the inclusion of well-known social protection regulations in labour law.

Company Mergers

Competition law is a discipline of public law which guarantees the proper functioning of markets for the benefit of consumers. Its main objective so far has been to prevent collusive agreements and excessive market concentration that enables certain companies to exploit their dominant position in the market. In recent decades, the relationship between competition law and the labour market has been 'controversial' to say the least. In the 1990s, at European level, competition rules played an important role in forcing states to authorise private employment services, which until then had been provided only by public employment services in many member states.[8] The CJEU also ruled that competition law prevented certain occupations from limiting access to the profession, as in the case of dockers, for example.[9] In recent years, opposition from the interpreters of competition law to self-employed workers being able to exercise collective bargaining rights has also been worthy of note. In this regard, while it is understood that workers are not companies and, therefore, are exempt from the antitrust rules of competition law (CJEU *Albany* case),[10] in the case of the self-employed, even if they do not have dependent workers, they are understood to be included in the prohibitions of Article 101 TFEU, preventing them from bargaining collectively (CJEU *FNV Kunsten* case).[11]

Thus, although the objectives of labour law and competition law seem to be at odds, the reality is quite different. In fact, collusive agreements between real companies and the dominant position of certain companies (or groups of companies), the abusive situation created by monopolies and oligopolies, which competition law seeks to prevent, not only harm consumers, but also harm employees (and other smaller companies and ultimately, their employees).

Amazon is a current case in point. The company is well known for pandering to its consumers. In many instances, when a customer who has purchased a product

[8] C Freedland, C Jacqueson and N Kountouris, *Public Employment Services and European Law* (Oxford, Oxford University Press, 2007).

[9] Ruling of the *Merci Convenzionali Porto di Genova v Siderurgica Gabriell* C-179/90, ECLI:EU:C:1991:464, [1991] ECR I-05889..

[10] *Albany International BV v Stichting Bedrijfspensioenfonds Textielindustrie* C-67/96, ECLI:EU:C:1999:430, [1999] ECR I-05751.

[11] *FNV Kunsten Informatie en Media vs Staat der Nederlanden* C-413/2013, ECLI:EU:C:2014:2411.

through Amazon wants to return it, the web platform refunds the customer before the product has actually been sent back. This is a very advantageous situation for the Amazon customer, but not so advantageous for the company that has sold the product. Obviously, Amazon imposes this condition on companies that want to sell their products on Amazon's website. The same applies to the commissions that Amazon charges companies for each sale, as well as the maximum home delivery times (thereby involving courier services as well). Of course, in a free market system, companies are at liberty to sell their products on other websites. However, if Amazon takes a majority of the online sales pie, small businesses have no real freedom to choose where to market their products.

Thus, one possible measure would be to regulate the commissions and conditions (e.g., maximum delivery times) that Amazon can impose on companies selling products on its website, as if there were minimum wages and maximum working hours. The main point, however, would be to prevent a monopolistic situation and the abuse of a dominant position on the part of the main company.

All this can be transposed to the labour market. Inequality between companies, contractors and subcontractors, company mergers and abuse of dominant positions by some companies impairs the efficiency of the labour market and worsens working conditions, as well as generating social conflict. Thus, labour theory must ensure that competition law institutions are not only concerned with consumers, but also with the inequality of power between firms (contractors and subcontractors) and the effects this has on the labour market.

Company Size

Economists point out that one of the factors most closely linked to productivity and firm stability is company size.[12] Indeed, medium-sized companies (between 50 and 250 employees) tend to have economies of scale that enable them to invest in new technologies, increase the professionalism of their managers, train their workers, access credit more easily, and withstand the impact of economic crises more effectively. Thus, labour productivity, competitiveness, work–life balance for employees, wages and employment adjustments will depend, to some extent, on encouraging the growth of firms towards an optimal size.

[12] B Van Ark and E Monnikhof, 'Size Distribution of Output and Employment: A Data Set for Manufacturing Industries in Five OECD Countries, 1960–1990' (1996) 166 *OECD Economics Department Working Paper*; D Snodgrass and T Biggs, *Industrialization and Small Firms Patterns and Policies* (San Francisco, International Center for Economic Growth, 1995); J Van Biesebroeck, 'Firm Size Matters: Growth and Productivity Growth in African Manufacturing' (2005) 53 *Economic Development and Cultural Change* 546; JR Baldwin, RS Jarmin and J Tang, 'The Trend to Smaller producers in manufacturing: A Canada/U.S. Comparison' (2002) 3 *Economic Analysis Research Paper Series*; FC Lee and J Tang, 'Multifactor Productivity Disparity between Canadian and U.S. Manufacturing Films' (2001) 15 *Journal of Productivity Analysis* 115; J Baldwin and W Gu, 'Plant Turnover and Productivity Growth in Canadian Manufacturing' (2003) 1993 *Analytical Studies Research Paper Series* 1205–9153.

In this regard, empirical studies have confirmed that larger firms have higher levels of labour productivity in both industrial[13] and non-industrial sectors.[14] According to Van Ark and Monnikhof,[15] industrial firms with 0–9 workers had 38 per cent less output per employee than the average-sized firm in the sector. Baldwin, Jarmin and Tang[16] found that the added value created per worker in firms with fewer than 100 workers was 31 per cent below the average value for the industry. Lee and Tang[17] reported that firms with between 100 and 500 workers were 15 per cent more productive than those with fewer than 100 employees.

Several factors explain this difference. Firstly, there are difficulties in obtaining finance. Small companies are viewed as being more unstable and more risk-prone by credit institutions, thus reducing their access to funding and, by extension, their capacity to invest.[18] In this sense, easy access to the financial market is closely linked to business productivity.[19] Essentially, this centres on the difficulties small firms encounter when trying to introduce technological and organisational innovations. In general, poor access to capital markets prevents them from acquiring and using the most efficient technology, makes it difficult for them to train their staff (managerial and non-managerial) and invest in innovative working methods.[20]

Secondly, firm size is linked to economies of scale. In fact, as a firm's output grows, its costs per manufactured unit fall. The more a firm produces, the less it costs to produce each unit, as the firm's overheads are spread over a larger number of units or services placed on the market. Thus, smaller companies incur higher costs.[21] In addition, small firm size prevents staff specialisation, as only a few workers carry out all the functions in the firm, reducing the options for specialisation and thus the productivity of each individual employee.[22] The division of labour proposed by Adam Smith is based precisely on dividing the tasks in a productive process to enable each worker to specialise in their own area and thus improve productivity. However, if the firm is not large enough, specialisation is impossible, and productivity suffers.

[13] JR Baldwin, 'Were Small Producers the Engines of Growth in the Canadian Manufacturing Sector in the 1980s' (1998) 10 *Small Business Economics* 349.

[14] Baldwin, Jarmin and Tang, 'The Trend to Smaller Producers in Manufacturing'.

[15] Van Ark and Monnikhof, 'Size Distribution of Output and Employment: A Data Set for Manufacturing Industries in Five OECD Countries, 1960–1990'.

[16] Baldwin, Jarmin and Tang (n 12).

[17] Lee and Tang, 'Multifactor Productivity Disparity between Canadian and U.S. Manufacturing Films'.

[18] A Kochar, 'An Empirical Investigation of Rationing Constraints in Rural Credit Markets in India? (1997) 53 *Journal of Development Economics* 339.

[19] Van Biesebroeck, 'Firm Size Matters: Growth and Productivity Growth in African Manufacturing'.

[20] K Lundvall and GE Battesse, 'Firm Size, Age and Efficiency: Evidence from Keynan Manufacturing Firms' (2000) 36(3), *The Journal of Development Studies* 146–63; Van Biesebroeck (n 12).

[21] R Dhawan, 'Firm Size and Productivity Differential: Theory and Evidence from a Panel of US Firms' (2001) 44 *Journal of Economic Behavior and Organization* 169.

[22] Banerjee and Duflo (n 3).

Thirdly, small and medium-sized enterprises cannot access international markets, with some exceptions.[23] Thus, all the 'advantages' of globalisation, including potential international markets, are off limits to firms that are not large enough to make the necessary investment. In addition, even if they do have the means to invest, they will only be able to do so if their size enables them to access a sufficiently large market share that lets them recoup their investment through the revenues obtained from internationalisation.

Of course, this does not mean that there is no limit to this link between firm size and productivity. As some economists have pointed out, excessive size can increase organisational complexity, leading to productivity issues.[24]

Productivity issues in smaller firms have direct effects on the quality of employment for workers in smaller businesses. Thus, as observed by Baldwin,[25] Brown, Hamilton and Medoff[26] and Morissette,[27] small firms pay lower wages on average than their larger counterparts in the same sector, as well as offering more unstable jobs with higher levels of seasonality and turnover.

In many cases, these smaller firms are simply divisions of larger firms that have been split off through subcontracting. In this sense, these poorer working conditions are not the result of the 'market' but of larger companies intentionally seeking to exert greater bargaining power over smaller companies. This, in turn, implies that there is an interest in keeping these SMEs from growing in size.

Finally, as Snodgrass and Biggs demonstrated,[28] there is a positive correlation between a country's per capita income and the number of workers in large firms. In other words, there are more workers in large firms in countries with high levels of per capita income, while in countries with medium or low per capita income there is a higher concentration of employees working in small and medium-sized firms. Hence, it has been argued that economic prosperity depends on a country's ability to grow its firms.[29] This makes the issue of firm size crucial to a country's growth, efficiency and improved working conditions.

[23] LD Satpathy, B Chatterjee and J Mahakud, 'Firm Characteristics and Total Factor Productivity: Evidence from Indian Manufacturing Firms' (2017) 11(1) *The Journal of Applied Economic Research* 77.

[24] OE Williamson, 'Hierarchical Control and Optimum Firm Size' (1967) 75 *Journal of Political Economy* 123; M Diaz and R Sánchez, 'Film Size and Productivity in Spain: A Stochastic Frontier Analysis' (2008) 30 (3) *Small Business Economics* 315.

[25] Baldwin, 'Were Small Producers the Engines of Growth in the Canadian Manufacturing Sector in the 1980s'.

[26] JT Hamilton, C Brown and J Medoff, *Employers Large and Small* (Cambridge MA, Harvard University Press, 1990).

[27] R Morissette, 'Canadian Jobs and Firm Size: Do Smaller Firms Pay Less?' (1993) 26 *Canadian Journal of Economics* 159.

[28] D Snodgrass and T Biggs, *Industrialization and the Small Firm. Patterns and Policies* (San Francisco, International Center for Economic Growth, 1995).

[29] D Leung, C Meh and Y Terajima, 'Firm Size and Productivity' (2008) 45 *Bank of Canada Working Paper*.

This relationship raises three elements of interest in the field of labour law. Firstly, given how damaging an excess of micro-enterprises can be for the economy, labour law should ensure that regulation does not encourage their excessive proliferation. Thus, a regulation which reduces the labour rights of workers in micro-enterprises or generally permits the non-application of collective bargaining in this type of enterprise could indirectly make them flourish, which would end up damaging the economy.

Secondly, the issue of company size leads us to analyse production outsourcing and subcontracting. Outsourcing is a strategy followed by companies to reduce their size and force others to take on economic risks inherent to their business. Labour regulations should ensure that company downsizing is not undertaken to exert market dominance of some companies over others. In other words, there should be penalties for companies that divest themselves of part of their manufacturing activity in order to outsource it, unless there are genuine production or organisational reasons for doing so. This means that regulations should ensure that subcontracting production is not carried out simply to reduce labour costs or because of the difference in bargaining power between the main company and the contractor, but that it is based on genuine specialisation of the subcontracted company. Several labour regulations can help to achieve this goal.

(i) Firstly, there should be mandatory equality of working conditions between the main company and the contractor, which would ensure that subcontracting is not used to worsen working conditions. Therefore, regulations should guarantee equal working conditions (wages, working hours, etc.) between employees in the main company and in the contractor, as well as guaranteeing that should the contract be terminated, the main company will bear the costs of dismissal.

(ii) Secondly, in terms of collective representation, the regulations should allow workers in subcontractors to elect representatives in the main company (on works councils, for example). This would be even simpler in the case of trade union representation, as the only safeguard would be to ensure that the workers in the main company and the subcontracting company are covered by the same sector.

(iii) Thirdly, the evidence about company size is at the heart of current policies that encourage self-employment. Indeed, there is no smaller company than a single self-employed worker. This form of self-employment has been widely promoted in recent years as a way of 'creating employment'. However, this type of strategy, which encourages everyone to become an entrepreneur, damages labour productivity and creates poor working conditions for the individuals concerned. The following graph on the percentage of self-employed people in OECD countries shows a clear link between economic development and the number of self-employed people in each country. Hence, the importance of the correct application of the concept of employee and the fight against bogus self-employment.

Figure 5.1 Self-employment rate in OECD countries

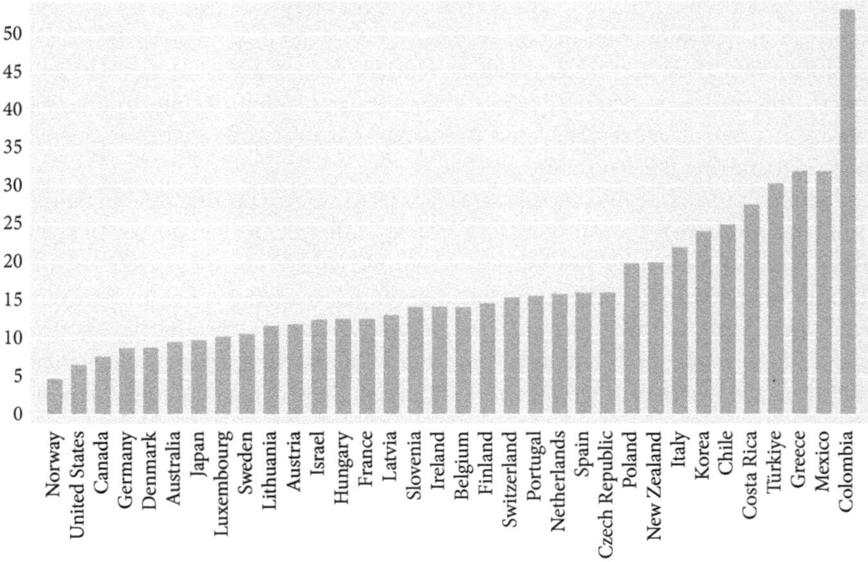

Source: OECD Statistics.

Thus, economic policy should help companies to increase in size so that they reach the optimum, either through internal growth or through the acquisition of other, less efficient companies. Accordingly, public loans, aid, capital investments and subsidies should centre on these types of companies and on promoting competitiveness.

It seems particularly important not to promote inefficient companies. Not only because of the negative impact they can have on the economy, but also because of their knock-on effect. Sustaining inefficient firms that take market share based on low wages and poor conditions will impede other efficient firms from growing and increasing their market share. Instead, economic policy and legislation should ensure that inefficient firms disappear from the market or are taken over by others that are in a better market position.

In short, given the advantages of firm concentration up to an optimum size, labour regulation and economic policy should encourage this type of production model, whilst removing obstacles that hinder company growth.

Corporation Tax Depending on the Number of Employees

As we have noted, one of the most obvious effects of the new wave of automation and digital transformation is a reduction in employment in the companies that implement these tools. Technology improves productivity, which makes it unnecessary to have as many employees in an organisation. In fact, this does not just occur in established companies. In recent decades, we have seen the emergence of new technological giants that obtain huge portions of national income with proportionally very few employees.

Both cases pose the same challenge for society. Until now, wages have been the major source of distributing wealth. That is, companies took in large amounts of income, but did not keep it in the form of profits. Instead, they roughly distributed it among the workers who had contributed to the company's success. In other words, through job creation, large traditional companies contributed not only to improving the lives of consumers with their new products and services, but also to redistributing their income through their employees' salaries. However, as technology advances and the need for workers to produce goods and services diminishes, the second beneficial effect for society, i.e., the distribution of wealth, disappears.

The most extreme scenario would be a society in which mainstream AI rules the roost (considered to be human-equivalent intelligence with the same capabilities)[30] and robots replace *all* human labour. In this scenario, the owners of capital could theoretically continue to produce goods and services by buying more robots without the need for human workers. Therefore, they could keep all the income earned without distributing it to its workforce. This would leave those who have no capital, and who live off their labour, with no way of earning a wage and no share of national income.

This poses the challenge of how to distribute wealth in a world without jobs, or rather in a world where jobs are progressively disappearing. The advantages and disadvantages of a basic income or a guaranteed employment programme will be discussed later in this book, but the problem of inequality comes first. If all income is kept by the owners of capital, inequality would be so great that democracy would hardly be sustainable.[31] Therefore, before we reach this point, it would seem pertinent to improve the existing formulas for redistributing wealth, as the share of income kept by capital grows and that of workers shrinks.

Thus, a not-too-disruptive approach would be to impose taxes on companies according to the number of workers in the company. Thus, firms that earned large amounts of income with few employees would continue to participate in the redistribution of wealth (and by extension, social welfare) by increasing their contributions to the State coffers. Along these lines, a progressive tax rate would have to be set that would not only depend on the income variable, but also on the employee variable. The tax percentage would increase as income rose in line with the number of employed workers.

[30] B Cantwell Smith, *The Promise of Artificial Intelligence: Reckoning and Judgment* (Cambridge MA, The MIT Press, 2019).

[31] JE Stiglitz, *The Price of Inequality*, (New York, W.W. Norton, 2012); OM Levin-Waldman, 'How Inequality Undermines Democracy' (10 December 2016) *E-International Relations*. Available at: www.e-ir.info/2016/12/10/how-inequality-undermines-democracy/.

This solution would have two additional positive effects (as well as better wealth distribution). First, firms would have a disincentive to downsize for reasons other than efficiency. Indeed, the decentralisation of production since the 1980s has shrunk the size of many firms, which have outsourced the ancillary and core tasks of their business model. In many cases, this decentralisation has not been carried out for reasons of efficiency, but to avoid labour regulations and reduce costs. Thus, this tax structure could improve the existing balance of power when it comes to making a decision to decentralise production.

The second positive effect would be to rebalance a tax system that currently encourages replacing workers with capital. Currently, tax laws impose higher taxes on the hiring of workers than on technology purchases. As Banerjee and Duflo pointed out,[32] whereas workers' wages are subject to social security contributions, AI is not. In turn, companies can offset technology purchases through tax deductions. In short, current tax legislation may be providing incentives for employers to automate tasks even though retaining an employee would have been more efficient.[33]

This means that even if a technology is no more productive than a human being, a firm may decide to switch over based on the tax savings obtained. To avoid this perverse incentive, some economists have proposed taxing the introduction of robots in a firm.[34] However, the problem is that most job losses do not come from a worker being replaced by a physical robot, but rather from automation through algorithms, digital transformation, AI and, in some cases, industrial robots. In other words, it makes little sense to attempt to identify which technological element specifically causes job losses if it is the latter that is to be discouraged. Therefore, instead of focusing on technology, it would seem more sensible to focus directly on the effect that we want to discourage: the depreciation of employment.

In short, a tax on business income depending on the number of workers who have produced this income would lead to a better distribution of the wealth generated in companies, either through salaries or through the State. In addition, it would discourage the downsizing of companies for reasons other than efficiency, and automation that is carried out for tax reasons rather than for productive reasons.

[32] Banerjee and Duflo (n 3) 233.

[33] D Acemoglu and P Restrepo, 'Artificial Intelligence, Automation and Work' (2018) 24196, *NEBER Working Paper* 1491.

[34] R Abbott and BN Bogenschneider, 'Should Robots Pay Taxes? Tax Policy in the Age of Automation' (2018) 12 *Harvard Law and Policy Review* 145. This was also proposed in the European Parliament in 2017 but was ultimately voted against. In South Korea, a plan has been set up to reduce tax subsidies for companies that invest in automation. This plan is combined with a tax on outsourcing to prevent the tax on "robots" from leading to an increase in outsourcing.

A Critique of Labour Law as a Regulator of the Labour Market

It is not an uncontroversial notion to include the governance of the labour market to improve efficiency as one of the justifications and functions of labour law. In fact, this could be criticised from both ends of the ideological spectrum. For example, the right could allege excessive interventionism and paternalism, while the left would frown upon the acceptance of labour as a commodity whose efficiency is to be enhanced. Indeed, while the right tends to support deregulation and the left the primacy of certain social values over efficiency, any justification that seeks *regulation* to improve *efficiency* is open to attack from both sides.

Paternalism

The quest for efficiency has historically been associated with conservative tenets. However, so has deregulation and a policy of laissez-faire. Thus, although it has been proven that wearing seat belts and not drinking at the wheel are measures that reduce traffic mortality rates, certain sectors criticise any restrictions on the freedom of adult individuals to make decisions. Along the same lines, regulation that restricts freedom of enterprise receives criticism, even if it benefits business owners.

According to this approach, employers and workers are adults who should be free to set their contractual conditions based on their own individual preferences, irrespective of whether this ends up with the most efficient solution or not. Anti-paternalism upholds the outcome of the individual's 'freedom', stating that it will always be better than trying to impose or promote an undesirable individual-level solution, even if it is wrong.

Criticism of state paternalism is mainly rooted in Anglo-Saxon countries, though in recent years, this way of thinking has also taken root in continental Europe and in some Latin American countries in line with the ideology that underpins dismantling the welfare state.

In this sense, it is often argued that the validity of the justification for state interventionism to enhance economic efficiency depends on individual and collective preferences as to an acceptable level of state intervention. This question is often connected to individual ideas over the legitimacy of the state to intervene in individual freedom for the sake of social welfare.

However, this assertion must be rejected on the grounds that it is based on an incorrect premise. It is true that paternalism criticises state intervention in the economy by calling for deregulation and 'non-intervention'. However, the reality is that there is no such thing as non-intervention in an economy. It is not an option. What is labelled as 'non-intervention in the economy' is actually a specific form of intervention that improves the economic situation of certain privileged groups, while advocating the disappearance of other state intervention that benefits the least disadvantaged groups. Hayek's work *Law, Legislation and Liberty*, in which he developed his theory of spontaneous order, was very clear on that. While he is highly critical of the welfare state, he defended the importance of law in shaping social institutions.

Let us look at three examples of economic policies that deliberately choose to reduce the total level of employment.[35]

Monetary policy. There is no such thing as a natural or neutral level of money creation in the economy. Economists almost unanimously agree that when central banks decide on the amount of money in an economy, they must choose between either producing inflation or increasing the level of employment.[36] According to the Philips curve, as inflation decreases, unemployment rises; conversely, as unemployment falls, inflation goes up. Thus, when central banks deliberately choose to keep inflation low, they are, in turn, automatically opting for higher levels of unemployment. Thus, those who advocate keeping central bank interest rates high, and support reducing the money supply, are voluntarily protecting those who have capital (inflation devalues the value of capital) over those who live off their labour (unemployment reduces the value of labour).

Even if someone wanted to defend the 'non-intervention of the economy' with the reductionist argument of 'the return to the gold standard' (central banks cannot create money beyond a country's gold reserves), this would still be an interventionist decision to leave the creation of a country's money in the hands of random events consisting of the 'discovery' of new gold mines in the world, with the catastrophic consequences that this would have for the economy.

Thus, without going into the rights or wrongs of this position, monetarist stances argue that central banks should continue to opt for low inflation over unemployment because of the negative consequences that high inflation has on the economy: what is not tenable is that this is the result of 'non-intervention' in the economy (there is always intervention).

Interest rate policy and trade deficit. Once again, central banks indirectly decide the value of a country's currency through interest rates. A strong currency (with high value) will make it cheaper to buy goods and services abroad and more expensive for foreign countries to buy domestic goods and services. Therefore, again, the decision to keep the value of a currency high provides an incentive, first, to buy abroad instead of buying locally and, second, to encourage domestic companies to produce in countries that do not have a strong currency because it is cheaper to do so. In other words, the creation of global production chains is encouraged, to the detriment of domestic workers who end up becoming unemployed. In short, this decision has a knock-on effect on the economy which leads

[35] D Baker, *Rigged: How Globalization and the Rules of the Modern Economy Were Structured to Make the Rich Richer* (Washington DC, Center for Economic and Policy Research, 2016).

[36] AW Philips, 'The Relation Between Unemployment and the Rate of Change of Money Wage Rates in the United Kingdom' (1958) 25 *Economica* 283–99.

to a reduction in domestic demand and a drop in employment, especially in the manufacturing industry.

Tax policy. Similarly, there is no such thing as a natural or neutral level of public spending. The insistence on pursuing a 'balanced' tax regime implies a decision to intervene in economic policy, which is again aimed at reducing inflation, thus leading to unemployment. Certainly, non-Keynesian positions argue that imbalanced public spending could end up causing more harm to workers, but what can hardly be contested is that keeping public spending low is a laissez-faire economic decision.

It is worth noting that those who advocate keeping interest rates high, not printing fresh money, reducing public spending, etc., do so on the grounds that the opposite would harm the economy and efficiency. Thus, it seems inconsistent to contend that such interventions in the economy are justified for the sake of efficiency, while at the same time arguing for 'non-intervention' in the labour market, when intervention in the labour market is done for the sake of this efficiency.

In short, and as shown, without state intervention, there is no economy (or it would be a similar economy to that which existed in the Middle Ages). Any arguments in favour of 'reducing state intervention in the economy' are simply a legitimate way of protecting private interests. Similarly, 'avoiding state paternalism' is not an option, since all decisions, even 'apparently' neutral ones, have an impact on the economy. The question is who benefits from these decisions?

In fact, given that full employment mainly improves the situation of lower- and middle-class workers, while rising inflation mostly undermines capital owners, it can be contended that economic policy decisions that are endorsed as 'non-interventionist' are actually strategies that aim to protect capital over labour.

As the following chapter argues, the factor that most reduces workers' bargaining power vis-à-vis the employer is the level of unemployment in a country, i.e., the higher the level of unemployment, the easier it is to replace a worker. Therefore, given the number of economic policy *decisions* that lead to lower employment levels, it would seem to make sense to focus some areas of economic policy, and specifically labour regulations, on redressing the imbalance created by state decisions.

Labour is not a Commodity

Originally, the aim of labour law was to prevent labour from becoming a commodity, i.e., taking labour out of the supply-and-demand equation[37] and making the labour market function on the basis of democratically decided principles other than those dictated by the 'invisible hand'. Thus, it is not surprising to note that

[37] P Davies and M Freedland, *Kahn-Freund's Labour and the Law* (London, Stevens, 1983).

voices supporting the use of labour law to optimise the labour market have been widely criticised (see especially Dukes[38] and Fudge[39]).

The justification and use of labour law as a cog in the labour market wheel has been criticised for two main reasons: firstly, because labour market regulation to date has been based on the assumption that market failures are specific and not a systemic problem of the economic model;[40] secondly, justifying labour law as a useful tool for improving efficiency overlooks the need for the State to grant certain rights to its citizens, *regardless of whether or not* this generates efficiency.[41]

If the objective, or one of the objectives, of labour law is to solve market failures, this requires accepting the validity of the neoclassical model that explains the functioning of the labour market. In fact, from the liberal perspective, market failures arise as one-off aberrations in the functioning of the market. However, part of the literature argues that market failures are not specific but systemic.[42] In this sense, it can be contended that the supply and demand model is so far removed from reality that using labour regulations to try to solve it would, firstly, legitimise the model and, second, be a waste of resources since one cannot 'improve' something that is basically flawed.

However, without going into which theoretical model is correct or detracting from the criticism, the fact is that state intervention can indeed improve efficiency. If these authors are right and market failures are systemic, labour law as an efficiency enhancer probably cannot fully address them. However, empirical studies show that there is room for improvement. Thus, without claiming to be an absolute solution, it would seem feasible to state that labour regulations can improve both efficiency and productivity and thus the economic situation. As Deakin stated,[43] labour law intervention does not provide an ideal solution to labour market issues, but it can improve the situation in comparison to the result obtained from labour 'deregulation'.

Criticism from the perspective of socially acceptable values deserves more credit. As will be discussed below, one of the standard justifications for labour law is the fact that without regulation the labour market reaches socially unacceptable equilibria for a democratic society (e.g., child labour, wages below subsistence level, deaths due to accidents at work).[44] Thus, the State has the right and the duty to intervene to correct socially unacceptable outcomes.

[38] R Dukes, 'Constitutionalizing Employment Relations: Sinzheimer, Kahn-Freund and the Role of Labour Law' (2008) 35 *Journal of Law and Society* 341–63; R Dukes, 'Hugo Sinzheimer and the Constitutional Function of Labour Law' in G Davidov and B Languille, (eds), *The Idea of Labour Law* (Oxford, Oxford University Press, 2011).

[39] J Fudge, 'Labour as a "Fictive Commodity"' in Davidov and Languille, *The Idea of Labour Law*, 120–35.

[40] Fudge, 'Labour as a "Fictive Commodity"', 125 and 131.

[41] Dukes, 'Hugo Sinzheimer and the Constitutional Function of Labour Law'.

[42] M Mazzucato, *Mission Economy* (London, Penguin Books, 2021) 172; Fudge (n 39) 125 and 131.

[43] S Deakin, 'The Contribution of Labour Law to Economic and Human Development', in Davidov and B Languille *The Idea of Labour Law*, 161.

[44] T Prosser, 'Regulation and Social Society' (2006) 33(3) *Journal of Law and Society* 364 developed the idea that employees' working conditions should not be decided by the market but should be the

From this perspective, to argue that child labour should be banned because it is inefficient for children to work since preventing them from receiving schooling will mean fewer educated workers in the future and less productivity for the country, is to overlook true democratic values. Therefore, 'efficiency' justifications are rejected. It should be remembered that, in a constitutional state, not everything should be left to the market. In other words, the State is legitimised to guarantee certain legal and constitutionally recognised rights, the justification for which comes directly from social preferences expressed through regulated procedures.[45]

Hence, the minimum wage is justified by the value of people for the simple fact of being people, regardless of whether or not this contributes to the efficiency of the economy. The same holds true for all other labour rights, as they are the result of democratically voiced expressions of social preferences, with their own legitimacy regardless of their economic utility.

The value-based critique is undoubtedly a sound one. It is difficult to sustain that the prohibition of child labour stems solely from the fact that it is inefficient to have children working. However, there is no need for a single justification. Thus, it seems reasonable, and even positive, that there is more than one type of rationale for a particular labour regulation. Thus, justifications based on social and democratic values or constitutional rights in force do not exclude the existence of other grounds.

In fact, the reality is that social values are a social construct (for want of a better use of words). Therefore, in order to be able to accurately establish its preferences, society requires all the information available. Therefore, in the end, the efficiency rationale is just another reason out of all those on the table for the establishment of legal and constitutional rights in the process of democratic deliberation. However, once this right has been established in the legal system, its legitimacy does not come from the value it seeks to protect, i.e., efficiency or the person as a human being, but instead from the 'rule of law'.

Finally, justifying labour law on the grounds that it promotes efficiency is not incompatible with the other values that labour regulations seek to safeguard. It is just another reason that justifies its existence. In a hypothetical situation, if there are conflicting values, the democratic process settles this problem and decides which one should prevail.

In short, I do not see why the value of efficiency as an argument for the social legitimacy of labour regulations should be monopolised by those who support the deregulation of labour markets, when in many cases, the opposite is true: the quest for efficiency requires strong labour regulations.

result of a democratic deliberative process. The author defends the existence of a series of values in society that can be distorted if working conditions are left to the free market. This justifies the existence of labour regulations.

[45] Dukes (n 38) 65.

Weak Grounds for Deregulation

Since the 1980s, economic and labour policy has been dominated by the so-called 'Washington Consensus'.[46] From this point, developed and developing countries focused on market liberalisation and labour market deregulation. This led countries to embrace a free market, *laissez-faire* approach to industrial and labour policy, whereby employers' unilateral decision-making power grew, and the costs of hiring and firing workers were reduced (the so-called external flexibility) and the costs of cutting wages and extending working hours (internal flexibility)[47] were lowered as the only way to achieve economic growth and efficiency. On top of this, labour law was directly accused of hurting those it was supposed to protect.[48]

This has resulted in a trade-off between economic efficiency and labour regulations,[49] and a contrived confrontation between economics and social issues that has been particularly detrimental to the latter. Thus, by suggesting that the only way to grow is by reducing labour protection and sacrificing the redistribution of wealth and equality in the imagination, voters and many political decision-makers have been forced to make a difficult choice, over an artificial conflict that 'forces' anyone who takes the premise at face value to choose growth. Thus, to people's dismay, it seemed that the only way to achieve economic efficiency, the desired productivity and economic growth was to opt for deregulatory measures in the labour market. This sentiment also served to unburden tormented consciences. Those who felt 'pity' for the dismal situation of many workers could fall back on the liberating sentiment that 'there is no other way' to achieve the necessary growth. This has made it relatively easy for deregulatory measures to be imposed as the only way forward.

In fact, this apparent incompatibility between economic growth and social benefits has also been used as an argument to defend positions at the opposite extreme. Thus, given that current growth models create poor quality jobs and destroy the environment, degrowth has been put forward as the only alternative to improve quality of life and the environment.[50]

However, the prevailing economic tenets and empirical studies differ considerably from this trade-off. Indeed, there is no trade-off or conflict between efficiency

[46] This term was coined by the economist John Williamson. The aim was to describe a set of relatively specific formulas, which he considered to create the reform package for crisis-stricken developing countries, in agreement with the institutions under US auspices, such as the International Monetary Fund (IMF), the World Bank, the International Monetary Fund (IMF) and the World Bank (WB); J Williamson, 'What Washington Means by Policy Reform', in J Frieden, M Pastor and M Tomz, *Modern Political Economy and Latin America* (Washington DC, Institute for International Economics, 1990).

[47] J Howe, 'The Broad Idea of Labour Law: Industrial Policy, Labour Market Regulation, and Decent Work', in Davidov and Languille *The Idea of Labour Law*.

[48] D Card and A Krueger, *Myth and Measurement: The New Economics of the Minimum Wage* (New Jersey, Princeton University Press, 1995).

[49] AM Okun, *Equality and Efficiency: The Big Tradeoff*, (Washington DC, Brookings Institute, 1975).

[50] PC Costa Morata, *Por el decrecimiento*, Libros de economía y empresa 1 (2010) 24–27.

and social protection. On the contrary, labour regulations are necessary to achieve a well-functioning labour market and much sought-after efficiency.

It should be remembered that the very concept of labour deregulation is fallacious: there is always regulation. Thus, the aim of so-called 'deregulation' is to return the employment contract to private control based on property law through civil law, i.e., an unbalanced scenario that overprotects capital owners against those who have no capital. Moreover, this regulation was unable to solve market failures and achieve efficiency in the labour market in the past and it has not been able to do so in the present either. Nor is it able to regulate an essentially collective relationship or reduce the social conflicts that arise in the labour market ('people are not melons').

Nor does economic theory *per se* promote the individualisation of labour relations. Quite the contrary, economic theories and the empirical studies analysed support collective solutions over individual ones, because they are more efficient (lower costs). Economic studies are especially concerned with standardising applicable rules. Thus, industrial collective bargaining agreements and the standardisation of safeguards enable firms to compete on the quality of their products and services rather than on low labour costs, which discourage training, investment in technology, and efficiency. By the same token, it would seem necessary for regulation to place the burden of risk on those who have the best incentives (and are best equipped) to reduce it. Therefore, if there is no regulation to prevent this, it will be in the company's interest to place the risk on the worker, who has no way of improving their productivity, since they have no capital to technologically enhance their production process, to train themselves, to prevent accidents at work, or to protect themselves against possible market contingencies.

The same conclusion is reached with the increase of unilateral employer power. Many of the labour reforms of recent years have advocated an increase in 'flexibility'. However, this flexibility means nothing more than increasing the unilateral power of the employer to dismiss, hire, reduce wages, and modify working conditions single-handedly. This is a different legal solution to the one mooted by the economic studies discussed in this chapter. Increasing the unilateral power of the employer does not guarantee efficiency, it is only a presumption. It is understood that employers, as rational people, will seek to maximise their profits and, if the law does not prevent them from doing so, they will act in a way that maximises efficiency. However, the reality is that people are not always rational, and the short term often prevails over the long term, while individual interests do not always dovetail with social interests. Thus, when empirical studies reveal that the behaviour of entrepreneurs does not lead to efficient optimisation, there are reasons to impose this behaviour on business owners, for the good of the economy. In this sense it must be argued that labour 'deregulation' harms the employer.

Thus, although employers may have a preference for temporary contracts, they should be discouraged by legislation as they have worse productivity outcomes than their big brother, the permanent contract. Employee profit-sharing should be imposed or sufficiently encouraged to reduce labour conflict, improve productivity, and boost firms' resilience in the face of economic downturns, among other things.

The necessary public intervention in the labour market provides major justification for the very existence of labour law, as well as a field of opportunities for new roles for labour regulations that reconcile the old purely protective functions with others that defend workers while making the labour market work, albeit ensuring fair distribution of the income earned to those who created it.

Improving productivity and competitiveness in this globalised world is essential for companies to survive in the marketplace, and this is a key factor in keeping workers in their jobs. Obviously, in the current economic set-up, the State needs competitive companies and employed workers to maintain the welfare state. It is therefore not a matter in which the State can turn a blind eye. Instead, boosting productivity has become a matter of public concern, which obliges the legislator to take action. Deregulation and mere promotion are unacceptable.[51] As Coase Theorem induce Efficient arrangement should prevail regardless of initial property rights or the relative bargaining power of the parties to the contract.[52]

Finally, as shown above, economic theory is not necessarily hostile to labour regulations, nor does it seek deregulation. This means that the sterile confrontation between 'economic' and 'social' values should be set aside to achieve harmonisation between, what are, in fact, two sides of the same coin.

[51] A Todolí-Signes, *Salario y productividad* (Tirant lo Blanch, 2017).
[52] RH Coase, 'The Problem of Social Cost' (1960) 3 *Journal of Law and Economics* 1.

6

Values: Unequal Bargaining Power and the Distribution of Wealth

Growth is not Everything

The inequality of bargaining power between employer and employee is, and always will be, in the DNA of labour law. This imbalance, which labour law seeks to redress through regulation, has an impact on the company level (working conditions) and on the economy as a whole (distribution of the income generated).

Although this is a standard justification for the existence of labour law and stems from the very origin of the discipline, the truth is that, in recent years, it has also gained traction with the most unexpected bedfellows. In fact, traditionally conservative institutions are increasingly concerned with the redistribution of wealth. Thus, the International Monetary Fund, the bastion of market ideology and of 'growth first', now recognises that growth at any price is bad policy. Sacrificing the most disadvantaged for the sake of economic growth leads countries towards instability and conflict. In fact, 'extreme' economic inequality is unsustainable in a democracy. Thus, either democracy succeeds in reversing inequality, or democracy is replaced by military dictatorships controlled by elites to maintain inequality. To prevent this, the International Monetary Fund now includes guidance on reducing inequality (and not just 'advice' on economic growth) when steering a country's economic policy in exchange for financial assistance.[1]

It should not be forgotten that the ultimate goal of any economic policy should be to improve the quality of life of the average and especially of the most disadvantaged citizens.[2] Thus, given that economic growth *per se* does not ensure an equitable distribution of income, there seems to be a need for rules that do not seek efficiency or growth but ensure these gains are fairly shared out among all concerned. Indeed, it is worth noting that welfare is improved not only through higher consumption rates, but also by guaranteeing human dignity, freedom of expression and the right to participate in matters that affect one's own life, among other principles. All these values are pursued by labour law, as will be discussed below.

[1] IMF, *Guidance Note for Surveillance under Article IV Consultations* (IMF, 2015).

[2] J Rawls, *A Theory of Justice* (Cambridge MA, Harvard University Press, 1971); A Banerjee and E Duflo, *Good Economics for Hard Times* (New York, Random House, 2019) 205.

Redressing the Balance of Bargaining Power

The recent history (since the origins of capitalism) of the world of labour has been shaped by a progressive, continuous loss of bargaining power by the owner of labour vis-à-vis the owner of capital.[3] Originally, artisans and farmers had all the elements they needed to trade in the market. However, over time, these elements were gradually lost as a result of the sacrosanct 'division of labour'. First, they were deprived of contact with their end customers through the traders or merchants who bought their goods to sell them on the market. Second, with the advent of technology, they lost the productivity battle against the big factories, which prevented their small workshops from being competitive. Thus, these workers, with no machinery to till their land or to make their own products competitively, had no choice but to sell their labour power. Indeed, one of the identifying elements of the weakness of bargaining power is precisely having *no alternative way of obtaining an income* other than by selling one's labour power.

This situation is excellently described in John Steinbeck's novel, *The Grapes of Wrath* (and its cinema adaptation with the same title brought to the big screen by the director John Ford). It tells the story of one of the thousands of farming families who lost their farmland as a result of mechanisation and were forced to move to California to find work that would help them subsist. Ten of thousands of other families were in the same boat, having been deprived of their livelihoods which had been built on farming the land. This mass exodus led to unemployment in the cities, pushing wages below subsistence level. It comes as no surprise that Steinbeck portrays the situation in his novel as all being part of the same 'plan': first, people are deprived of their livelihood by artificially creating an excess of labour supply, which then drives down the wages of those who have no alternative but to accept poor working conditions.

The same happened with the petty bourgeoisie who, after the 1929 crash, lost their capital income from agriculture, investments and real estate, which had previously given them a comfortable life with economic stability. This does not mean that this urban petty bourgeoisie did not work before the loss of this income. However, if they did, it was easy to bring in some extra revenue. Thus, photographers, journalists, lawyers, and doctors worked, although these jobs were not their primary source of income. Hence, working was not imposed on them, as they had alternative incomes that came from their capital, but they did provide services as a means of participating in society. This also implied that any loss of work would not entail any financial hardship, since their economic stability was assured.

The disappearance of these sources of economic security as a result of the 1929 crash and the Second World War changed the paradigm, forcing the petty

[3] BE Kaufman, 'Labour's Inequality of Bargaining Power: Changes over Time and Implications for Public Policy' (1989) 10(3) *Journal of Labor Research* 285; BE Kaufman, 'Labor's Inequality of Bargaining Power: Myth or Reality? (1991) 12(2) *Journal of Labor Research* 151.

bourgeois to work and accept the imposed labour conditions as their only means of subsistence.

In reality, there is no need to travel back in time to expose 'financial necessity' as the origin and reason for the supply of labour. Observational studies in countries with poor working conditions show that young people refuse, or delay, entering the labour market until they can no longer depend on their parents, or want to start a family and need the resources.[4] We are talking about young well-educated university graduates who do not take up the jobs on offer or leave them shortly after they start working. If we analyse the reasons given by these young people, most of them coincide in that the job conditions were poor: too much work, excessive working hours, low salaries, etc. Obviously, the fact that they can refuse this kind of work (and have some bargaining power) comes solely from their parents' ability to support them (and probably also from the lowering of these young people's expectations for an independent life). That is, these young people who do not have alternative sources of income (parents without sufficient resources, a substantial inheritance, alternative income, etc.), will have to accept the kinds of jobs which others in a better position turn down.[5] In general, whenever a firm uses imbalances in bargaining power to try to impose wages below what workers are willing to accept (reservation wage), this will lead to unemployment.[6]

Thus, the main reason for the inequality of bargaining power, and the lack of real free will, requiring the intervention of labour law, stems from the lack of alternative sources of subsistence (not having capital) beyond the sale of one's labour power, i.e., living off one's work.

This issue also explains the weakening of labour law. The golden years of economic growth substantially improved the positions of many employees. Good salaries and economic security enabled people to buy properties to rent out, to invest in stocks and shares, and in investment funds or in small businesses, which spared many citizens from having to work as their sole source of income. As a result, some employees (the 'upper' part of the working class) may see the existence of labour law as being unnecessary, since these alternative sources of income now provide them with the economic security that was previously provided by the welfare state and labour law. This is tantamount to a kind of 'death by success' of labour law, which enjoyed its greatest moments thanks to the fall from grace of the petty bourgeoisie. Thus, the recovery of this part of society's economic status, thanks precisely to labour law, may have ironically caused it to lose ground today.

[4] A Banerjee and G Chiplunkar, 'How Important are Matching Fictions in the Labor Market? Experimental and Non-experimental Evidence from a Large Indian Firm' (2018), *Working Paper*, cited in Banerjee and Duflo, *Good Economics for Hard Times* 197.

[5] In some cases, the public policy tries to force this people to abandon 'voluntary unemployment'. This takes the form of measures within social security law, for example, withdrawing benefits from individuals who refuse to accept jobs offering low-standard terms and conditions of employment. The British experience is a good example, see S Deakin and F Wilkinson, 'Labour Law, Social Security and Economic Inequality' (1991) 15(2) *Cambridge Journal of Economics* 125–48.

[6] OECD, *Competition in Labour Markets* (Paris, OECD, 2020).

This is in line with how people vote, as mentioned above. Many voters know that conservative policies can harm their status and rights, yet still vote for them as workers because these parties protect their 'other' agenda. Thus, citizens' disinterest in labour regulations as a key factor in determining their vote and the consequent indifference of political parties (including progressive parties) may stem from the emergence of alternative sources of income that voters wish to protect (income from real estate and investments, untaxed inheritances, etc.).

This effect is the outcome of a well thought out plan of action. In 1976, at the height of the ideological confrontation with the USSR, the congressional Joint Economic Committee presented a report to the US Congress, which advocated encouraging the majority of US citizens to become owners of part of their business capital as a way of bringing them into the capitalist system.[7] The idea to increase the number of 'owners' was seen as a retaining wall against communism. Irrespective of the success or failure of this plan, it became clear that citizens who were employees as well as owners (of shares, real estate) were likely to believe they had conflicting interests if the 'economic' and the 'social' were perceived as antagonistic.

It therefore seems plausible that this 'upper' part of the working class (which had more contacts in politics than the rest of the working class) would decide to make political demands that differed from those of the bulk of the working class, given that its financial security was guaranteed by other means.

However, there are other causes that weaken workers' bargaining position vis-à-vis the capital owner. As authors have pointed out on many occasions,[8] capital is more liquid and flexible, which gives the owners of capital better control over the demand for labour. Conversely, workers cannot accumulate their labour, nor can they save it for a time when the market situation is more favourable. Labour is supplied or wasted. Thus, the pressure to 'sell' labour, since it is otherwise wasted and cannot be recovered, weakens the bargaining position of all workers, even those who hypothetically have alternative sources of income.

Yet these two reasons are not the only ones that trigger the existence of unequal bargaining, there is a third factor. Let us think for a moment about the case of an elite football player like Messi. He is a worker who has no alternative sources of income and whose job is less permanent than any other because he is forced to retire before the age of forty. Messi knows that whatever he does not earn for his services as a footballer during his youth, he will never earn afterwards. This situation should put him in a very weak negotiating position. However, if this player

[7] US Congress, Joint Economic Committee, *1976 Joint Economic Report, Senate Report No 94-690, Congress 2nd session* (Washington DC, US Government Printing Office, 1976) 100.

[8] S Deakin and F Wilkinson, 'Justifications and Techniques of Legal Regulation of the Employment Relation', in H Collins, P Davis and R Rideout (ed), *Legal Regulation of the Employment Relation, Kluwer Law International* (London, Collins, 2001) 42; RD Blair and JL Harrison, *Monopsony in Law and Economics* (Cambridge University Press, 2010) 81; G Mundlak, 'The Third Function of Labour Law: Distributing Labour Market Opportunities Among Workers', in G Davidov and B Languille, (ed), *The Idea of Labour Law* (Oxford, Oxford University Press, 2011) 318.

is known for one thing, it is for his astronomical earnings, which means that he does have bargaining power. The third factor that removes any potential redress in the balance of bargaining power between capital and labour is precisely the fact that workers are not Messi, i.e., the fungibility of workers. Thus, while Messi is a unique player, there is just one of him; most workers (99 per cent) can be replaced by someone else. The easier it is to replace workers with another comparable colleague, the less bargaining power they have.

The expendability of an employee reflects another fact brought about by economic and technological change. First of all, high fungibility stems from the worker's anonymity in the market. Thus, when the end customer of a product or service does not value the identity of the worker who does a job (probably because they do not even know who they are) the employer will find it very easy to replace them if they so wish. Thus, historically speaking, from the moment traders and distributors took on the role of marketing others' goods, workers' bargaining power began to wane. This situation has now worsened given the importance consumers now attach to brands.

Market developments are increasingly moving towards the use of uniform brands and trademarks, removing everything else from the equation, including the provision of the specific service the brand sells. In today's highly competitive globalised world, the most important asset (the capital) of any business is undoubtedly its customers. Small entrepreneurs struggle as they are unable to gain a foothold in the market when competing against large, well-known brands that use economies of scale in advertising and marketing.

In this context, the small business owner is forced to work under another company's letterhead in order to remain in the market; his survival depends on customers, who prefer a well-known brand name (and a certain standardised way of doing things) and choose this company over others. Small enterprises can only survive in this globalised world by paying a high price: anonymity in the marketplace. This brings them even closer to a position of unequal bargaining power that has traditionally been suffered by employees. Basically, workers are 'anonymous' in the eyes of the end customer. The customer trusts a brand (that is what marketing is for) and, from the customer's perspective, the worker is replaceable.

Secondly, technology also makes it easier to replace workers. Whereas artisans were highly trained individuals with long apprenticeships that made it difficult to replace them, machine operators often need less than two weeks of training to be able to do their job. This implies that, from the employer's perspective, anyone is a potential surrogate, thereby increasing their bargaining power to impose contractual conditions on the employee who wants or needs to keep their job.

Finally, this easy interchangeability is further enabled by another factor: structural unemployment. As Marx explained in *Capital*, a permanent rate of unemployment (an industrial reserve army) makes the threat of dismissal plausible if a worker objects to or complains about being replaced. In addition, the mere existence of high levels of unemployment is a permanent reminder of the difficulty of finding a new job and the need to keep one's current position. This situation weakens bargaining power.[9] Full employment brings the opposite situation; the worker knows that they will easily find a new job, while the employer will fear not being able to find a replacement. This is no small matter, since the level of unemployment as a factor affecting the individual bargaining power of workers, the justification for labour law (and the need for it) depends precisely on the unemployment rate in a particular country. Countries with non-existent unemployment have higher levels of bargaining power, making labour safeguards less essential than in countries with high unemployment rates.

The inequality created by the factors we have just seen, the lack of alternatives to obtain resources, the impossibility of stockpiling labour for the future and the ease with which workers can be replaced (together with other factors such as workers' risk aversion (fear of unemployment), the cost of finding alternative employment, the lack of job opportunities in the market) imply that there is no real negotiation between the parties. The worker is *economically subordinate* to the point of not being able to consider that they have given their free consent to working conditions (a cornerstone of any contractual relationship).[10] From an economic perspective, these 'frictions'[11] in the labour market have been considered as factors that lead to employers having monopsony power (or bargaining power) that leads to inefficiencies: (i) reduction of total employment; (ii) reduction of output; and (iii) higher prices in the product market.[12]

From a legal perspective, this economic subordination gives the employer discretionary power to dictate working hours, wages, occupational health and safety conditions, etc., which the worker cannot object to for fear of losing their job. As if this were not enough, economic subordination puts at risk all the other rights that a worker may have as a citizen, including constitutional rights. As such, dignity, freedom of expression, association, thought and privacy are affected in the employment relationship, unless limits are set. These are liberal values inherent to individuals that disappear if the employment relationship is left in the hands of supply and demand.

Thus, restricting and regulating the employer's unilateral power becomes a central objective of labour law as a way to reduce the imbalance of bargaining power. Since it is unfeasible to consider the worker's consent as valid, due to their unequal bargaining position, legal alternatives must be sought to legitimise the contractual relationship. Thus, labour law seeks to redress the balance of bargaining power with a view to providing greater equilibrium[13] and

[9] D Baker, *Rigged: How Globalization and the Rules of the Modern Economy Were Structured to Make the Rich Richer* (Washington DC, Center for Economic and Policy Research, 2016) 33.

[10] F Valdés Dal-Ré, 'Descentralización productiva y desorganización del derecho del trabajo' (2001) *Revista Universitaria de Ciencias del Trabajo* 45.

[11] P Basu, 'Understanding Labour Market Frictions: An Asset Pricing Approach' (2009) 61 (4) *Bulletin of Economics Research* 305.

[12] S Naidu, EA Posner and G Weyl, 'Antitrust Remedies for Labor Market Power' (2018) 132 *Harvard Law Review* 554; A Manning, *Monopsony in Motion: Imperfect Competition in Labor Markets* (New Jersey, Princeton University Press, 2003) 4; OECD, *Competition in Labour Markets*.

[13] P Davies and M Freedland, *Kahn-Freund's Labour and the Law* (London, Stevens, 1983) 8.

reducing the monopsony power (bargaining power) of the employer. In fact, the OECD[14] suggests that regulations are needed to address the distortions created by the accumulation of bargaining power in the hands of employers. Specifically, it states that collective bargaining and minimum wages may represent a solution.

Criticism of Unequal Bargaining Power to Justify Labour Law

Some authors have criticised the use of unequal bargaining power to justify labour regulations.[15] On the one hand, others have argued that there are always different degrees of interest in any exchange, i.e., one side is always more interested than the other in participating. However, *per se*, this does not mean that the exchange cannot benefit both sides. On the other hand, and along the same lines, it is claimed that nobody 'forces' an employee to accept the conditions offered in the labour market, and that if the employer offers unsatisfactory conditions, the worker can simply look for another job.

This criticism errs in equating the formal ability to give consent with real free will and autonomy. It is one thing to be able to theoretically refuse a job or resign to look for a better one, but it is quite another for this option to actually be feasible for a worker who lives off his labour power. Firstly, it presupposes that real employment alternatives are available and that workers can find them easily and cheaply. However, in economies with high rates of unemployment or informality, the real chances of finding a job for certain (poorly trained) profiles are low and, in any case, very costly in terms of time spent looking for a job, loss of income while looking, etc. As it has been said 'standard microeconomic models of labor markets almost always implicitly assume conditions of full employment'[16] which most of the cases make them of little use.

In addition, this theory is based on a person having perfect information and being totally rational, i.e., it assumes that the worker knows that they can find a better job and that they will leave their current job. As we have already said, the first drawback is that this hypothetical job may not exist or may be too costly to find. However, even if this is not the case, a worker in a poor situation may not want to take a gamble with his livelihood and that of his family, preferring instead to settle for poor conditions as opposed to ending up in a worse situation. In this way, fear (however irrational) or workers' typical risk aversion may prevent them

[14] OECD (n 6) 47.

[15] A Alchian and W Allen, *University Economics* 3rd edn (Belmont CA, Wadsworth, 1972) 427.

[16] BE Kaufman, 'The Old Institutionalists', in Kaufman (ed), *Government Regulation of the Employment Relationship* (Madison WN, Industrial Relations Research Association, 1997) 49.

from accessing better working conditions. In particular, the study by Cardoso et al.[17] showed how misperceptions about unemployment rates and the state of the labour market affected workers' willingness to accept lower wages.

In general, empirical studies confirm the low degree of worker mobility in order to obtain the 'deserved' wage (equivalent to marginal productivity). Several studies have shown that workers do not respond to wage decreases by seeking other jobs, as they would if the market worked efficiently.[18] The main reasons given were: workers' preferences, mobility costs, lack of information about job opportunities and workers' risk aversion.

In short, the difference in bargaining power, based on replaceability (level of unemployment and market anonymity) and the lack of alternatives in terms of earning income (no capital), justifies the need for and existence of labour regulations, mandatory minimum standards set by the legislator and rules that promote collective bargaining as a way of redressing the imbalance. What does not seem feasible, however, is to justify poor working conditions on the grounds that the worker could hypothetically find a better job, which is easier in theory than in practice.

[17] D Card et al, 'Firms and Labor Market Inequality: Evidence and Some Theory' (2016) Working Paper 22850 *NBER* 17.

[18] A Sokolova and T Sorensen, 'Monopsony in Labor Markets: A Meta-Analysis' (2018) Discussion Paper Series 11966 *IZA Institute of Labor Economics*; B Hirsch, T Schank, and C Schnabel, 'Differences in Labour Supply to Monopsonistic Firms and the Gender Pay Gap: An Empirical Analysis Using Linked Employer-Employee Data from Germany' (2010) 28 (2) *Journal of Labor Economics* 291; DA Webber, 'Firm Market Power and the Earnings Distribution' (2011) CES-WP *US Census Bureau Center for Economic Studies* 11.

7

The (Pre)Distribution of Wealth

Increasing Inequality in the Distribution of Wealth

Unequal bargaining power between employers and workers leads to abusive, degrading and dangerous working conditions, which are far removed from any notion of real consent on the part of the worker who has no choice but to accept them, and also triggers imbalances at macroeconomic level, i.e., social inequality.

Wages are the main tool to distribute the wealth created in an economy. Thus, a decrease in workers' bargaining power will lead to an increase in social inequality, by polarising society between those who have capital and those who do not.

This effect has been very visible in recent years. The demise of labour law in Western economies has coincided with a steady, permanent reduction in the share of income generated in an economy (or in a particular company) that is paid to employees. From 1970 to 2019, in the USA, employees' share of national income fell by 6%. The same applied to Spain, where this figure fell from 62 to 55 per cent, and to Italy, where the figure dropped from 59 to 52 per cent. In other countries such as Germany and France, the reduction was smaller, down from 66 to 64 per cent in the first case and from 65 to 62 per cent in the second.[1]

There are many possible explanations for this reduction in the income received by wage earners over the last 40 years.[2] Two factors will be discussed here: firstly, labour law as an effective means of redistribution, and secondly, the increase in automation and globalisation as factors that eat further into workers' bargaining power, thereby increasing the imbalance.

Labour Law as a Means of Income Redistribution

In the capital-labour conflict, i.e., in the division between those who live off income generated by capital and those who have no capital and therefore have to sell their

[1] All data taken from the Saint Louis Federal Reserve Bank. See www.stlouisfed.org/.

[2] For a summary of the factors explaining the increase in wage inequality, see K Stone, *From Widgets to Digits: Employment Regulation for the Changing Workplace* (Cambridge, Cambridge University Press, 2004) 261 and following.

labour power, wages are the main way in which income is distributed.[3] Hence, they are no longer a simple 'wage condition', but a form of redistribution of the wealth generated in a country. This redistribution, far from being purely merit-based, responds to the bargaining power of each of the parties involved.[4]

In fact, although orthodox economic theory holds that the wage paid by employers is equal to the product of the marginal value of the worker's productivity,[5] the reality is very different.

According to this theory, the employer pays a wage based on the exact output that each worker produces for that employer. In a competitive market, where companies need to minimise costs to stay in business, employers will only grant wage increases when the worker's productivity increases.[6] This economic theory holds that if employers were to pay more than a worker's marginal productivity, the company would be priced out of the market because its products would incur a cost premium that would drive up prices, causing consumers to reject them. In turn, this theory also states that if an employer pays less than the marginal value of the worker's productivity,[7] employees will leave their jobs and go to another firm that pays them their marginal value (marginal productivity).

However, this theory does not reflect reality.[8] As noted above, there are many reasons why employees do not 'go to another company' that would pay them the full value they bring with their labour. The first reason is that there may not be better job opportunities. Secondly, the employee may not know the true value that their work brings to the organisation. Thirdly, the fear of unemployment may prevent the employee from asking the company for what they are entitled to.

This is demonstrated by empirical studies. For example, according to an ILO study,[9] over the period 1999–2013, the increase in average labour productivity was twice as high as the increase in average wages. The OECD also supports these findings by stating that average real wages in developed countries between 1995 and 2013 grew annually by an average of 0.8 per cent while labour productivity

[3] However, there are others, such as subsidies, social inclusion income, etc. In other words, the state, through capital taxes, can subsequently redistribute the income generated through transfers to those without capital.

[4] On how wages are set in the economy or in a company see Todolí-Signes, *Salario y productividad* (Tirant lo Blanch, 2017).

[5] JB Clark, 'The Possibility of a Scientific Law of Wages' (1889) 4 *Publications of the American Economic Association* 39. For a detailed study of this theory see J Tobin, 'Neoclassical Theory in America: JB Clark and Fisher' (1985) 75(6) *American Economic Review* 28.

[6] RL Heneman and JM Werner, *Merit Pay: Linking Pay to Performance in a Changing World*, 2nd edn (Greenwich, CT, Information Age Publishing, 2005) 34.

[7] A worker's marginal productivity refers to how much the worker's output increases by adding an extra hour of work.

[8] A Manning, 'The Elusive Employment Effect of the Minimum Wage' (2020) *Journal of Economic Perspectives* 3–27.

[9] International Labour Organization, *Global Wage Report 2012/2013* (Geneva, 2013) 48–49, graph 36.

increased by 1.5 per cent.[10] In other words, while the value that a worker contributed to the company doubled, wages did not, and the owner of the capital retained all the profits from these labour productivity increases. In short, the reality is that workers' wages hinge on negotiation (and not on any objective factor) and on the power of each of the parties in the bargaining process.

Therefore, given the imbalance between the bargaining power of the employer and the worker, as we have seen, the latter will usually obtain much less than the value they contribute to the company and to the economy. Hence, the weakening of labour regulations over the last forty years has been a key factor in both the decline in the amount of income received through wages and the polarisation on this issue.

A number of empirical studies have confirmed the positive impacts of minimum wages and collective bargaining protection as effective instruments for improving workers' bargaining power.[11]

In particular, the vast majority of empirical studies show that raising the minimum wage through legislation leads to real improvements in the pay received by workers.[12] This increase has been criticised by orthodox economic theory on the grounds that it also leads to an increase in unemployment. This criticism is consistent with the principles of neoclassical supply and demand. That is, if the price of something is artificially increased (by law or collective bargaining), people will buy less of that product, generating a surplus. In the 1980s and 1990s, economists[13] recommended scrapping minimum wage laws, in line with this theory. Even highly respected economic institutions such as the OECD,[14] in a report on desirable labour market policies, advised countries to 'reassess the role of statutory minimum wages as an instrument to achieve redistributive goals'. However, over the years, and following a notable increase in the number of studies that have failed to prove the validity of neoclassical theory, there is now growing interest in the role of the minimum wage as a way to redistribute bargaining power across countries.

[10] OECD, 'Decoupling of Wages from Productivity: What Implications for Public Policy?' (2018) 20(2) *OECD Economic Outlook* 51.

[11] P Denice and J Rosenfeld, 'Unions and Non-union Pay in the United States, 1977–2015' (2018) 5 *Sociological Science* 541; B Western and J Rosenfeld, 'Unions, Norms, and the Rise in U.S. Wage Inequality (2011) 76(4) *American Sociological Review* 513–37; BT Hirsch, 'What Do Unions Do for Economic Performance?' (2004) 25 *Journal of Labor Research* 193–237; D Card and A Krueger, *Myth and Measurement: The New Economics of the Minimum Wage* (New Jersey, Princeton University Press, 1995); SJ Nickell and M Andrews, 'Unions, Real Wages and Employment in Britain 1951–79' (1983) 35 *Oxford Economic Papers* 183; F Jaumotte and C Osorio Buitron, 'Inequality and Labor Market Institutions' (July 2015) *IMF Staff Discussion Note*; Y Abdih and S Danninger, 'What Explains the Decline of the U.S. Labor Share of Income? An Analysis of State and Industry Level Data' (Washington DC, 2017) *IMF Working Paper* (WP/17/167); I Álvarez et al, 'Missing Links in the Inclusive Growth Debate: Functional Income Distribution and Labor Market Institutions' (2011) *International Labour Review* 337–62.

[12] Manning, 'The Elusive Employment Effect of the Minimum Wage'.

[13] C Brown, 'Minimum Wage Laws: Are They Overrated?' (1988) 2 *Journal of Economic Perspective* 133.

[14] OECD, *Jobs Study* (Paris, 1994).

A joint report by the IMF, the World Bank, the OECD and the ILO[15] stated that statutory minimum wages that were set at an appropriate floor level increased workers' income share without affecting the demand for labour. This was especially true for employees with the poorest working conditions. The OECD also seems to have embraced a much more positive view of the potential of the minimum wage than it had before. Specifically, a report by this international organisation[16] argues that the minimum wage can help to ensure fair rewards for work and prevent job cuts if it is moderate and well designed.

In recent years and following a wealth of empirical studies showing that increasing the minimum wage does not destroy jobs,[17] there has been a major shift on this issue, from scrapping it to debating what is the appropriate figure for it. In fact, the key seems to reside in the floor of the minimum wage. When wages are too low, as firms are able to take most of the profit due to their strong bargaining position, an increase in the minimum wage ensures better redistribution, without having a negative impact on employment as firms will still make enough profit per worker. Thus, as the above-mentioned reports point out, the minimum wage brings better distribution of the profits generated in a business without leading to unemployment.

In this sense, the EU seems to be in favour of establishing a minimum wage directive to guarantee or encourage countries to introduce a statutory minimum wage. According to the European Commission, this regulation is justified because in recent years low wages have not kept pace with increases in other higher wages. This is due to an increase in wage polarisation.[18] In fact, it is clearly specified that this minimum wage regulation is necessary because collective bargaining, hitherto the guarantor of equal pay, has been weakened in many EU countries. Thus, in the absence of strong collective bargaining, the law must take action by introducing a minimum wage. More interestingly, these EU reports suggest that the optimal minimum wage should be 60 per cent of a country's full-time median wage. That is, the EU specifies that an amount below 60 per cent of a country's median wage cannot be considered a *living wage*, and thus implies the need for a ban on this type of low pay.[19]

[15] ILO, OECD, IMF and WORLD BANK, *Boosting Jobs and Living Standards in G20 Countries* 12. Available at: www.oit.org/wcmsp5/groups/public/---dgreports/---dcomm/documents/publication/wcms_183705.pdf.

[16] OECD, *Employment Outlook* (Paris, 2018) 72.

[17] Manning (n 8); M Reich, K Jacobs, A Bernhardt and I Perry, 'The Proposed Minimum Wage Law for Los Angeles: Economic Impacts and Policy Options' (March 2015) *UC Berkeley ILRE*; M Chletsos and GP Giotis, 'The Employment Effect of Minimum Wage Using 77 International Studies since 1992: A Meta-analysis' (2015) Paper 61321, *MPRA University of Munich*; Card and Krueger, *Myth and Measurement: The New Economics of the Minimum Wage.*

[18] European Commission, *Consultation Document. Second phase consultation of Social Partners under Article 154 TFEU on a possible action addressing the challenges related to fair minimum wages* (Brussels, 2020).

[19] European Commission, *Consultation Document. Second phase consultation of Social Partners under Article 154 TFEU on a possible action addressing the challenges related to fair minimum wages.*

In addition, other mechanisms, such as limits on unilateral dismissal, can have the same counterbalancing effect on bargaining power. Since fear of dismissal can be a powerful deterrent on workers seeking the wages they deserve according to the value they have contributed, effective protection against arbitrary dismissal improves workers' bargaining position. Similarly, a maximum limit on working hours protects employees from overexertion, job-sharing and the resulting drop in unemployment lessens employees' likelihood of being replaced, which again enhances their bargaining power.

Technology and Globalisation as Factors that Reduce Bargaining Power

Workers have participated in the growth generated in the economy over the last 40 years, yet ironically their purchasing power has been reduced. That is, despite the fact that the economy has grown and generated wealth, workers' real wages (purchasing power) have been frozen, and in the case of non-university graduates, wages have been slashed by between 10 and 20 per cent.[20]

While some economists point to political and regulatory changes in recent decades (let us not forget that the downward slide began precisely during the Reagan-Thatcher era),[21] others point to structural shifts in the economy as the culprit for this deterioration in workers' incomes.[22]

It is argued here that the decline in wages also coincided with two key challenges in the labour market. Firstly, globalisation.[23] In 1978, China embarked on a market orientation policy, and in 1984, India began liberalisation. These two countries have become a source of labour for the entire world market, increasing the fear of production relocation and job losses. Indeed, globalisation (and globalisation of labour with platforms such as Amazon Mechanical Turk) has brought a new perspective to the replaceability of workers as a factor that undermines bargaining power.

On the concept of decent work see, JL Gil, 'Concepto de trabajo decente' (2012) 15 *Relaciones Laborales: Revista Crítica de Teoría y Práctica* 77; A Sen, 'Trabajo y derechos' (2000) 119(2) *Revista Internacional Del Trabajo* 129.

[20] D Autor, 'Work of the Past, Work of the Future' (2019) 25588 *NBER Working Paper*.

[21] T Piketty, *Capital in the Twenty-First Century* (Cambridge MA, The Belknap Press, 2017). In addition, D Howell, ('Theory-Driven Facts and the Growth in Earnings Inequality' (1999) 31 *Review of Radical Political Economics*) analysed countries that have seen the same type of technological change but have experienced major differences in income distribution. Thus, for example, France has seen a much smaller decline in the income share of workers than the USA, pointing to policy and regulatory differences between the two countries.

[22] A Banerjee and E Duflo, *Good Economics for Hard Times* (New York, Random House, 2019) 243; Katz ('Industry Studies of Wage Inequality: Symposium Introduction' (2001) 54 *Industrial and Labor Relations Review*) argued that changes in business organisation are a relevant factor in explaining income inequality in recent years.

[23] B Hepple, *Labour Laws and Global Trade* (Oxford, Hart Publishing, 2005); C Kaufmann, *Globalisation and Labour Rights. The Conflict Between Core Labour Rights and International Economic Law* (London, Bloomsbury, 2007).

Empirical studies[24] have demonstrated that the prospect of delocalisation, or the mere threat of manufacturing delocalisation, leads to a loss of bargaining power for workers who accept wage reductions to avoid losing their jobs. These authors reported that, in the cases studied, not even the coordinated, collective action of all the workers in a company or a country has been able to prevent this. Globalisation has thus become one of the main causes of the loss of employees' bargaining power in recent years.[25]

In addition, we need to factor in the effects of automation and digital transformation. The 1970s and 1980s were also the beginning of the race to computerise the economy (IBM launched its first personal computer in 1981). Again, the effects of automation have not been kind to those who only own their labour power. Thus, manufacturing firms have laid off large numbers of workers, and the threat of job losses (thanks to machines) has contained if not directly reduced wages for the rest of the workforce.[26]

Hence, automation and digital transformation have a twofold effect on workers' bargaining power. First, the increased value of capital over labour: the better the technology (i.e., the more productive it is) the more value given to the capital that can buy it. Imagine the extreme case in which AI performs all the intellectual and physical tasks of a human. At this extreme, humans would be unnecessary for production, resulting in zero bargaining power for workers. Obviously, we are a long way from this point, and we may never get there,[27] but as technology moves forward, capital owners gain more bargaining power.

Second, the mere threat of automation can deter wage increases. If workers demand wage increases, even if only to maintain their purchasing power, the firm may decide to invest in automation. Thus, workers may decide not to ask for wage increases or may accept wage reductions to at least keep their jobs.

Returning to the question of what has driven wage reductions and widening inequality in the distribution of wealth; the reality is that both facts point to the same outcome. Thus, the debate over whether it has been caused by policy changes (reduction of labour protection and taxes) or structural changes in the economy (globalisation and automation) is of little interest since, whatever the root cause, the reality is that they both have had the same effect: shrinking bargaining power. Thus, unless the aim is to reverse globalisation and automation, the only factor that

[24] G Epstein and J Burke, *Threat Effects and the Internationalization of Production* (Amherst: University of Massachusetts, PERI Working Paper Series n. 15, 2001).

[25] JC Messenger and N Ghosheh, (dir), *Offshoring and Working Conditions in Remote Work* (Geneva, ILO, 2010).

[26] D Acemoglu and P Restrepo, 'Robots and Jobs: Evidence from US Labour Markets' (2017), *NBER Working Paper 23285*; D Acemoglu and P Restrepo 'Secular Stagnation? The Effect of Aging on Economic Growth in the Age of Automation, American Economic Growth in the Age of Automation' (2017) 107(5), *American Economic Review Papers and Proceedings* 174.

[27] According to many of the world's leading experts on the subject, interviewed by M Ford, *Architects of Intelligence: The Truth About AI from the People Building It* (Birmingham, UK, Packt Publishing, 2018).

could be changed is the political one. Therefore, empowering labour regulations that restore the bargaining power lost by workers would appear to be necessary to bring back workers' bargaining power and rebalance income sharing. As Polanyi argued in *The Great Transformation*,[28] the underlying the regulation of labour market was the need to protect social structures from the disruptive consequences of fast changing economic situation.

However, returning the status of labour law to its 1980s' heyday does not seem sufficient to reach this goal. Firstly, because the problems facing workers today are very different. Secondly, because globalisation and automation have eroded bargaining power to a much greater extent than the pre-Reagan-Thatcher era. Thus, there is a need for stronger regulation, probably at international level, to curb the erosion of purchasing power and the conditions of those who make a living from their labour.

Meritocracy and Distributive Justice

The value of meritocracy, understood as the justice of everyone receiving what they deserve, is deeply rooted in our society. It is a value that responds to two different objectives. First, meritocracy ensures fair allocation of incentives. In fact, if the economic system assures market agents that they will receive the benefits of what they have produced or created, they will be motivated to produce. Conversely, in a society where individual efforts are not rewarded, there will be very little incentive to create anything.

Second, one of the basic principles in the justice theory[29] is 'receiving what one deserves'. A society can only be fair (regardless of the incentives it creates) if it ensures (or tries to ensure) that each citizen gets a share of what he or she has helped to create or build.

In this way, by failing to distribute profits fairly, deregulation in the labour market can be criticised from two perspectives: firstly, for not generating the right incentives to add more value, and secondly, for not distributing income fairly according to the value contributed by each individual.

Classical economic theories were particularly concerned about ensuring that 'rent extraction' by the unproductive sectors of society did not impede economic growth. François Quesnay (1694–1774), often regarded as 'The Father of Economics', divided society into three classes. Firstly, there was a productive part composed mainly of farmers who worked the land. Secondly, the part that transformed this production, such as artisans and merchants, and thirdly, the unproductive or 'sterile' class, which included landowners, the nobility and the clergy. In this distribution of society, Quesnay warned that if the unproductive

[28] K Polyani, *The Great Transformation* (New York, Reinhold, 1944).
[29] J Rawls, *A Theory of Justice* (Cambridge MA, Harvard University Press, 1971).

members of society kept too much of what was generated, the economy would grind to a halt. That is, if in the distribution of wealth, the unproductive actors kept too much of the pie, producers would have little reason to continue to make or create anything.[30]

Adam Smith took up this idea of rentiers as the unproductive part of society.[31] In this sense, Smith, who wrote at a time when capitalist societies were beginning to emerge as opposed to the mainly agricultural world of Quesnay, added a new factor. He thus understood that there were three ways of distributing the wealth generated by society: (1) the part taken by workers in the shape of wages; (2) business profits taken by the capitalists; and (3) the rent taken by landowners.

Smith separated the concepts of 'rent' and 'profit' precisely because of the idea of value contribution. Smith understood that capitalists added value by starting a business and risking their capital to acquire new machinery and innovate, while the rentier only extracted value from those who generated it, i.e., workers and capitalists. In other words, once again, the need to 'deserve what one puts in', and to share the profits generated based on merit, was present in classical economic theories.

However, even then, Smith saw that it was not only landowners who were unproductive rent extractors. Smith considered that the problem of rent and value extraction could be extended to other agents such as monopolies. Thus, benefiting from a monopolistic situation could lead people to obtain more income than they deserved, which would turn them into rentiers by gaining income (rents) over and above the value actually created.

It is not difficult to establish a connection with worker-employer bargaining positions based on this concept of value creation and extraction. Indeed, an acute imbalance in bargaining power that leads to workers being paid less than their 'deserved' wages will turn the employer into a rentier (receiving more than they generate) on the one hand and reduce incentives to work productively on the other.

Building on this belief, other economists have applied the ideas of value extraction to the behaviour of capitalist entrepreneurs and investors. Thus, Marshall[32] considered that the profit made from machines could be considered as a 'quasi-rent' or unearned rent, i.e., any return obtained by an investor, which was above the market return on capital, and did not come from genuine entrepreneurial risk-taking.

All this makes even more sense today, in a context in which vertically 'dismantled' companies are taking on less and less financial risk by making other agents shoulder it, either through subcontracting (trading companies without bargaining power are forced to take responsibility for financial risks) or through dismissals,

[30] H Higgs, *The Physiocrats: Six Lectures on the French Economists of the 18th Century* (London, Macmillan and Co, 1897) 27–49.

[31] A Smith, *The Wealth of Nations: An Inquiry into the Nature and Causes*, 1st edn 1776 (Eireann Press, 2023).

[32] A Marshall, *Principles of Economics*, 8th edn (London, Macmillan, 1947) 74.

substantial changes in working conditions, non-application of collective bargaining agreements, etc.

In short, an imbalance of bargaining power, left to the free market, can easily turn into rent extraction, precisely because whoever has the bargaining power can keep the lion's share of the profits, while at the same time forcing the powerless party to take on the economic risks of the business.

This outcome has little to do with the sought-after meritocracy. Thus, these unbalanced positions of power can be (and are) used to prevent other agents from receiving the reward they deserve for the value generated, or for the risks taken, begetting rentiers who extract more value than they create. This can be criticised on the grounds of distributive justice theories, and on the grounds of values that are more akin to market freedom.

The market maxim is that economic operators should be rewarded according to their contribution and effort. Thus, when this result does not occur, it is because we are dealing with a market failure.[33] It is true that market mechanisms are primarily designed to generate efficiency and growth and not to distribute it later, but the truth is that without meritocratic distribution of the profits obtained, growth will rapidly disappear.

As neo-liberal thinkers regularly remind us, if investors do not receive a return on their investment, they will not invest. In fact, one of the most repeated maxims in recent years is that if the state imposes excessive taxes there will be no growth because no one will have an incentive to work or invest. All of this is based on the same idea: the wealth generated must be distributed according to the contribution made. Well, the same applies, and must apply, to workers. If they do not receive a share commensurate with their input and involvement, their incentive to invest their labour power will disappear.

This is confirmed by empirical studies. When there is no correlation between the amount of effort invested and the rewards received, workers generally reduce their overall input.[34] Thus, unequal bargaining power, without a counterbalance, quickly leads to lack of motivation and poorer productivity among workers. Hence, it is economically justified for the legislator to impose limits on the use of unilateral employer power to safeguard productivity growth.

This is not just an economic issue. As in many other cases, there is a social value that justifies labour regulation to ensure (or attempt to ensure) that workers are compensated according to the profit generated to reduce the feeling of injustice.

Thus, besides safeguarding fair distribution of wealth between capital and labour (through minimum wages, stronger collective bargaining, etc.), there are other regulations that are justified on the grounds of distributive justice. Thus, for example, arbitrary dismissal (without cause or reason) clashes head-on

[33] G Davidov, *Distributive Justice and Labour Law. Philosophical Foundations of Labour Law* (Oxford, Oxford University Press, 2018) 143.

[34] A Engellandt, and RT Riphahn, 'Evidence on Incentive Effects of Subjective Performance Evaluations' (2011) *IRL Review* 241, 256.

with the concept of merit.[35] Of course, dismissal for no reason does not actually exist. What happens is that the so-called dismissal 'without cause' is based on non-work-related justifications or on grounds that are discriminatory or violate other rights, i.e., they are reasons that are not deemed to be valid in a system that assesses whether dismissal is deserved or not. Thus, depriving an employee of economic support when they have not behaved in a manner that warrants this is socially reprehensible from a justice perspective. Therefore, this justifies public legislation that prevents depriving someone of economic support when they have not done anything to deserve it (dismissal without cause).

From a purely rational economic perspective, it could be argued that no employer would dismiss a productive worker. However, this is not the reality. The fourth season of the series *Fargo* shows how, in the USA, the director of a private hospital refuses to treat a man who is bleeding to death because he is Italian. When offered more than enough cash to pay for any expenses incurred (and make a substantial profit) in his medical treatment, the director still refuses, referring him instead to a public hospital that treats his 'kind'. The same idea emerges, almost parodically, in another scene in which, in the 1950s, several Minnesota banks rejected the 'invention' of the credit card as a financial instrument because it came from a person of colour. Ultimately, the show's excellent storytelling conveys the point that business owners have prejudices and interests which are not centred on maximising efficiency, i.e., for some, exercising power over others may be more useful than economic gain. Hence, the importance of not leaving certain decisions in the hands of the unilateral power of the employer, especially those related to workers, given that they will not only harm the employer, who would end up without a genuinely productive employee (reducing productivity),[36] but they will also break with the principle of justice based on merit, hurting those who do not deserve it.

However, for the ideal of meritocracy to prevail in the labour market, the ban on dismissals without cause must be *effective*. The fact that dismissal without cause is 'illegal' on paper (though in practice there are no truly compensatory consequences for this breach of the law), does not seem to be sufficient to reach the objective of meritocratic justice. For this reason, dismissal without cause must be ruled out by law through legal consequences that discourage its use, on pain of calling into question a society based on merit and reducing the productivity generated by workers who know that, no matter how hard they try, they can still be dismissed, whether they deserve it or not.

[35] Davidov, *Distributive Justice and Labour Law* 151.

[36] Several studies have proved the segregation on labour markets and the link between discrimination and the loss of efficiency, see GS Becker, *The economics of discrimination*, 2nd edn (University of Chicago Press, 1971); DM Gordon, R Edwards and M Reich, *Segmented Work, Divided Workers* (Cambridge, Cambridge University Press, 1982); JI Bulow, LH Summers, 'A Theory of Dual Labor Markets with Application to Industrial Policy, Discrimination and Keynesian Unemployment' (1986) 4(3) *Journal of Labor Economics* 376.

Efficiency versus Distributive Justice

Distributive Justice

As pointed out repeatedly in this book, economic growth goes hand in hand with distributive justice. Without fair or meritocratic distribution of profits, cooperation will quickly disappear, generating conflict and impeding growth (not to mention threatening democracy). Hence, it is argued in this book that the dichotomy between 'the economic' and 'the social' is an artificial and fallacious construct designed to force voters to choose the former. However, it must be acknowledged that this dichotomy may sometimes exist. In other words, rules or regulations which may undermine growth in the short or long term for the sake of redistribution. Ignoring the potential existence of this situation in this book would be as reductionist a view as the one that argues that this conflict always occurs.

However, precisely because growth and distribution are commonly understood to be at odds, there is a large body of literature that deals with this conflict of interest and attempts to resolve it. Rawls' *theory of justice*[37] is built around the defence of individual rights versus efficiency. Rawls' principle of justice is primarily aimed at protecting individual freedom, to pursue what each individual regards as 'a good life', as opposed to the maximisation of efficiency. In this sense, he argued that the provision of basic elements (food, shelter, education, etc.) should be guaranteed even if they cause inefficiency.

The argument used by this author to choose this option as the 'fairest' is the following. Before each person's position in the system is determined (the intellectual, physical and health capacities that each one is born with, race, nationality, wealth or debt inherited, etc ...), it is reasonable to accept certain minimum conditions for everyone. In other words, if we were unaware of our personal situation (a condition called 'the veil of ignorance'), it would be rational to accept certain inefficiency in exchange for insuring ourselves against the risk of 'falling' into misfortune. Thus, all the rules we would be willing to accept to correct the 'lottery' of life would be justified.

Rawls sets out a number of examples that support his theory. First, he considers it reasonable to accept that all important decisions should be made democratically, as well as stating that coercive power should only be exercised in accordance with pre-established rules. Indeed, not knowing whether we will be born a monarch with absolute power or a peasant, we would be unlikely to accept life in an absolute monarchy without the rule of law.

In any case, Rawls' aim is not to establish what specific minimum standards must be set for a fair society, but to dictate the grounds on which these standards must be set.[38] Thus, through this theory, Rawls justifies that fair laws must improve

[37] J Rawls, *Political Liberalism* (Oxford, Oxford University Press, 1972).

[38] In any case, a variety of authors argue that regulatory intervention in the field of contractual relations is implicit in Rawls' theory. On this, see GA Cohen, 'Where the Action Is: On the Site of

the situation of the most disadvantaged, given that the improvement of those who are worse off in society is a reasonable axiom to accept under the 'veil of ignorance'.

This rule of the 'veil of ignorance' can easily be applied to the world of work.[39] Given that we do not know whether we will be the owner of capital or a worker without capital when we are born, it seems fair to establish rules that balance out the power between the two, even if this leads to some inefficiency (anti-discrimination rules that guarantee equal treatment, wealth distribution, occupational health and safety, social protection against unforeseen events such as illness, accidents, disability, retirement, and maximum working hours that enable workers to have a private life, in short, respect for dignity and other fundamental rights).

However, the reality is that the theory of the veil of ignorance does not always lead to the justification of labour regulations.[40] Indeed, Rawls' objective is a maximum one, that is, to establish conditions that enable the so-called 'pursuit of individual happiness'.[41] This means that, if there are other valid solutions to achieve this objective and they do not lead to a reduction in efficiency, they will have to be chosen.

Guaranteed Employment or Minimum Income

Those who recognise the need for fair wealth distribution proffer different approaches to achieve this goal. A clear case in point is the European Union's commitment to the so-called 'flexicurity'. The report on 'Jobs, Jobs, Jobs', known as the Wim Kok Report,[42] introduces the concept of flexicurity[43] (although it does not expressly mention it), which focuses on 'finding the right balance' between flexibility and security. The aim is to protect workers' employability and not their jobs. The rol of the state appears to be confined to offering its citizens 'competitiveness' as proxy for the 'security'.[44] In addition, the concept of flexicurity includes increasing income security during job transitions (preferably through social security coverage), updating the skills of the unemployed (active labour market policies) and increasing social security coverage.

Distributive Justice' (1997) 26 *Philosophy and Public Affairs*: L Murphy, 'Institutions and the Demands of Justice' (1999) 27 *Philosophy and Public Affairs*.

[39] On the justification for the minimum wage as a means of preventing income disparities, see A Kronman, 'Contract Law and Distributive Justice' (1980) 89 *Yale Law Journal* 472.

[40] H Collins, 'Theories of Rights as Justifications for Labour Law', in (ed) *The Idea of Labour Law* (Oxford, Oxford University Press, 2011) 145.

[41] From the US Declaration of Independence: Life, Liberty and the Pursuit of Happiness.

[42] W Kok, (Dir) *Facing the Challenge. The Lisbon Strategy for Growth and Employment* (Luxemburg, EU, November 2004).

[43] This report introduces the idea into the European debate, though the concept of flexicurity was introduced by the Dutch sociologist Hans Adriaansens, who was the first to put the term into circulation, describing it as a set of policies capable of reconciling flexibility measures with security actions, the beneficiaries of which were to be precisely the workers affected by those measures, F Valdés Dal-Ré 'Flexiseguridad y mercado de trabajo' (2010) 9 *Relaciones Laborales* 129.

[44] S Deakin, *Renewing Labour Market Institutions*, (Budapest, Central European University, 2004) 4.

This flexicurity policy, which had many supporters during the early 2000s, was largely shelved as it did not produce the desired effects. The unemployment toll from the 2008 economic-financial crisis made it clear that the chances of those who had been made redundant finding a new job were simply unrealistic. Therefore, on 3 March 2010, the European Commission published a new document entitled *Europe 2020. A Strategy for Smart, Sustainable and Inclusive Growth* in which it (partially) corrects the previous flexicurity strategy and opts for internal flexicurity.[45]

In any case, the idea of reducing labour safeguards (labour rights) to achieve an equivalent result by other means has continued to be pursued.

Based on the perspective that work is a means to an end, i.e., an income, a variety of ways have been proposed for the state to ensure an income for all citizens, usually as a way of justifying the reduction of labour safeguards.

Basic income (in all its possible shapes and forms, of which there are many) has garnered considerable success between the two political and economic extremes. Firstly, neo-liberalism sees it as a way of deflecting criticism of the unemployment brought by globalisation and digital transformation, as well as a way of reducing state intervention in the economy. That is, the welfare state stops directly providing education, health care, etc., in exchange for handing over a cheque to citizens so that they can purchase these services on the free market. In turn, labour safeguards would cease to be necessary since if workers are dismissed rightly or wrongly, they would still be guaranteed a minimum income. The more progressive view justifies giving a cheque to citizens as a form of wealth redistribution. In other words, taxing higher incomes to give a share of wealth to everyone just because they are human beings.

If we imagine a world in which widespread artificial intelligence has been created and human labour is completely unnecessary, basic income, or a similar redistribution mechanism, which taxes capital to share it out to those who lack capital, seems indispensable (within a democratic capitalism). Indeed, in a world where labour has no productive value (because it is unnecessary), taxation and redistribution are essential. However, given that we are not at this stage (and may never get there), the disappearance of state intervention in favour of a single form of redistribution such as a basic income may be open to criticism.

Criticism of Basic Income

First, as previously discussed, labour regulations do not merely redistribute existing wealth, they increase it. The primary and secondary objective of many labour regulations is to address labour market failures to improve efficiency. Thus, replacing labour regulations (e.g., minimum wage, dismissal safeguards) with a

[45] S Ruesga Benito (Dir), *Instrumentos de flexibilidad interna en la negociación colectiva* (Ministerio de Empleo y Seguridad Social, 2012) 49.

minimum income would lead to a labour market riddled with inefficiencies and failures requiring a solution. The idea of flexicurity conjures up a recent example of the consequences of reducing dismissal safeguards in exchange for social welfare improvements during job transitions. In fact, labour deregulation in favour of greater unilateral company power to dismiss workers (flexibility is a euphemism) led to millions of redundancies that made it impossible for people to find another job quickly in a period of economic crisis. This increased the burden on unemployment benefits which, in turn, had to be reduced. Thus, weaker dismissal safeguards restored one of the failures of the labour market: the externalisation of dismissal costs, probably leading to more redundancies than necessary and, in turn, triggering a vicious circle of redundancies which made it impossible to maintain the promised unemployment benefits.

Secondly, maintaining a basic income in the long run can be problematic from a social point of view. It can divide and antagonise society rather than bring it together. Ronald Reagan, in his campaign for the US presidency, caricatured the poor as 'the welfare queen' alongside those who needed the welfare state to survive, in order to subsequently slim down the welfare state and reduce protection. In other words, there is a very real danger that those who are unemployed and are protected by a minimum income will be 'undervalued' by those who work, creating division among citizens. In fact, this situation of conflict may not be a 'natural' outcome but can be provoked. Basic income needs to be financed by taxing higher incomes, but what prevents these fortunate people from deciding to use their wealth to lobby against this minimum income instead of handing it over in the form of taxes? Thus, even if a basic income could be secured, it might not last very long.

Thirdly, there is a real likelihood that people whose jobs are replaced by a minimum income will lose skills, training and leverage that will push them out of any political involvement. The concept of the Roman 'bread and circuses' is well known. This strategy was based on the idea of maintaining a system of castes (patricians and plebeians) in which the former continued to own the means of production (land) and their political capacity and intervention, while the latter were only given the 'crumbs' to prevent uprisings. However, although the plebeians had the right to vote, they had no real political power, nor was there any real upward social mobility.

Thus, even if a minimum income lasted over time, it would only freeze the status quo, impeding social change or improvement for the most unfortunate and their descendants, thus doing away with upward social mobility and meritocracy.

Finally, work should not only be seen as a means to earn an income. For many wage earners, employment fulfils other primary needs such as self-esteem and self-respect, and it is a way to learn new skills and socialise.[46] In fact, in experiments where a basic income (through a 'negative income tax') was provided, workers

[46] Collins, 'Theories of Rights as Justifications for Labour Law' 149.

rarely reduced their working hours, i.e., they continued to work even though this was not necessary for them to live off.[47]

Even if most workers received a minimum income, they would prefer to continue working. In fact, in a survey by Banerjee et al,[48] 87 per cent of workers chose to continue working even when they received a basic income. Indeed, the evidence suggests that most people prefer to work, not because they need the money, but because work brings meaning to life, a sense of belonging, dignity and of being useful.[49] In fact, as already mentioned in this book, unemployment after a certain age (after collective redundancy) shortens life expectancy and increases the likelihood of alcoholism, addiction, pain and depression.[50] Thus, a minimum income does not seem to be the best solution for those pushed out of work by globalisation and technology, at least in the medium term.[51]

Other Tools: Work-Sharing and Guaranteed Employment

Instead, there seems to be a need for other types of measures that are much more closely related to labour regulations, e.g., shorter working hours for a better work–life balance and job sharing. Indeed, improvements in business productivity resulting from the use of technology imply that a company will be able to produce more products or services with fewer working hours. This reduction in hours can either take the form of redundancies, i.e., by keeping hours constant, fewer workers are needed to produce the same amount, or by reducing all the employees' working hours.

Another option, to prevent the damage caused by globalisation and technology that causes anger and conflict among the disadvantaged population in developed countries, is through guaranteed job programmes.[52] In fact, in the USA, when Vice President Kamala Harris was running for president during the primaries, she

[47] PK Robins, 'A Comparison of the Labour Supply Findings from Four Negative Income Tax Experiments' (1985) 20(4) *Journal of Human Resources* 567.

[48] A Banerjee, et al, 'Me and Everyone Else: Do People Think like Economists?' (2019) *MIMEO, Massachusetts Institute of Technology*.

[49] Advocates of basic income argue that its implementation means that people will seek other ways of obtaining satisfaction from life. While this is possible, it will undoubtedly require a change in mindset that will not occur in this generation. Another alternative is to engage in voluntary work. However, at least at present, this is not happening. In fact, people with more free time (retired people, unemployed people, do less volunteering than those who are in the labour market. (Banerjee et al 'Me and Everyone Else: Do People Think like Economists?' 301).

[50] D Sullivan, and T Von Wachter, 'Job Displacement and Mortality: An Analysis Using Administrative Data' (2009) 124 (3) *Quarterly Journal of Economics* 1265.

[51] At least not before changing social perceptions of people as being valuable in themselves and not conditioned by what they contribute to society.

[52] See more in M Hernández-Bejarano, 'Empleo garantizado y sus posibles yacimientos: atención a la dependencia como propuesta' (2020) 38 *Trabajo: Revista Iberoamericana de Relaciones Laborales* 101; JM Morales Ortega, 'Trabajo garantizado: luces y sombras sobre su régimen jurídico' (2020) 38 *Trabajo: Revista Iberoamericana de Relaciones Laborales* 51.

proposed a federal jobs guarantee (as did other candidates such as Bernie Sanders, Elizabeth Warren and Cory Booker). That is, the promise that anyone who wanted to work would be given a good job by the federal state. These are jobs that subsequently provide positive externalities to society and that can seldom be carried out by machines, such as care for the elderly, work in education, nursery schools, etc.

Finally, as Banerjee and Duflo argued,[53] a minimum income can be useful to end poverty in developing countries where governments are not able to roll out more complex programmes. However, this is not the case in European countries or in the USA, where governments can put together programmes that guarantee other values beyond the redistribution of wealth. Piketty[54] agreed, pointing out that taxes (and the transfer of money) cannot solve all social problems or guarantee all democratic values. Mazzucato[55] is also an advocate of *pre-distribution* of income through good working conditions and not only through traditional ex-post redistribution via taxation. She argued that while income redistribution aims to fight inequality after it has been created, *pre-distribution* focuses on achieving better distribution conditions from the outset. Thus, in accordance with the idea that value and rents are obtained collectively (in the firm) through collective effort, all those involved in this effort should obtain their fair share of what is obtained. This, in my opinion, is where labour law comes in. This regulation, which takes a much finer line than the simple transfer of money, not only guarantees the economic rights of those who lack capital (e.g., a minimum wage), but also brings a series of other values that are desired in a democratic society, such as freedom of expression, participation in the economy and in business management (collective bargaining), meritocracy, job security, real equality and non-discrimination, the prohibition of the arbitrary, as well as correcting market failures (externalities, imperfect information, etc.).

[53] Banerjee and Duflo, *Good Economics for Hard Times.*
[54] Piketty, *Capital in the Twenty-First Century.*
[55] M Mazzucato, *Mission Economy* (London, Penguin Books, 2021) 167 and 189.

8

Liberal Values, Human Rights and Labour Law

Liberal Values in the Employment Contract

From the outset, the employment contract has existed within an authoritarian structure that is at odds with the values inherent to any liberal society, such as freedom, equality and respect for privacy. In fact, both the economic and legal subordination involved in standard employment contracts jeopardises certain commonly accepted individual rights. Firstly, workers' rights could be violated without specific regulation on the grounds that the lack of economic security prevents the practical enforcement of liberal values, Secondly, the employment contract is based on the employer's power of management and supervision, which comes into direct conflict with the supreme value of freedom.

If we take privacy as an example, which is a basic, fundamental right in any liberal society, this is reduced in the labour context given the company's right to monitor and check on employees. This corporate power of surveillance and control over the worker would be difficult to tolerate in a democratic state governed by the rule of law in any other sphere. In fact, this kind of control of one citizen over another, e.g., within a marriage (or in a relationship between state and citizen), is considered unacceptable. Thus, the limitation of liberal values is inherent to today's production model, and thus it can be stated that the employment contract is built on weak foundations in modern society.

In general, it could be argued that the deprivation of liberal values under the employment contract is necessary to maintain production levels and thereby give the worker economic security. However, it should not be forgotten that fundamental rights and liberal values are not a commodity to be bought. Liberals should oppose such exchanges, at least in principle.[1] Indeed, as soon as the market can buy and sell values, fundamental rights cease to be inherent to the individual and become available only to those who have the economic means to enjoy them. If workers cannot make ends meet, they will have no choice but to 'sell' their fundamental rights.

[1] H Collins, GL Lester, and V Mantouvalou, 'Introduction: Does Labour Law Need Philosophical Foundations?' in *Philosophical Foundations of Labour Law* (Oxford, Oxford University Press, 2018) 50.

This idea is far from being pure fantasy. In Sweden, a company offers workers a bonus if they agree to have a chip implanted in their bodies that can be used to record their employment activity.[2] Firstly, if the worker needs money to make ends meet, it is difficult to refuse. Secondly, even if the employee does not need the money, they may fear that refusal will make it difficult for them to move up in the company or put them at the top of the list if some employees have to be made redundant. Thus, even if they do not need the extra money, the fear of retaliation may eventually cause them to give in.

The company could argue that this is necessary to optimise production efficiency or even that it is done for the employee's well being. This would not be the first time this has happened. One of the most common effects of technology is its 'normalisation'. In the 1960s, video surveillance cameras were considered an extremely dangerous intrusion into people's intimacy and privacy,[3] but today they are accepted relatively naturally. The López-Rivalda judicial doctrine[4] from the ECHR is a good example of this. The same has happened with satellite navigation systems, and implanted chips will probably become progressively more normal. We will find out in 50 years' time.

Therefore, irrespective of the technology or the method used, the main issue is that the employment contract contradicts liberal values, at least from a philosophical perspective, but often also from a practical standpoint.

As Collins pointed out,[5] there is a high risk that an employer can use the employment contract to violate liberal values and civil liberties. This is not based on the inherent danger of any citizen or the state violating these rights, but that the employment relationship itself, based on hierarchy and legally sanctioned authority, causes permanent conflict and tension between the two rights. Therefore, specific labour regulation is needed to address this specific risk.

This is not the first time this argument has been raised. One clear example is that referring to the cross-cutting regulation in Europe on data protection (GDPR). Although this regulation is fully applicable to labour relations and employment contracts, the European legislator was not thinking specifically about this situation.[6]

European regulation decrees data protection rules from the perspective of consent without taking into account the conventional, well-documented objections of lack of consent in the employment relationship. Thus, it is important for the protection of liberal values (such as privacy, as well as others like equal

[2] J Mcgregor, 'Some Swedish workers are getting microchips implanted in their hands' (2017) *The Washington Post*. Available at: www.washingtonpost.com/news/on-leadership/wp/2017/04/04/some-swedish-workers-are-getting-microchips-implanted-in-their-hands/.

[3] This is why a novel like George Orwell's *1984* was so successful.

[4] CJEU Ruling of *López Ribalda v Spain* (2018) ECHR 14.

[5] Collins, Lester, and Mantouvalou, 'Introduction: Does Labour Law Need Philosophical Foundations?', 60.

[6] M Rodríguez-Piñero Royo and A Todolí-Signes, *Vigilancia y control en el Derecho del trabajo digital* (Cizur Menor, Aranzadi, 2020).

treatment, and freedom of expression), to be specifically regulated from an employment perspective, failing which generic doctrinal constructions will be made that neglect the peculiarities and risks inherent to the employment relationship.

Finally, labour law needs to ensure that the practical authority of the employer (in employee supervision and control, as well as in dismissals and decisions on bonuses, promotions, etc.) is constrained by strict, mandatory limits so that workers' civil rights are not breached.[7] At the same time, these limits must not be the generic ones applicable to relations between citizens, between state and citizen or between companies and consumers. This is because of the specific nature of the employment contract, which gives the employer wide-ranging powers, the nature of which endanger liberal values.

Human Rights and Labour Law

In a liberal society, it is not easy to completely separate liberal values from human rights. Although there are philosophical foundations based on the moral imperatives, universality and timelessness of human rights that liberal values lack,[8] the reality is that human rights are imbued with liberal values. Thus, the main applicable difference is the definition of human rights (also considered fundamental rights when they are enshrined in a state constitution) as a right and establishing them as such in the legal system).

If a right is established as being fundamental, it is protected vis-à-vis other lower-ranking interests as well as creating a powerful narrative for those who exercise it. From a hierarchy of rights perspective, it is not the same for a dismissal to violate employees' human or fundamental rights as it is to violate their legal rights. Indeed, once a right is considered a human right, other values, such as maximising efficiency, would (or should) be pushed into second place. In addition, human rights are inherent to the individual from birth, which would prevent (at least, in theory) their exclusion based on purely contractual considerations such as applying labour or civil law to a service contract.

Given the power of the language of human rights, and its ability to defeat efficiency arguments, part of the discipline has begun to use human rights to address the interests of workers and trade unions.[9] The connection of labour law with

[7] Collins, Lester, and Mantouvalou (n 1) 66.

[8] On the concept of human rights see, J Nickle, *Making Sense of Human Rights*, 2nd edn (Oxford, Blackwell, 2002).

[9] RJ Adams, 'From Statutory Right to Human Right: The Evolution and Current Status of Collective Bargaining' (2018) 12 *Just Labour: A Canadian Journal of Work and Society* 137–55. J Fudge, 'The New Discourse of Labour Rights: From Social to Fundamental Right?' (2007) 29 *Comparative Labor Law and Policy Journal* 29–66; P Alston, *Labour Rights as Human Rights* (Oxford University Press, 2005); G Mundlak, 'The Right to Work: Linking Human Rights and Employment Policy' (2007) 146 (3–4) *International Labour Review* 189; G Mundlak, 'Human Rights and the Employment Relationship: A

human rights is seen as the solution to a twofold problem: on the one hand, the reduction of safeguards that concede ground to other interests and, on the other, how to extend labour protection to the self-employed and thus put an end to the 'flight from labour law'.[10]

It must be said that using labour law as a human rights instrument is relatively straightforward, based on the Universal Declaration of Human Rights (1948). This document, which is a world benchmark, expressly includes a large part of the values and contents of labour law:

> Article 23
>
> Everyone has the right to work, to free choice of employment, to just and favourable conditions of work and to protection against unemployment.
>
> Everyone, without any discrimination, has the right to equal pay for equal work.
>
> Everyone who works has the right to just and favourable remuneration ensuring for himself and his family an existence worthy of human dignity, and supplemented, if necessary, by other means of social protection.
>
> Everyone has the right to form and to join trade unions for the protection of his interests.
>
> Article 24
>
> Everyone has the right to rest and leisure, including reasonable limitation of working hours and periodic holidays with pay.

In addition to these labour-related articles, there are others that are directly or indirectly applicable to labour relations, such as the prohibition of slavery (Art 4), the right to life, liberty and security (Art 3), the right not to be discriminated against (Art 7), freedom of expression (Art 19), the right of assembly (Art 20) and the right to social security (Art 22).

Thus, as national legal systems reduce labour protection for the sake of supposed efficiency gains, it seems logical to resort to international standards and principles which have invariably provided for and protected these rights for more than half a century as a way of justifying the need to maintain and uphold labour law.

There is a simple argument: labour law protects values included in human rights, therefore, it cannot be scaled down or disappear from the domestic legal system at the risk of becoming a country that violates human rights. In this sense, linking a labour right to a human right would be sufficient justification to uphold it.

The right to life, liberty and security justifies the enforcement of effective standards for health and safety at work, but also for rest breaks, maximum working hours, family care leave, and so on.

In general terms, everyone's right to liberty protects the capacity for the individual to pursue their own concept of what is a life worth living. Amartya Sen

Look Through the Prism of Juridification' in Daniel Friedmann and Daphne Barak-Erez, (eds) *Human Rights in Private Law* (Oxford, Hart Publishing, 2001) 297–330.

[10] Rodriguez-Piñero, 'La huida del derecho el trabajo', *RL*, 1996.

(1999), in *Development as Freedom*, grounds his thesis in freedom, which he describes as the capability to lead the kind of lives that people have reason to value. According to Sen, freedom includes well-being, as a personal situation that is individually regarded as positive, and the ability to exercise one's own choices as a way of achieving these positively valued states.

For this reason, the right to freedom is infringed if the pursuit of one's choices is impeded by physical or economic restrictions. According to this view, a legal system that does not permit work to be compatible with a full life (in one's concept of what one considers a full life, e.g., having children, having hobbies, pursuing personal projects) is a system that does not comply with due respect for human rights.

In addition, given the link between health problems and the lack of rest and disconnection at work, the regulation of maximum numbers of working hours and minimum rest periods is connected to the human right to health. A question which, in any case, is mentioned in Article 24 of the UDHR (Universal Declaration of Human Rights), establishing limits for working hours and paid holidays.

However, if the rights to collective bargaining and to strike were not fundamental rights that are protected as such, human rights such as freedom of association, freedom of expression and the prohibition of forced labour could be violated.[11] Along the same lines, both the right to form trade unions and the right to political participation included in the UDHR are closely linked to the right to collective bargaining, and the right to information and consultation with trade unions in the company. They could even justify other types of participation that are characteristic of industrial democracy, such as co-determination.[12]

The right to work, recognised in Article 23.1 of the Universal Declaration, includes effective safeguards against unjustified dismissal as part of the right to work. Deprivation of work without justification, in this sense, violates the right to work, thus justifying the existence of labour standards that effectively curb such practices.

Compliance with the Human Right to 'just and favourable' remuneration (UDHR, art 23.3) justifies national regulations such as collective bargaining and the minimum wage.

Finally, the right to work, the right not to be discriminated against and the right to dignity justify a series of labour safeguards that are protection if these rights are to be upheld. History has taught us how the deregulated labour market leads to poor working conditions far removed from any concept of human dignity. Thus, if society wants to prevent the recurrence of these patterns of precariousness and social conflict, labour law has been and remains the answer.

[11] J Atkinson, 'Human Rights as Foundations for Labour Law' in *Philosophical Foundations of Labour Law*, (Oxford, Oxford University Press, 2018) 133.

[12] There are also studies which link more industrial democracy and co-determination to higher productivity rates, J Cable and F FitzRoy, *Cooperation and Productivity: Some Evidence from West German Experience* (Coventry, University of Warwick, 1979).

The use of human rights to justify labour law has its drawbacks. Collins,[13] pointed out that when one compares, for example, the right not to be tortured with the right to fair pay, they look like different kinds of rights. While the former requires strong, urgent moral rejection that is applicable to every person and in every country, the latter does not have the same force and applicability. In fact, this author argues that human rights are considered timeless while the labour rights included in the Universal Declaration are only applicable at a particular time and may evolve according to the production system and the division of labour.

In short, critics seem to argue that, although labour rights are formally included in the Universal Declaration of Human Rights they are not protected as such, meaning that countries can make them disappear from domestic law if they so wish.

In my view, these arguments need to be reconsidered. The ultimate aim of the labour regulations set out in the UDHR is to enable human beings to have lives worth living, including the right not to die of starvation or exhaustion. While it is true that the UDHR could have simply stated 'the right not to starve', it was decided to be much more specific in labour issues.

Indeed, the difference between the first type of morally more reprehensible declarations (e.g., prohibition of torture) and the second (e.g., right to just and favourable remuneration) is specificity. If torture were a common activity, which most people suffered on a daily basis, the UDHR would probably have given much more space and interest to detailing all the types of torture that are forbidden to ensure its eradication. In that scenario, with such a detailed list, there would probably be authors willing to point out that some forms of torture are not as painful as others, therefore they should not all be included in the UDHR, since the prohibition of some kinds of 'torture' (because they require less moral rejection) could be considered as mere ordinary rights. However, as torture is not an everyday activity, the UDHR pays less attention to its prohibition, which does not mean that it is of less interest. However, as work is a daily activity, the chances of dying from exhaustion due to work fatigue or from starvation due to insufficient pay are much greater. Hence the UDHR devotes more space to detailing what intermediate rights should be established in order to achieve the right to life.

In this sense, it is probably the special interest and importance of work in people's lives that made the UDHR go into so much detail about how to protect it. Thus, the argument should be the opposite: the fact that the UDHR goes into such detail on labour regulations responds to the social importance of work as a way of ensuring a free, dignified life for people. In addition, it is also a guarantor of peace. Indeed, as the foreword to the UDHR indicates, the rights enshrined therein are proclaimed with the conviction that their preservation will be a guarantee for peace. As has been pointed out in this book, labour deregulation, and workers'

[13] H Collins, 'Theories of Rights as Justifications for Labour Law' in (ed) *The Idea of Labour Law* (Oxford, Oxford University Press, 2011) 142.

subjugation to market laws, have historically been the cause of social conflict and violence. Indeed, its dismantling (and that of the welfare state in general) creates anger and causes extreme politics, conflicts between countries (US–China) and division (Brexit).

The UDHR was written just after the end of the Second World War, at a time when the commodification of labour and the rise of fascism had caused major bloodbaths. The conviction was that only respect for these rights (including labour and social security rights) could guarantee that these events would not be repeated. The times we are living in are the best proof that the authors of the UDHR were right. Deregulation, and the disregard for human rights by governments over the last 40 years, has once again led to social conflict and extremism. It is a return to a world in which freedom is merely superficial and there is no substantive freedom; a world in which people lack the economic and legal capacity to actually lead a life worth living, which will inevitably lead to social conflict once again. The recipe against this evil is written in human rights: the only thing we need to do is to respect them.

9

Distribution between Workers: Equality

New 'Priorities'

So far, we have seen the two main functions of labour law: (1) regulating the labour market to achieve efficiency gains; and (2) distributing profits and evening out the balance of bargaining power between capital and labour. However, within this second function, or as a third one,[1] we also need to point out that labour law is also in charge of distributing profits between workers.

In recent years, most of the labour regulations that have created new rights have sought to regulate the inequality that exists between some workers and others. Thus, anti-discrimination regulations based on gender, origin, and disability; European directives on equality between temporary and permanent workers; part-time and full-time workers; regulations to protect maternity rights, etc., are rules that do not aim to rebalance the power between capital and labour, but to improve the situation of those workers who are worse off than others. Four factors have driven the growth of these new labour regulations:

Labour Market Fragmentation

The large-scale incorporation of women into the labour market over the last 40 years, increased migration due to globalisation, widespread outsourcing and the emergence of 'first' and 'second' class companies with bargaining power imbalances between companies, the digital divide and its effect on educated and uneducated workers, and the growing divide between booming and declining sectors due to technology and globalisation have fractured the working class by creating (or increasing existing) different interests. It could be argued that, in the past, society was much more divided than it is today, yet the bargaining power of certain groups (totally removed from the labour market) was so low that any specific improvements to help them were not even taken into account. Thus, individual interests were homogenised as 'working class' concerns as if they were all the same.

[1] G Mundlak, presents this as a third function in 'Corporatist and Pluralist Labor Laws', in *Fading Corporatism*, (Ithaca, NY, Cornell University Press, 2007).

In recent years, the film industry has tried to portray this much-sought unity on several occasions. The film *Pride* (2014) shows how the strikes of the National Union of Mineworkers in Great Britain in 1984 were supported by pro-rights associations of gays and lesbians, despite the social and economic differences of those involved. Even more striking is the story of Fred Hampton, leader of the Black Panthers in Chicago, as depicted in the film *Judas and the Black Messiah* (2021). Again, the film, in addition to telling his story, draws attention to the fact that the leader sought the betterment of the working class over and above any differences in skin colour.

There is no doubt that part of the success of social improvements for all stems from the quest for (real or contrived) working-class unity. At present, however, this unity seems to be broken. First, certain groups that were previously willing to compromise in exchange for improvements for all are no longer willing to do so, instead demanding that their own specific interests be taken care of.

Second, there are now major salary differences (wage polarisation) between groups that did not previously exist (e.g., between skilled and unskilled workers). Let us consider the situation brought about by COVID-19. While low-skilled workers lost their jobs (because of the need to be on-site) or risked contagion, other more skilled workers were able to telecommute, thus protecting themselves and maintaining their income.

In addition, wage differences increased for the same work depending on the sector or company. On the one hand, productive decentralisation and the creation of 'first' and 'second' class companies has created inequality between similar tasks, depending on the company in which they are carried out. In addition, globalisation and technology have also increased inequality between 'winners' and 'losers' in each country. One of the phenomena that has most influenced industry polarisation was the COVID-19 pandemic.[2] This saw technological sectors and online distribution (Amazon, delivery platforms) grow their revenues, whilst traditional sectors such as local commerce, the hotel and catering industry and passenger transport were severely affected. This phenomenon has undoubtedly increased the inequality between workers in different industries, not only because of the type of skills required in each one (skilled in the first group, unskilled in the second) but also by the mere fact of belonging to one sector rather than another.

The Inability to Recognise and Reconcile Differences

As noted above, many of the differences between the situation of some workers and others have existed since the golden age of labour law. However, labour regulations have not been up to the task. As the film *Made in Dagenham* (2010) excellently

[2] International Labour Organization, *Monitor on the World of Work. Tenth edition Multiple Crises Threaten the Global Labour Market Recovery* (Geneva, 2022).

portrays, historically, trade union support for minority causes has left a lot to be desired. This film chronicles the struggle of 200 female workers in 1968 in England who aimed to gain recognition as skilled workers and receive the same pay as their male counterparts in a car factory where the vast majority of employees were men. Given the very low representation of women, the works council, while supporting the women, was unwilling to bring their demands to the negotiating table, fearing that the company would reduce other benefits that would affect the rest of the workforce. Indeed, the majority principle on which trade union elections are based poses the same problems as this principle when applied to democracy: minority interests can be excluded from protection. In essence, this is simply the expression of differences in bargaining power between different groups of workers.

Moreover, as Weiss pointed out,[3] collective bargaining is not designed to protect employees in 'new forms of work'. In fact, for matters of representation, workers in subcontracted companies, temporary employment agencies, the self-employed and the unemployed have little chance of being protected by collective bargaining alone. An example of this is some trade unions' and works councils' acceptance of double pay scales.[4] That is, collective agreements that sanction paying lower wages for the same work depending on when people joined the company. Thus, workers' representatives accept that new workers in the company (who are not represented by the works council which signed the agreement) have worse working conditions, thereby protecting only those workers it represents.[5]

Individualisation of Rights

One of the features of the socio-political context of recent years is the increasing prevalence of the individual over the group.[6] In this environment, standardising interests becomes more complex. In fact, as the individual is placed above collective interests, individual interests, even of a small collective, override the interests of a larger group. Differences outweigh common interests, making standardisation problematic. While it is not clear whether this is a cause or effect situation, the fact is that the legal system has shifted towards the individualisation of rights. In other words, as collective labour rights have been weakened by the state, the power of individual workers to impose their will on the common interest has increased.

[3] M Weiss, 'Re-inventing Labour Law?', in G Davidov and B Languille (eds), *The Idea of Labour Law* (Oxford, Oxford University Press, 2011) 47.

[4] A Todolí-Signes, 'El principio de igualdad y las dobles escalas salariales' (2015) 383 *CEF* 47.

[5] This situation has been declared unlawful in certain cases by the Spanish Supreme Court on the basis of the principle of equality applicable to rules and collective agreements of a regulatory nature. The Supreme Court understands that the collective agreement cannot establish wage differences based on a non-relevant fact such as the date the employee joined the company, see Todolí-Signes, 'El principio de igualdad y las dobles escalas salariales'.

[6] B Hepple, 'Factors Influencing the Making and Transformation of Labour Law in Europe', in G Davidov and B Langille (eds), *The Idea of Labour Law* (Oxford, Oxford University Press, 2011) 34.

In turn, the rise of the equalising function between workers is promoted by despondency among progressive parties. These parties, which have been incapacitated by neo-liberal theses to improve workers' conditions through regulation (wealth distribution) focus their attention on rules that improve the conditions of a part of their electorate, i.e., redistribution between workers. Thus, as labour law, and its ability to deliver on its functions of redistributing wealth between capital and labour, becomes weaker, new rights are created that redistribute bargaining power between workers. In this way, although the working class is worse off, certain groups see their demands for equality being met. The problem is that equality has been on the decline in recent decades. As Fudge pointed out,[7] while shifting the focus from redistribution between capital and labour to horizontal equality within the labour force, the first type of inequality has increased to levels not seen since before the Second World War.

Furthermore, as this book has shown, labour law, as a redistributor of bargaining power between employers and workers, has ceased to interest a certain part of the 'upper' working class. However, equality issues, especially gender-equality issues, continue to be relevant. In fact, while a highly qualified woman may not need labour law to redress her situation vis-à-vis her employer, she will still feel that she is discriminated against when compared to male workers at the same level, or that she is subjected to a kind of harassment that her male counterparts are not. Labour law, based on individual rights, can help her in this respect.

An Interest in Creating Division

A dictum in politics is that the more you talk about one issue, the less you talk about another. Hence the importance of getting the media to focus on what is of interest to a particular political party. What is not spoken about does not exist. Thus, the greater the emphasis on inequalities and injustices within the working class, means there is less time spent on highlighting the inequalities between capital and labour. In this way it is in the interests of business (or at least it does not harm them) to highlight the differences between workers so that common goals are swept under the carpet.

In fact, equality rights are often quite well accepted by the employer. The employer is willing to negotiate on the company's total wage bill, yet how it is subsequently distributed among its employees is of secondary importance.[8] Thus, as long as rights are limited to ensuring fair redistribution of wages between workers themselves, but not to increasing the total amount of wages paid, the employer is not likely to raise too many objections.

[7] J Fudge, 'Labour as a "Fictive Commodity"', in Davidov and Langille (eds), *The Idea of Labour Law*, 124.

[8] G Mundlak, 'The Third Function of Labour Law: Distributing Labour Market Opportunities among Workers', in Davidov and Languille *The Idea of Labour Law* 322.

Creating a divide between types of workers is a strategy used by employers to reduce labour rights. Since it is controversial to reduce the rights of those who already have them, the decision has been taken not to grant any more to those who entered the labour market after a certain point in time. Thus, the new generations, or those who are currently unemployed, will be worse off when they enter the labour market as it is a relatively common tactic in times of crisis to lay off workers so that they can be rehired by contractors of the main company, with poorer working conditions and fewer rights.[9] Firstly, this succeeds in separating some workers from others, breaking workers' future solidarity. Secondly, distinctions can be made between new workers who carry out the same tasks as older colleagues.

Subsequently, the very existence of inequalities between some employees and others is used as an argument to reduce labour safeguards. The so-called 'duality' of the labour market, whereby some workers are protected (insiders) and others are not (outsiders) is often used by advocates of deregulation to reduce the rights of the former.[10]

Recognising Inequalities

Making the rebalancing of bargaining power between workers an objective of labour law carries intrinsic risks. However, not doing so does not improve the situation. Denying this reality (the difference in bargaining power between some workers and others) for fear of diluting the strength of the 'working class' can cast aspersions on the legitimacy of labour law. The reality is that labour regulations influence not only the distribution of power and income between capital and labour, but also between workers themselves.

In fact, as inequalities between workers grow, this factor will gain in importance. Apart from the fact that the disparity in income between executives and average workers has grown exponentially since the 1970s and today is at epic proportions,[11] one of the most profound effects of globalisation and digital transformation (including the effects of the pandemic), in conjunction with the reduction of workers' bargaining power, is the polarisation between skilled and unskilled workers. Even when automation does not lead to a reduction in the level of employment in the economy (because new jobs are created in new sectors) it tends to reduce the number of professions requiring average skills (e.g., clerical workers) by increasing the need for highly skilled workers (e.g., computer

[9] D Weil, *The Fissured Workplace, Why Work Became So Bad for So Many and What Can Be Done to Improve It* (Cambridge MA, Harvard University Press, 2014).

[10] Mundlak, 'The Third Function of Labour Law: Distributing Labour Market Opportunities among Workers' 324.

[11] K Stone, *From Widgets to Digits: Employment Regulation for the Changing Workplace* (Cambridge, Cambridge University Press, 2004) 7.

programmers) or totally unskilled workers (e.g., dog walkers) as these are much more difficult to replace.[12] This polarises the working class as a result.

As Cowen rightly predicted in his famous book *Average is Over*,[13] digital transformation and global production chains are killing off the middle class in developed countries. However, as Baker pointed out,[14] this is not the result of hard 'economic' facts, but the effect of specific regulatory policy. According to this author, developed countries are deliberately agreeing to free trade agreements that make it very easy for domestic industrial firms to produce their goods in developing countries (with the job destruction that this implies in developed countries) by sending the finished products back to developed countries. In addition, they do little to reduce the migration barriers that prevent skilled personnel from these third countries from freely entering developed countries to provide services. Thus, while workers in industry compete for jobs globally, national (or supranational in the case of Europe) borders continue to restrict competition between workers in the knowledge economy, such as doctors (at least for the time being, as telecommuting may soon change this in the service sector/knowledge economy).

In this context, the 'losers' of globalisation will develop resentment and hatred towards those who reap profits without wanting to share them. As inequality within the working-class increases, division will give way to political radicalism. In the Trump campaign, one of the most viral slogans was the fight against the 'elites' and the 'establishment', which is nothing more than reinforcing the sense of institutions' neglect of certain social classes. In the same way, Reagan, in his election campaign, also attacked the 'Welfare Queen' to pit those who 'contributed' against those who, in his opinion, lived off state aid.[15] Thus, redistribution centred on taxation alone generates division among the working class, resulting in the same extremisms that capital–labour inequality can generate.

Conversely, labour law pre-distributes wealth, understood as the distribution carried out when the value is created, which reduces polarisation and limits 'divide-and-rule' discourses.

The fact is that economic polarisation of the working class, which has been a constant in recent decades, can be reduced through labour regulations. The minimum wage and collective bargaining flatten wage variance in the firms and sectors where they are applied, i.e., they reduce wage polarisation.[16] We are not talking

[12] A Banerjee and E Duflo, *Good Economics for Hard Times* (New York, Random House, 2019) 232.

[13] T Cowen, *Average is Over* (New York, Plume, 2013).

[14] D Baker, *Rigged: How Globalization and the Rules of the Modern Economy Were Structured to Make the Rich Richer* (Washington DC, Center for Economic and Policy Research, 2016) 6.

[15] W Brown, *In the Ruins of Neoliberalism. The Rise of Antidemocratic Politics in the West* (New York, Columbia University Press, 2019).

[16] See J Dinardo, MF Nicole and T Lemieux, 'Labor Market Institutions and the Distribution of Wages, 1973–1992: A Semiparametric Approach' (1996) 64(5) *Econometrica*; DS Lee, 'Wage Inequality in the United States during the 1980s: Rising Dispersion or Falling Minimum Wage?' (1999) 114(3) *Quarterly Journal of Economics* 977; D Autor, A Manning and LS Christopher, 'The Contribution of the Minimum Wage to US Wage Inequality over Three Decades: A Reassessment' (2016) 8 (1) *American Economic Journal: Applied Economics* 58.

about banning technological progress or globalisation, but about regulating its most negative consequences.

Finally, if labour law (and other economic policy instruments) does not curb excessive differences between workers (not justified by merit in the generation of value, but by factors such as 'luck', inherited education, gender, country of birth, etc.), it will not only fail to serve its purpose to reduce social conflict (differences in income can provoke as much conflict and anger as differences between capital and labour), but it will also lose its social legitimacy as a vehicle for pre-distributing wealth.

Merit-based Justifications

Let us take merit as an example. It is difficult to advocate rules that encourage fair distribution of merit-based income between working capital and the contribution made by each individual if there is no corresponding merit-based distribution between workers.

The excessive salaries of certain types of highly valued workers (e.g., computer engineers) to the detriment of others does a disservice to labour regulation as a means of redistributing wealth and rebalancing bargaining power. Labour regulations should limit abuses of power both by capital over workers without capital, and the abuse of other workers who, privileged by a favourable bargaining position, leave mere 'crumbs' for the rest of the workers.

In this sense, economists suggest that one of the reasons why real wages have been frozen for 40 years is the removal of limits to infinite wage growth for some workers. In particular, they claim that reducing the higher personal income tax rates (marginal rates of 70 and 80 per cent) that were common in the 1960s and 1970s to much lower rates (e.g., 25 per cent in the US in 2020) has led to a boom in the salaries of corporate managers.

According to economists, these increases have had another indirect effect: workers' wages have been frozen. It is argued that when marginal income tax rates were much higher, managers had no incentive to raise their pay to excessive levels since much of that pay would go to the state and not to them. Thus, these executives chose other types of benefits, such as improving the salaries of their workers, which made them popular within the company, while at the same time reducing the complexity of their job by increasing workers' cooperation. However, now that upper salary limits have disappeared (in the form of a drastic reduction in personal income tax), today's executives negotiate for their own benefit at the expense of the salaries of the rest of the company's workers.[17] That is to say, whereas in the past middle and top management were willing to sacrifice part of their salary (of which

[17] Banerjee and Duflo, *Good Economics for Hard Times*.

they only received a small part due to high taxation) in exchange for increasing the salary of their subordinates, thus making their job easier, today they prefer to keep that part of their salary, even if they have to 'crack the whip' in order to achieve the objectives that make them worthy of the bonus or salary increase.

This permissiveness in the infinite growth of high incomes can also lead to unemployment. It is more or less common in large corporations for department heads to ask the company management for more staff for their area in order to meet targets. Again, the company can make the large bonuses for area managers conditional on the achievement of targets without increasing the number of staff. In other words, the department manager is offered part of the income that the company saves by not hiring more employees. Again, without a cap on individual wage growth, the area manager has an incentive to accept the trade-off, thereby reducing the number of employees hired by the company, even if he must then 'put pressure on himself and his already hired subordinates' to do so. In addition, if there were wage ceilings (via income tax or collective bargaining), the result would be different: either more workers would be hired to share out the work, or the income would be shared more equally among all workers.

This shows that the conflict between workers is real and the bargaining power of some can be used to prevent others from getting the share they actually deserve.[18] Hence the need to build regulations that rebalance bargaining power between workers.

Corrective measures based on merit or contribution seem perfectly applicable in horizontal redistribution. According to Miller,[19] merit-based distributive justice implies, firstly, that decisions based on criteria which are obviously irrelevant from the point of view of merit should be prohibited (e.g., based on race, gender, religious affiliation, non-labour reasons, etc.). This would justify anti-discrimination rules and the application of the principle of equality to temporary agency workers, subcontracted workers, part-time workers, temporary workers, workers from different companies within a group of companies, etc. All these reasons should not be considered sufficient to justify the worsening of working conditions as they are not based on merit. Indeed, a wage difference between two workers performing the same functions, and achieving the same level of productivity, because they have a temporary contract or formally belong to a subcontracted company, etc., is not acceptable.

Conversely, merit does permit differences in treatment based on objective criteria. Thus, distributive justice does not imply treating all workers equally, but allowing differences only on the basis of an objective, justified and proportionate reason (e.g., work performance, productivity, income generated, added value, etc.).

[18] Baker, *Rigged: How Globalization and the Rules of the Modern Economy Were Structured to Make the Rich Richer* 147.

[19] D Miller, *Principles of Social Justice* (Cambridge MA, Harvard University Press, 1999) 151–55.

Finally, genuine meritocracy requires the application of the principle of equality to individual relations by only accepting differences, either when faced with objectively diverse situations, or when faced with *de facto* identical situations whose cause for differentiation is reasonable (related to work and merit and not based directly or indirectly on a traditional stereotype) and proportionate.

Back to Protecting Efficiency

In 1975, Okun, in his famous book *Equality and Efficiency: The Big Tradeoff*, set out one of the dominant economic principles that has taken root in today's economic theory. This study, which reviewed historical data, sought to demonstrate that the most equal societies were the most inefficient.[20] Based on this principle, regulatory policy began to move away from any regulations that encouraged egalitarian societies (e.g., progressive taxation, minimum wages, or collective bargaining). However, without entering into the debate on how harmful a society with strong economic inequalities can be for a true democracy, the fact is that this economic principle has since been economically challenged. Thus, in 2014, as part of the IMF's research, a study entitled '*Redistribution, Inequality and Growth*'[21] was presented in which, using more data than that used by Okun thirty years earlier, it was shown that, contrary to popular belief, social equity and economic efficiency go hand in hand. In other words, there is a positive correlation where more equal societies are more efficient societies.

This economic conclusion is consistent with the reasoning of this book. Thus, a society that does not reward workers fairly for their efforts to generate wealth will discourage effort, thereby reducing efficiency. Indeed, without labour regulation to rebalance the bargaining power between capital and labour, and between workers, the party wielding greater bargaining power will be able to use that power to extract more income than it deserves, thereby discouraging effort and cooperation (and creating social disaffection), resulting in poorer efficiency and economic growth.

Thus, several theories support the IMF's findings. Adams' equity theory[22] states that an employee's incentive to work hard not only depends on how much they are paid, but also on what the other workers with whom they compare themselves are paid. In this sense, the theory explains the role comparisons play in worker motivation.[23] This theory holds that when employees understand that there is a fair

[20] AM Okun, *Equality and Efficiency: The Big Tradeoff*, (Washington DC, Brookings Institute, 1975).
[21] JD Ostry, A Berg and CG Tsangarides, 'Redistribution, Inequality and Growth' (2014) *IMF Staff Discussion Notes*.
[22] JS Adams, 'Inequity in Social Exchange' in LR Berkowitz (ed) *Advances in Experimental Social Psychology (Vol. 2)* (New York, Academic Press, 1965) 267–99.
[23] RL Heneman and JM Werner, *Merit Pay; Linking Pay to Performance in a Changing World*, 2nd edn (Greenwich, CT, Information Age Publishing, 2005) 29.

relationship between what they contribute to the company and what they receive from the company (including salary, bonuses, social recognition, status, etc.) they will be motivated. However, opinions vary greatly as to what fairness and equity mean in terms of pay. There are no absolute, objective and universally accepted units of measurement of fairness.[24] Therefore, this theory assumes that workers compare themselves to other workers, both in their own company and in other companies, to establish the ratio of fairness between what they contribute and what they receive.

According to this theory, if an employee feels under-rewarded compared to their peers, or to their own perception of what they deserve, they will decrease their performance to re-establish a balance between what they receive from the company and what they give to it. Furthermore, according to Adams, this also occurs if the worker feels over-rewarded. In this case, the theory holds that workers who receive more than they feel they deserve will feel guilty about what they earn compared to their colleagues and will therefore not be motivated to do their best at work.[25] That is, in order to ensure employee cooperation and motivation for the benefit of efficiency, wage systems need to be non-discriminatory and based on objective criteria.

Several experiments support the validity of this theory. The extreme case among the possibilities of subjective (as opposed to objective) wage-setting is reflected in so-called surprise bonuses. These wage bonuses are given irregularly by the employer or middle management to workers, without any preconditions and without justification or motivation.

In this system, supervisors have an annual budget to spend on bonuses on a discretionary basis, and they can reward their subordinates until the budget allocated for this purpose has been used up. In this way, workers do not know which behaviours the supervisor will reward, and the supervisor does not have to justify these bonuses, nor do they have to follow a pattern (i.e., the supervisor can give a bonus to some workers and not to others, even though these employees behave in the same way).

Empirical analysis of these types of bonuses has shown a reduction in the effort of all the workers involved in the plan, both among those who receive the bonus and those who do not. The justification comes from the lack of foresight and the feeling of injustice. Workers who receive the bonus have no incentive to repeat the behaviour because they do not know the reasons for it; and, if they do, there is no guarantee they will receive it again if they repeat the same behaviour. In addition,

[24] DS Belcher, *Sistemas de retribución y administración de salarios* (Ediciones Deusto, 1978) 21.

[25] Empirical studies confirm that the feeling of being over-remunerated appears only in extreme cases, H Garland, 'The Effects of Piece-rate Underpayment and Overpayment on Job Performance: A Test of Equity Theory with a New Introduction Procedure' (1973) 3 *Journal of Applied Social Psychology* 325.

workers who do not receive the bonus feel unfairly treated, which causes them to lose motivation and reduce their efforts.[26]

In short, the perception of fairness, predictability and absence of favouritism play a crucial role in the effectiveness of wage incentives.[27]

Finally, regulatory intervention, when there is an imbalance in bargaining power between workers, can be justified on two grounds. Firstly, in terms of wage fairness, whereby nobody should receive more than what they deserve for their efforts. Secondly, intervention is also necessary to prevent arbitrary or subjective distribution of income from discouraging hard work and reducing efficiency.

Therefore, transparency is required so that workers are aware of what their colleagues who perform the same tasks are paid, so that the company is forced to justify wage differences, only accepting the justifications related to merit and which do not lead directly or indirectly to discrimination based on historical stereotypes or non-work-related issues. In addition, for this labour regulation to be successful, the scope of application of the principle of 'work of equal value, equal pay' and of the rules of transparency and wage accountability must be broader than that of the business sphere. If the mere intervention of a different legal personality (different company) can restrict the application of equality in working conditions and of the principle of merit when making differences, its effectiveness will be negligible.

Finally, if these principles are to be effective, they must be applied at industry level or at least to all the companies that make up the same economic sector, including subcontracted workers, temporary agency workers, employees working for other companies within the sector, employees from different agencies within the main company, and franchises. Otherwise, a whole host of employment contracts will appear enabling the principle of equal pay and merit to be circumvented, making it impossible to apply.

[26] A Engellandt, and RT Riphahn, 'Evidence on Incentive Effects of Subjective Performance Evaluations' (2011) *IRL Review* 241, 256; E Breza, S Kaur and Y Shamdasani, 'The Morale Effects of Pay Inequality' (2018) 133(2) *Quarterly Journal of Economics* 611.

[27] E Fehr and KM Schmidt, 'Adding a Stick to the Carrot? The Interaction of Bonuses and Fines' (2007) 97(2) *American Economic Review* 177.

PART III

The Concept of 'Genuine Business Owner' as a Determinant of Labour Law

Adapting labour law to the twenty-first century should begin with a profound reflection on who it should apply to. The business-production model and employees (now much better educated) are very different from the time when labour law first came into being.

Increasingly, companies only retain the assets that have high added value (what is economically valuable) and decentralise everything else. This results in the legal separation of the company's brand name and infrastructure on the one hand, and the workers or workforce (including supervisors) on the other, who are given commercial contracts (service contracts, agency contracts, industrial leases, franchises, etc.). The aim of these strategies is none other than to push the risks inherent to the business and the parts considered to add little value further down the chain. These almost always include labour-intensive work.

The only way to ensure workers' rights and the effectiveness of labour market regulation in the light of this strategy is to impose labour obligations on those who have the resources to meet them. Therefore, it would seem wise to move away from the traditional concepts that define salaried work along the traditional lines of industrial work with set hours, and working hours determined by the business owner and conducted in a physical space owned by the employer. The financial reality of workers who are economically dependent on their employer due to lack of other resources, lack of their own brand, and a lack of sufficient capital goods will be what identifies twenty-first-century workers. In short, workers who lack their own independent productive structure will have to be salaried employees.

In this third part of the book, it will be argued that the change in the forms of business organisation has made the current concept of a worker obsolete, thus impeding labour regulations from doing what they are supposed to do. The restrictive scope of application of their rules excludes a large part of the workforce and is an obstacle to improving efficiency (mainly through unfair competition and lower labour costs) and to achieving a more merit-based distribution of wealth. Thus, an interpretation of the concept of worker is proposed based on the current economic and productive reality of the labour market, which can be applied to all subordinate workers in the twenty-first century. This is achieved by defining what a genuine business owner is, which is the only service provider that should be excluded from labour law.

10

The 'Self-Employed' Do Not Exist

Eliminating Legal Dependence as a Defining Criterion for Labour Regulations

Globally,[1] the main characteristic that gives rise to the application of labour regulations is the existence of a subordinate relationship. In fact, the current model of protection revolves around the existence of legal dependence in the provision of services as one of the two main features of the employment contract.[2]

However, if we want to modernise labour law and adapt it to the new types of business organisation and make it a useful instrument for economic policy, the first thing that must be done (and is already being done[3]) is to do away with the requirement of legal dependence on the employer as the gateway to labour law.

The employment contract, born at the onset of the industrial revolution, was intended to protect workers in large factories and in vertically integrated companies.[4] These workers had two main characteristics. The first was legal dependence, understood, first, as belonging to an organisational structure owned by the employer and second, as the hierarchical dependence of the worker on the employer or their representative. That is, the employer could legally dictate orders and instructions, including working hours, the working day, the way tasks were to be carried out and, in turn, supervise that this work was carried out in accordance

[1] International Labour Organization *Employment Relationship Recommendation* (2006, No 198). Article 4(a) specifically states that member states should 'provide guidance for the parties concerned, in particular employers and workers, on effectively establishing the existence of an employment relationship and on the distinction between employed and self-employed workers'.

[2] In Spain, Art. 1 of the Worker's Statute includes both legal dependence and economic dependence. However, over time, the first has reduced in importance. In the USA, the courts mostly apply the 'right to control test' to determine whether subordination exists and to classify the worker as an employee: R Sprage, 'Worker (Mis)Classification in the Sharing Economy: Square Pegs Trying to fit in Round Holes' (2015) 31 *ABA Journal of Labor & Employment Law* 16. In Italy, Art 2094 of the Civil Code regulating the standard employment contract refers to subordinate work. In the Netherlands, the employment contract is regulated in Art 7:610, para 1 of the Civil Code, where the placing at the disposal of another person to provide services is the only qualifying factor, and so on.

[3] A Todolí-Signes, 'The End of the Subordinate Worker? Collaborative Economy, On-Demand Economy, Gig Economy, and the Crowdworkers' Need for Protection' (2017) 33(2) *International Journal of Comparative Labour Law and Industrial Relations* 241–68 (IJCLLIR).

[4] K Stone, *From Widgets to Digits: Employment Regulation for the Changing Workplace* (Cambridge, Cambridge University Press, 2004).

with those wishes. The final dictate included disciplining the worker (including dismissal) if they failed to comply with these instructions.

The second characteristic was that of the employee's subordination (similar to economic subordination). This feature has several facets:[5]

(i) non-ownership of the means of production, given that the worker was not the owner of the factory, nor of the machinery;
(ii) non-ownership of the risks, understanding that the worker was not involved in the company's fortunes, with the employer being the one who bore any losses or received any profits from the business;
(iii) non-ownership of the fruits of labour, the result of the employee's work being the property of the employer; and
(iv) non-ownership of the market, meaning the worker cannot offer their labour directly to clients, in other words, the clients belong to the employer.

Given that nineteenth-century workers who were to be protected at the time had these two distinctive characteristics, the applicability of labour standards was contingent on compliance with these two conditions.[6] This decision could have been criticised at the time (as being misguided), but today can have very damaging effects on the labour market.

In fact, even at the time, when the main objective of labour law was solely to redress the balance of bargaining power between the parties in terms of the employment contract, the requirement of legal dependence as a condition for its applicability differentiated between those who needed protection and those who received it. The main reason behind unequal bargaining power and the lack of real autonomy of the will on the part of the worker, which makes labour law necessary, does not stem from the worker having to carry out the employer's orders, rather it comes from not having any means of production, something which was available to the employer.

The fact that the worker does not have sufficient capital (brand, technology, infrastructure) to provide services directly to the market is the reason why he has to offer his labour power to those who do have this capital. It is precisely the right of ownership which enables capital owners to exclude (dismiss) employees who do not comply with what is required of them, and forces workers to comply with the instructions and orders given by the employer. Thus, what we call legal dependence today was initially a *consequence* of the provision of industrial services (and of workers' economic conditions) and not a *prerequisite*. For this reason, requiring

[5] GK Dow, 'The New Institutional Economics and Employment Regulation', in Kaufman (ed), Government Regulation of the Employment Relationship (Madison WN, Industrial Relations Research Association, 1997) 58.

[6] S Deakin, 'The Evolution of the Employment Relationship' in P Auer and B Gazier (ed), *The Future of Work, Employment and Social Protection: The Dynamics of Change and the Protection of Workers*, (International Institute for Labour Studies, 2002); Stone, *From Widgets to Digits: Employment Regulation for the Changing Workplace.*

legal dependency as a necessary criterion for the applicability of labour regulations may exclude many from their scope of protection.

Historically, this has not been overly damaging since the majority of employers' organisations were vertically integrated and extremely hierarchical. This meant that the majority of workers who had no means of production were *also* subject to the strict orders of the employer and were therefore covered by labour law. In recent decades, however, this has changed. Today, if we insist on the requirement of legal dependence as the necessary defining criterion of labour law, labour regulations will not be able to serve their purpose in rebalancing bargaining power. Furthermore, labour law will not be able to comply with its function of regulating the labour market to achieve the desired efficiency.

Evolution of the Economic Model and its Connection to the Reduced Legal Dependence of Employees

Business theorists have raised the question as to what makes employers decide whether they are interested in managing fewer or more activities within their organisation and thus in employing more or fewer workers. The answer to this question was given by a young Ronald Harry Coase, then a lecturer at the London School of Economics in 1937,[7] who pointed to *transaction costs* as the key concept. This explanation, together with other research, won him the Nobel Prize for Economics. This economist and lawyer, considered one of the founders of the economic analysis of law, argued that a business organisation defines the breadth of its optimal scope so that it maximises the economies of scale that can be obtained within it. The more it minimises costs by carrying out tasks in-house, thanks to the prevailing hierarchy within the organisation, the more it will grow. Thus, large industrial companies that perform all the tasks involved in producing goods in-house (the typical example is a car factory) do so because this hierarchical integration option has cost advantages over buying the intermediate products (engines, wheels, dashboards, windows) on the market, which must be assembled into the final product.

However, production chains as we know them today, even in the automotive sector, are characterised by more market transactions between different types of suppliers, and between these suppliers and the assembler that lends its name to the vehicles. Moreover, many of these exchanges take place across borders, through truly global production chains. The reason for these changes (outsourcing of production phases and globalisation of chains) is that a hierarchical relationship within a single company is sometimes no longer the most advantageous option for minimising production organisation costs. Nor is it the best way to check

[7] RH Coase, 'The Nature of the Firm' (1937) 16(4) *Económica, New Series* 386.

manufacturing processes: markets are more reliable than they used to be and monitoring technologies have improved enormously, thanks to the tools offered by information technology and telecommunications. The upshot is that the transaction costs of market trading have been greatly reduced, while the advantages of cutting these costs through planning and hierarchy within firms are no longer clear-cut in many cases.

The transaction costs of operating in markets are the main reason why firms prefer to do the work themselves in a service organisation.[8] In the nineteenth and twentieth centuries, companies were aware that getting work done by staff outside the firm was expensive. Information travelled slowly and much productivity was lost by *subsequently* having to check the quality of the work performed. Therefore, companies preferred to have their own (dependent) staff to do the work; staff trained by the company to ensure the quality of the product or service it provided; staff subject to intake controls (job interview and selection processes); work quality controls (supervision by middle management), and dismissal control (disciplinary power). These criteria led to the growth of salaried employment in the organisations most able to exploit their potential advantages.

All this changed when new technologies reduced the transaction and monitoring costs of external staff to the same level as those of salaried employees. New digital technologies are bringing reductions in transaction and monitoring costs in markets that were unimaginable until a few decades ago. This can only be achieved by using alternatives that are effective in the above-mentioned areas: provision of abundant, reliable and cheap information; control of the quantity and quality of work or products; mechanisms for worker selection and ex-post monitoring, etc.

As market transaction costs fall, companies have fewer incentives to maintain large organisational structures. We can all see that decentralisation is increasing, tasks are being outsourced and scattered production chains and networks are being created. Thus, with the reduction of transaction costs, what makes a company competitive is no longer the ability to perform multiple production tasks with shared synergies. Instead, what is important is specialisation in certain tasks and phases of industrial production, especially those that add the most value to the chain. The rest can be outsourced if markets offer attractive alternatives, i.e., they can be acquired anywhere.

As technologies improve and transaction and monitoring costs fall, the outsourcing of tasks can break down to very specific tasks in the market.[9] Some of them can be performed by individual workers on a competitive basis.[10] Financially,

[8] Coase, 'The Nature of the Firm'. Recently they have also been called external costs and coordination costs, A Sundararajan, *The Sharing Economy, The End of Employment and the Rise of Crowd-based Capitalism* (Cambridge MA, MIT Press, 2016) 85.

[9] JR Mercader Uguina, 'Nuevos escenarios para el Estatuto de los Trabajadores del siglo XXI: digitalización y cambio tecnológico' (2020) 63 *Trabajo y Derecho: Nueva Revista de Actualidad y Relaciones Laborales*.

[10] However, self-employed workers are often only competitive because they reduce the price of their work, not because they are more efficient or because they are not subject to certain regulations such

there are two conditions for this to be feasible: mechanisms are available to check the tasks performed by these workers; and the workers have the necessary equipment, either because it is supplied by the company or because it requires low investment that is within their reach (e.g., personal computers, smartphones).

Salaried workers, hired by a company as employees, were introduced to ensure standardisation of the product or service offered by a brand through specific instructions. This ensures quality goods or services for many potential consumers,[11] thanks to the company's ability to centralise the information garnered from their experience. As a result, a well-known brand reduces consumers' search and choice costs by anticipating the quality of the transaction.[12] The brand owner which decentralises and diversifies its production does not sacrifice the value of its brand. In fact, the brand is an intangible asset that the company retains, and the service provider (or employee) does not have. This circumstance makes them economically subordinate to the company for which they work. In this sense, the fact that this is a commercial relationship or agreement on paper does not mean that all the parties involved are equal: subordination and hierarchy often persist, but in other ways. There are also certain economies of scale, now partly linked to the major brands.

One of the implications of this trend towards lower market transaction costs is that companies hire fewer permanent employees, and their business model can draw more on individual service providers who are not permanent employees or salaried workers but are formally self-employed. However, as we have seen, these workers are still controlled by and subordinate to companies, as are the businesses that supply the companies spearheading the value chains in the different industries.

The conclusion is that the decentralisation of production chains and individual supplier fragmentation of the manufacturing market does not eliminate the hierarchy, or the control exercised by the main company. Above all, it does not remove the non-ownership of assets (economic subordination) that gave rise to the need for labour law, given that these individual service providers do not have the manufacturing infrastructure (capital) to operate in the market without the support of the main company. In short, this means these self-employed workers are totally dependent on the main company.

Thus, in many of these cases, we are not dealing with truly self-employed people who are independent and have the capacity to make decisions on relevant business issues and self-management. We are actually dealing with workers whose dependence is manifested, not by the classic signs of subordination, but by new forms of subordination given that technology and new organisational methodologies enable work to be subordinated differently than in the past. Thus, if only

as the minimum wage or even because the employer saves certain costs in terms of social security contributions.

[11] Coase (n 7).

[12] PH Rubin, 'The Theory of the Firm and the Structure of the Franchise Contract' (1978) 21(1) The *Journal of Law and Economics* 223.

traditional signs of subordination continue to be used, much of the subordinate work may go unnoticed, thus preventing the application of labour law to these truly dependent relationships.

In addition, better training and cultural levels among workers and lower information-sharing costs thanks to new technologies have led to the vertical disintegration of companies, the reduction of middle management and an overall decline in instructions and monitoring of workers by companies. This has increased workers' autonomy and self-control (or control by clients and co-workers). Thus, nowadays, the aim is for employees to do what they have to do without having to be told to do it. Through the 'threat' of dismissal and the granting of salary bonuses, traditional hierarchical control has been replaced with employees' own self-control in which legal dependence is no longer necessary, since the economic subordination of the employee serves the same purpose, i.e., the employee serves the interests of the employer without being told what to do or being strictly controlled.

This means, firstly, that the worker's freedom and autonomy only exists on paper and is not real and, secondly, that if we persevere with legal dependence as a criterion for defining labour regulations, these will not apply to all those who make a living from their labour.

As regards the first issue, when instructions, timetables and working hours are eliminated, yet safeguards against dismissal (free dismissal) are reduced, workers will have to exercise self-control to keep their job. In this sense, the freedom of the employee to choose their working days and hours, which can be seen as a source of freedom and independence, may mean that they are responsible for carrying out the tasks assigned to them regardless of the time needed to do so. Again, if they do not deliver, they will be dismissed. The same applies to the freedom to choose one's place of work or teleworking. The company is not interested in checking where or how the job is done. It is simply interested in ensuring that it is completed to the expected quality standards (the disappearance of effective safeguards against dismissal means that it is not necessary to dictate instructions or check the work, just the result). Thus, anywhere and everywhere are ideal for work, which precludes the separation of work from one's personal life. In other words, when there is *economic subordination*, there cannot be true independence or freedom (understanding economic subordination as a *high level of replaceability* (non-brand ownership) and the existence of a real inability to refuse work *because there are insufficient alternative sources of income*). However, where the worker, hypothetically, has real autonomy or freedom to accept or reject orders from the employer, to choose their working hours and working day, etc., this cannot be seen as a criterion for the inapplicability of labour law, but precisely as a labour 'victory', just like the eight-hour working day and the minimum wage.

The film *Modern Times* is famous for its humorous portrayal of labour alienation caused by workers' lack of autonomy. This lack of freedom and autonomy has always been an issue of workers' demands as well as a source of conflict between trade unions and employers. In fact, one of the reasons behind changes in company organisation, which led to employees being given more freedom, was precisely that the lack of autonomy at work and excessive supervision was a constant source of conflict in the workplace. Thus, achieving success in labour grievances should never be a reason to exclude the application of labour law. The opposite would lead to a meaningless cycle, whereby workers improve their conditions thanks to labour law, only to have their situation worsen because of the non-application of labour regulations, which would make their application necessary again.

Workers' freedom and autonomy in the way they do their jobs has been a traditional labour demand and has been partly successful thanks to workers' increased education and cultural levels. However, it should not lead to the non-application of labour law as a result.

In the comparative sphere, there are already examples of regulations which do away with legal dependence as a necessary defining criterion for the employment contract. In other words, they advocate the application of all labour regulations, even if the worker is legally independent. This is the case in the State of California, where the AB5 law stipulates that for a self-employed individual (worker) not to be considered as an employee, the employer must demonstrate the following three conditions:

(a) that they are free from company control and management;
(b) that they provide services that are not performed by the ordinary business of the company that hires them; and
(c) that the self-employed person has an independent business structure.

Thus, if the company which hires the formally self-employed worker is unable to prove these three conditions simultaneously, the worker will be deemed to be an employee. This means that it is perfectly feasible for an employment contract to exist in which the service provider is totally free from the control and management of the company as long as one of the other two conditions is met.[13] Therefore, it would not seem unreasonable for other countries to follow the same line by applying the employment contract to individual service providers who have complete and absolute autonomy.

It is a different matter if new technologies and the level of workers' education and training give them greater freedom and autonomy, which may justify changing certain labour regulations (their content), but not excluding them from the application of labour law. As Cruz-Villalón pointed out, the bulk of labour law revolves around regulating company power, whether of an organisational, performance or disciplinary nature, which is designed on the premise of legal dependence. Thus, this author stated that, technically speaking, it is unfeasible to transfer these regulations to the sphere of self-employment where this power in favour of the 'client' does not exist. Should this happen, it would lead to 'rigid rules

[13] A Todolí-Signes, 'El ámbito subjetivo de aplicación del Estatuto de los Trabajadores ante las nuevas formas de trabajo: la nueva ley de California (AB5)' (2020) 66 *Trabajo y Derecho* 2020.

that are not easily adaptable to an economic model that requires the corresponding amounts of organisational flexibility'.[14]

In this sense, in *The 'Gig Economy': Employee, Self-Employed or the Need for a Special Employment Regulation*?',[15] I mentioned that work on digital platforms, where technology means workers can choose their own timetable and working day, could come into conflict with certain labour regulations regarding a guaranteed hourly wage.[16] If so, labour law (or preferably collective bargaining) should establish legal mechanisms to resolve this issue. However, this possible conflict in the applicability of a specific rule does not seem to justify the outright exclusion of these workers, and their autonomy and freedom, from labour regulations.

In other words, the requirements or criteria for the applicability of labour law should not be confused with regulatory content. If a certain specific rule (material content of labour law) cannot be applied to self-employed workers, it can be amended through special labour regulation or a particulat type of employment contract (as has been done with teleworking)[17] or collective bargaining, but this should not be a reason for exclusion from labour law.

Finally, it must be concluded that there can be no real freedom if there is economic subordination (non-ownership of property, market and the fruits of one's labour) and that no matter how much theoretical freedom (working hours, working day, freedom to refuse tasks, how and where to carry out the work) the self-employed person has, the reality is that they will have to comply with the wishes of the person who commissions the task or work (expected quality of the service provided, maximum delivery times, quantity of work to be carried out as decided by the company) if they want to continue receiving orders and the income they need (threat of dismissal). In addition, even if this were not the case, the fact is that the existence of legal dependence is not a relevant criterion for examining the need for labour protection and the applicability of labour law so that it can serve its purpose.

Thus, what will enable labour law to accomplish its objectives of labour market regulation, wealth distribution and equality is for it to apply to anyone who *provides services without being a genuine business owner*, irrespective of whether they do so in a legally dependent or independent capacity.

[14] Cruz Villalón, 'El debate en torno a la adaptación o superación de la subordinación como elemento referencial del Derecho del Trabajo ante las nuevas formas de trabajo. Un debate global desde la perspectiva española' (2020) 6(2) *Labour & Law Issues* 32.

[15] A Todolí-Signes, 'The "Gig Economy": Employee, Self-Employed or the Need for a Special Employment Regulation?' (2017) 23(2), *Transfer: European Review of Labour and Research* 193–205.

[16] However, some authors argue that there is no 'incompatibility' but that companies must adapt their business model to the current legislation on working hours, see A Ginès I Fabrellas 'El tiempo de trabajo en plataformas: ausencia de jornada mínima, gamificación e inseguridad algorítimica' (2021) 2(1) *Labos* 19.

[17] M Rodríguez-Piñero Royo and A Todolí-Signes, *Trabajo a Distancia y Teletrabajo: análisis del marco normativo vigente* (Cizur Menor, Aranzadi, 2021).

Scope of Application of Labour Law for it to Serve its Purpose

The problem of excluding workers from labour law and social security protection is undoubtedly one of the main reasons why labour law cannot serve its purpose (along with the existence of ineffective rules).

However, it would be naïve to think that this is a completely new issue. Labour market developments in recent years have seen an increase in the replacement of an in-house labour force with 'self-employed' labour. In fact, extreme flexibility in the use of labour, and the transfer of risk from the company to the service provider by using the self-employment tag, have become the norm for a large part of the labour force.[18]

Accordingly, the doctrinal proposals to modernise labour law that have been made in recent years all seek to broaden the personal scope of the discipline so that it can comply with its remit. This does not mean broadening the definition of the employment contract in all cases. Instead, it means delinking labour regulations from the ties of the employment contract as the basis for the scope of application. In fact, in one way or another, the proposals advocate that labour law should not be constrained by the definition of the employment contract, but that its scope should be extended to the entire 'world of work'.[19] The primary consequence of this would be that personal work, whether carried out in a dependent or independent capacity, would continue to be subject to protective regulations.

Positions obviously differ within the discipline on how this extension should be implemented and on the type of protection that should apply to personal employment relationships that come within the scope of labour law.

The European Commission, in a report drafted under the leadership of Alain Supiot,[20] aimed to reshape labour law in such a way as to free it from the restrictions of subordinate work under an employment contract. The central idea in the Supiot Report was to recognise and raise awareness of the existence of a wide range of situations in which citizens work even though they do not have an employment contract. In fact, the Supiot Report extended the personal scope of the discipline to 'non-subordinate work', as well as to 'unpaid work' (e.g., intra-family care and unpaid household activities). The ambitious proposal outlined a 'professional status', which included all those providing labour services. However, in this proposal, this status was limited to the granting of social security rights. In other words, Supiot advocated separating social security protection from the

[18] V De Stefano, 'The Rise of the 'Just-in-Time Workforce', On-demand Work, Crowdwork and Labour Protection in the Gig-Economy' (2016) 37 (3) *Comparative Labour Law and Policy Journal* 471.

[19] C Freedland, C Jacqueson and N Kountouris, *Public Employment Services and European Law* (Oxford, Oxford University Press, 2007) 21.

[20] A Supiot et al, *Beyond Employment. Changes in Work and the Future of Labour Law in Europe*, (Oxford, Oxford University Press, 2001).

existence of an employment contract. Indeed, one of the first problems encountered by the self-employed is their lack of social security protection compared to their employed counterparts. This is the area where most progress has been made in recent years, even though significant differences still remain.

In his day, Lyon-Caen[21] also advocated the integration of personal employment relationships other than the employment contract into labour law. In this respect, he proposed 'a labour law for workers other than those contemplated in the labour law model'. At the same time, he stated which legal principles should be applicable to workers who were not subordinate workers.

For their part, Ewing, Hendy and Jones,[22] in their *Manifesto for Labour Law* and its follow-up *Rolling Out the Manifesto for Labour Law*,[23] also suggested the need to broaden the national construct of the personal scope of labour rights through their proposed definition that any person engaged by another to provide labour and not genuinely operating a business undertaking on his or her own account is defined as an employee.

In addition, Dockés[24] and other French authors have also defended broadening the scope of application of labour law in France.

In a similar vein, the proposal made by Freedland and Kountouris is also of interest.[25] These authors also advocated dropping the notion of subordination to define the scope of labour law. It should be noted that these authors do not suggest modifying the personal scope of the employment contract (which would continue to be limited to legal dependence). They instead propose to include other personal employment relationships which are currently found in private law within the scope of labour law.[26]

This is based on the idea that we are currently faced with a binary system of personal employment services: first, the employment contract (regulated by labour law) and second, all other employment services covered by private law. However, this division is based on the false idea that all employment services governed by civil law are identical. This argument is reinforced by the fact that civil law regulation does not differentiate between the provision of personal and non-personal services.[27] In fact, the regulation applicable to a contract for the provision of services between a company and a self-employed worker is the same as the one between two companies. Against this background, these authors suggest that labour law should extend its scope to all the work an individual performs personally. The aim

[21] G Lyon-Caen, *Le droit du travail non salarié* (Sirey, Paris, 1900) 7–9.

[22] KD Ewing, J Hendy and C Jones, *A Manifesto for Labour Law: Towards a Comprehensive Revision of Workers' Rights* (Liverpool, IER, 2016) 35.

[23] ibid, 36.

[24] E Dockés, (ed), *Proposition de Code du Travail* (Paris, Dallorz, 2017).

[25] M Freedland and N Kountouris *The Legal Construction of Personal Work Relations* (Oxford, Oxford University Press, 2011).

[26] ibid, 38.

[27] ibid, 289.

is to shift the focus of labour law from the employment contract to 'people who work'.[28]

This doctrinal position is echoed by Countouris and De Stefano[29] who stated that labour law should not be restricted to subordinate work, since all those who 'live off their labour' require protection. Although these authors do not stipulate a specific level of protection in their report, they do establish that everyone should have the right to freedom of association and collective bargaining (also referring to other individual rights, though without specifying which ones) at the very least. Indeed, it is argued that labour law should apply to all those who perform personal work, i.e., who perform the work themselves, as opposed to others (who would be excluded) who either have employees who perform the work for them, or whose work is capital- or technology-intensive and is owned by those workers. In other words, according to these authors, labour law should apply to all those who personally provide services, irrespective of whether they are carried out under direct instructions. Thus, only those who provide services through other hired individuals who perform them on their behalf or those who do not provide services personally would be excluded, since they are owners of significant capital (in the shape of technology or assets), which is essential to perform the service.

Finally, in comparative theory, there is a drive towards redefining the scope of application of labour law. Although there are differences between the proposals, they all have a common aim: to adjust the application of this discipline to encompass all those who require protection. To this end, the starting point is the hypothesis that many individuals who are not really business owners are currently excluded from labour law. In other words, it is understood that the limits of labour law should lie at the door of a genuine business owner. Instead, with the current definition of subordination as a way of attributing labour rights, the effect is that there are many individuals who are excluded from labour law, although they are not genuine business owners.

In other words, there are legally dependent workers, self-employed workers and business owners. These authors argue that, under current legislation, only legally dependent workers are protected, while self-employed workers are not, although they lack sufficient bargaining power to protect themselves (they are *economically subordinate*). For this reason, the proposals all involve broadening the scope of

[28] ibid, 316. However, this doctrinal proposal does not advocate equating the rights and duties of all 'people who work' with the rights and duties of the employment contract, but instead suggests that differentiations should be made with regard to mandatory content according to the needs of each legal relationship. In short, these authors propose an extension of the personal scope of labour law through the establishment of what could be called a list of special employment relationships, which would not be limited to dependent employment relationships, but would also include those that are not dependent. The authors thus establish a list of personal employment services that should be included in labour law, as a guideline. These include the liberal professions, the self-employed, external consultants, and business agents.

[29] N Countouris and V De Stefano, 'New forms of employment' (2019) *Syndicat Europeaen Trade Union*.

labour law, extending it to people who work (and who are not genuinely business owners) even if they are not strictly controlled by the employer.

As we will now explain, labour law also needs to be applied to workers, even if they are truly independent, so that it can serve its purpose of (i) resolving market failures; (ii) distributing wealth between capital and labour; and (iii) distributing wealth between workers themselves.

Minimum Wage

When labour remuneration is low, there is little incentive for firms to innovate (to improve technology, work methods and processes). Moreover, the fact that inefficient firms can survive in the market because of such low wages consequently reduces the incentives for other firms to invest in innovation, since they will not be able to earn the returns they deserve because they have to compete with firms that have lowered their prices not because they are efficient, but because they pay their workforce too little. This market failure is equally detrimental whether it applies to dependent or self-employed workers. Thus, to promote innovation, labour regulations cannot allow firms to get away with paying less than minimum wages simply by hiring self-employed people.

By the same token, low wages for workers also inhibit purchasing power in society, driving a downward spiral of decline and unemployment and damaging the economy. Collective bargaining and minimum wages are an economic policy response that put a stop to this. However, regulation needs to apply to the entire workforce without opening up loopholes based solely on whether the worker earns their income on the basis of service provision freely or under instructions from the employer, if this goal is to be reached.

Collective bargaining and the minimum wage help to distribute wealth better and reduce labour polarisation. Again, this should be guaranteed by labour applying to dependent and self-employed workers alike. In fact, when a company has a monopoly in the labour market, the abuse of this position affects both dependent and self-employed workers equally, implying that legislative solutions should apply to both types of workers.

Job Stability and Protection against Dismissal

Job stability is not only an individual worker's interest to obtain economic security. It also has a positive impact on the economy through staff training, improved expectations, and incentives for employee involvement: all of which lead to better productivity.

In fact, in short-term relationships, or those with few expectations of continuity, workers will have little incentive to acquire company-specific training, and high turnover will reduce on-the-job experience and the motivation to work hard. Legislation advocates permanent over temporary contracts so as to promote labour productivity, and this rule is equally applicable to the self-employed. The freedom to choose how to perform tasks should not exclude the need to guarantee the employee a minimum of job stability if they need to acquire company-specific skills, gain experience in the tasks acquired and be motivated to perform them.

Likewise, for macroeconomic purposes and the stability of the economic cycle (economic policy decisions), regulations are required to discourage redundancies. If at the onset of a mild downturn companies decide to lay off workers, this will eventually lead to a much larger decline in demand, leading to a worsening of the recession. Hence, there are compelling economic reasons to discourage redundancies on economic grounds, unless they are really justified (essential). This deterrent must apply equally to employees and self-employed workers (as long as they are not genuine business owners) if this proposal is to work properly and have any real effect. If companies (or some of them) can reduce numbers by laying workers off without sufficient economic justification simply because they are self-employed this will worsen any economic downturns.

In turn, the individual suffering (in the shape of alcoholism, depression, pain and addiction) experienced by redundant workers over a certain age, does not seem to be exclusively related to the loss of a legally dependent job, but instead applies to the loss of earning a living through work, regardless of how this was carried out. Thus, if these situations are to be mitigated (and if the company is to internalise the social cost of its actions) it would seem appropriate to legally penalise the arbitrary or unjustified dismissal of self-employed workers who work for the same company on a regular basis.

Finally, it should be remembered that protection against unjustified dismissal also responds to the principles of merit and protection of other fundamental and general rights. In fact, dismissal without cause breaks with the principle of justice by depriving employees of their livelihood without justification that warrants this punishment. In addition, this type of employer behaviour leads to poorer motivation, and less effort and cooperation on the part of the employee. Effective protection against dismissal is the only way to ensure the other rights of citizens and workers. In this sense, employees who fear that the company will retaliate by terminating their contract if they exercise a right (or negotiate a wage increase) will end up using self-restraint (self-control) by not exercising their rights. This endangers both human rights and liberal values.

As shown, both the principle of merit and the need to protect legal rights mean that these safeguards must be applied across the board to service provision. Precisely because we are dealing with individual service providers, and not with genuine business owners, their behaviour is similar to that of a worker and their rights will correspond to those of any physical person (including the application of human rights) with the legal dependence aspect once again being irrelevant.

Collective Disputes

One of the characteristics of the new business organisation consists of companies offering services that are not provided by employees, but by self-employed workers. Thus, there are large numbers of self-employed workers waiting to receive an order from the main company. In these cases, the traditional characteristics of collective disputes can be seen once again. The workers (whether legally dependent or self-employed) have the same interests in terms of the working conditions established by the main company for both groups (wages/salary per job, remuneration for the time spent waiting for a job, occupational health and safety in service provision, costs incurred by the service, etc.). In fact, their interests are so similar that the main company usually draws up general terms and conditions for hiring these self-employed workers that cannot be negotiated. In other words, self-employed workers can agree to the conditions established by the main company or not work, but they cannot negotiate, modify or adapt them, even slightly, to their preferences. Consequently, it is clear that there is also a need for the self-employed to obtain collective representation which enhances their bargaining power and gives them a voice in the process of determining working conditions that affect them all.

There is no room for arguing that each worker has individual bargaining power (which would hypothetically exclude the need for collective representation) when it is clear that they all have the same working conditions (mainly the same salary and type of job). If the company has a general framework agreement for all self-employed workers providing services, the only way to ensure that workers can participate in the negotiation of those working conditions is through collective representation. Indeed, it is the very existence of general terms and conditions that demonstrates that workers can be easily replaced by the company and implies the lack of individual bargaining power which leads to the need for the application of labour law, at least in its collective aspect.

Similarly, from the company's perspective, it is more efficient to negotiate just once with the workers' representatives than to negotiate individually with each self-employed worker. It is a different matter if the company does not wish to negotiate either individually or collectively, preferring instead to establish a blanket contract in which the 'self-employed' worker's only option is to accept or reject it. However, the second option (neither individual nor collective bargaining) reveals the bargaining weakness of the self-employed, which is precisely why they should be placed under the umbrella of labour law.

Collective bargaining has historically been the way to address bargaining weakness by empowering workers to participate in shaping their working conditions. Collective bargaining is the response to the democratic deficit in the relationship between capital and labour, which is detrimental to the latter[30] and is increasingly

[30] G Davidov, *A Purposive Approach to Labour Law* (Oxford, Oxford Monographs on Labour Law, 2016).

seen as an inherent right of the individual that cannot be removed merely by providing services in a legally independent capacity.[31] The fact is that what makes the application of collective rights necessary is not the way in which the work is performed (dependently or self-employed) but the fact that the work is performed by an individual without bargaining power.

However, collective rights alone are not sufficient to redress the balance of bargaining power between the parties. As mentioned above, if workers are afraid to retaliate because of the fear of dismissal, they are unlikely to exercise individual or collective rights. Thus, effective protection against unjustified dismissal needs to be implemented so that collective rights take root and workers are not afraid to elect union representatives and initiate collective bargaining processes.

Occupational Health and Safety (OHS)

One of the most astonishing features, from an efficiency and fundamental rights perspective, is the exclusion of the self-employed from the occupational health and safety protections available to workers. The private liability system has failed to reduce accidents[32] because, in this system, the company, which is best placed economically to reduce the risks of accidents, has little incentive to do so as it can pass on the costs of accidents to society. The main objective of the private liability system is to repair damage, but when we are talking about the life and health of people, the objective should not be to 'repair damage' but to prevent it. This principle (and an occupational health and safety system) should be applicable to both legally dependent and self-employed workers, as long as they are individuals, not genuine business owners.

One possible objection is that independent ways and times of work may make it difficult to hold the employer liable for accidents that occur. Indeed, one of the foundations of the employer's responsibility in terms of occupational health and safety stems from the fact that the employer determines the way work is done and should therefore be liable for accidents that occur in this context. This is not the case when the worker is truly free.

However, it should be remembered that it is companies that have decided to change the way work must be done over the last forty years to give workers more freedom. This should not exonerate them from protecting the worker who performs tasks for their benefit.

From an efficiency perspective, the responsibility must be placed on the party that is in the best position to reduce occupational hazards. In this case, it is the

[31] V De Stefano, 'Non-Standard Work and Limits on Freedom of Association: A Human Rights-Based Approach' (July 2017) 46 (2) *Industrial Law Journal* 185.

[32] H Collins, 'Justification and Techniques of Legal Regulation of the Employment Relation' (2000) 3 *WG Hart Legal Workshop Series* 19.

company that is in an economic position to protect workers, whether they are employees or self-employed. If the responsibility for protecting health is placed on the shoulders of the self-employed, it is very likely that they will be unable to bear the planning and costs that OHS requires, thus leading to accidents. There seems little point in arguing that workers will incorporate these OHS costs into the price of their services which, in the end, would be paid for by the employer who benefits from them. There are two reasons for this.

Firstly, the lack of bargaining power will prevent the company from factoring in this cost, as it will be the party deciding the price of the service provision. The 'self-employed' party only has the power to accept or reject the price offered.

Secondly, even if there is a residual amount of bargaining power and the worker can incorporate these costs into the final price of their work, the reality is that in a world as competitive as today's, if the company has several offers on the table (from several workers) it will choose the cheapest, i.e., the one that does not factor in the costs of occupational health and safety to the price of the service on offer.

In both cases, the outcome is the same: if the individual worker is made solely or preferentially responsible for their own occupational health and safety, the system will not work.

In addition, it should be remembered that the worker, whether dependent or independent, provides services for the benefit of the employer, so that any accidents they suffer should be borne by the party that benefits from that work, so they do not externalise these costs to society.

Again, from the perspective of human rights and liberal values, the right to life and physical integrity cannot be contingent on the way in which services are provided.

Social Security

From an economic perspective, compulsory social security addresses the so-called problem of 'economic myopia'. This occurs when people underestimate the risks to which they are subject, leading to the acquisition of low levels of coverage for those risks, when they are given the choice to acquire this protection. The answer to this is the obligation to purchase a minimum level of cover for all service-providing citizens in the shape of social security. In fact, compulsory insurance schemes to cover disability, retirement and death risks are particularly necessary for those who have no alternative sources of income, i.e., those who live off their labour, as they are usually the ones who acquire the lowest level of cover when they are not obliged to do so, because they need their meagre income to subsist.

Thus, once again, the reasons cited, which justify the need for a social security system for workers, do not differentiate between dependent and self-employed people, but should apply equally to both.

In fact, the opposite is true. The literature argues for compulsory coverage to be the same for all workers to prevent optional exclusion from coverage from becoming an element of rivalry between hired workers.[33] Indeed, one of the main reasons why companies currently decide to hire self-employed workers and not dependent workers is because of the lower social security costs involved. This prevents workers from being properly covered against the risk of loss of income.

Hence it is essential for all dependent and self-employed workers to have the same compulsory coverage, because if workers could choose not to have social security coverage at the cost of exposing themselves to risk (non-compulsory coverage), employers would hire these cheaper workers, leaving the others unemployed. This would lead to a 'race to the bottom' in which all workers would have to forego coverage in order to get work.

Business Risks Taken on by the Employer

The imbalance in the parties' bargaining position can easily lead to certain risks or errors being passed down to the bottom of the chain, i.e., to the worker. In factories and in agriculture, where piece-rate or performance-related pay was common, workers bore the cost of delays, lack of supplies and other types of administrative disruption caused by the company, including planning, task organisation, the training of company managers and technological innovation. Thus, when production could not take place in the factory, due to company 'errors', the worker was at the disposal of the employer, but did not get paid. Over time, the law legislated to regulate this type of situation, preventing the company's errors or inefficiency from being passed on to the worker.

In economic terms, this regulation is justified in terms of efficiency. If the employer can pass on the business risks to employees, there will be no incentive for them to improve. This transfer of business risks may mean less training for the company's managers, less production planning work, less methodological innovation and even less technological innovation, all resulting in lower labour productivity. In general, the fact that the firm can transfer business risks to the worker, together with low wages, will imply an increase in the use of labour but lower productivity per worker. In other words, more workers will be used, although each worker will be less productive, moving us away from the production model of industrialised countries and closer to that of developing nations. Legislation must force companies (which have the capital and the investment potential) to take on the business risks so that they have the right incentives to invest in the company.

In fact, one of the major problems in terms of classifying workers as employees or self-employed has been the understanding that taking on risks should be seen as an indication of independence. The fact is that, in many cases, the main company,

[33] F Pérez García et al, *Cambios tecnológicos, trabajo y actividad empresarial: el impacto socioeconómico de la economía digital* (XXI ESC Research Award, 2019); B Suárez, 'The 'Gig' Economy and its Impact on Social Security: The Spanish Example' (2017) 19(4) *European Journal of Social Security* 307.

with its bargaining power, will have incentives to transfer these business risks to its service providers without this implying that they are independent. The opposite is true. They are so subordinate that they cannot refuse to take on risks that should be borne by the main company, as this would mean losing the opportunity to work. In fact, the employee's 'immunity' from the risks of the business is a consequence of applying labour regulations and should not, therefore, be considered as a criterion for their classification.

Thus, labour law protects national productivity which can be affected if these regulations are not applied by the simple fact of considering certain workers as independent.

Competition Based on Labour Costs – Social Dumping

The minimum wage, collective bargaining, compulsory social security and occupational health and safety regulations all have a common objective: to ensure that companies do not compete with each other by reducing lower labour costs, but by improving productivity and the quality of the product or service provided.

Companies can grow and gain market share in two main ways:[34] firstly, by improving their products, and secondly, by reducing their costs. In this second option, cost savings can come from productivity improvements, lower input costs (raw materials, suppliers, etc.) and/or lower labour costs (wages, social security, occupational health and safety, etc.).

The aim of labour regulations is to level the 'playing field' for all companies so as to prevent them from competing on labour costs and ensuring they compete via all the other costs. It must be stated that labour legislation (preventing labour-cost-based competition) serves both the interests of workers and of companies.

Firstly, the fact that some companies compete on labour costs forces other firms to do the same, spiralling down to a point where no company stands to benefit. They will all be equal at the bottom of the pile, with all businesses finding themselves in the same situation they were in before they started the 'labour cost war'. Secondly, wage decreases across the board weakens domestic consumption, making it difficult for firms to grow. Third, lower labour costs trigger conflict and anger, making it difficult to uphold social order and, in the worst case scenario, democracy (hence the UDHR's insistence on the importance of labour rights). Fourthly, it undermines method, process, and technological innovations. In other words, if inefficient companies can survive in the market because they pay low wages, this reduces the incentives for other companies to invest in innovation, as they will not be able to earn the returns they deserve because they have to compete with firms that can sell their products at lower prices (not because they are efficient) but because they pay their workforce too little.

[34] M Porter, *Competitive Strategy: Techniques for Analyzing Industries and Competitors* (New York: Free Press, 1980).

In short, as we can see, there are powerful economic reasons, in addition to distributive justice, to prevent part of the workforce from being excluded from labour law simply because they are self-employed (as long as they are not genuine business owners). If the use of independent labour is allowed without enforcing labour regulations, it opens the door to allowing companies to compete on labour costs, resulting in a detrimental impact on the economy.

Company Size

One of the conclusions reached in this book is that economic policy and legislation should help companies to grow to their optimal size and not encourage companies which, due to their small size, cannot access the resources they need to be efficient, do not have the economies of scale to reduce costs per unit produced and, moreover, are unable to access international markets.

In this sense, the ultimate expression of these inefficiencies as a company is the self-employed individual. Obviously, as this book argues, these self-employed individuals are not genuine business owners. However, in any case, legislation should not consider them as such either, for the sake of productivity. The reality is that these so-called business owners do not have the capacity to invest in their own training, in technology, in contingency cover, or in occupational health and safety. This is why the law should impose this obligation on the company that benefits from their work, just as it does for salaried employees. The law should discourage individual self-employment as a job alternative, as it is more inefficient. If the main company wishes to subcontract part of its production process, it should do so through another genuine business owner, not through an individual worker condemned to inefficiency. The mere fact that labour regulations do not apply to self-employed workers encourages their proliferation (as a way for companies to reduce labour costs) thereby damaging the country's labour productivity.

In short, if labour law is to be the 'law of the labour market' and protect all those who lack bargaining power (who have no real free will), its scope needs to be extended to include all those who receive an income in return for their *labour*.

Hyde[35] argued that market failures affect all personal services, regardless of whether they can be legally classified as subordinate. Thus, to address these market failures, and to promote efficient regulation, labour law must apply to all workers. Indeed, to combat these failures, all workers must be able to organise and bargain collectively, as well as have minimum working conditions that cannot be relinquished (minimum wage, social security, restrictions on child labour, occupational health and safety regulations, among others). In short, social rights are a prerequisite for a well-functioning labour market,[36] which includes all types of

[35] A Hyde, 'What is Labour Law', in G Davidov and B Langille (eds), *Boundaries and Frontiers of Labour Law* (Oxford, Hart Publishing, 2006).

[36] S Deakin and F Wilkinson, *The Law of the Labour Market: Industrialization, Employment, and Legal Evolution* (Oxford, Oxford University Press, 2005) 290–303.

workers, whether dependent or self-employed, as long as they are not genuine business owners.

In turn, if certain social rights cannot be contravened for workers, why is this acceptable for the self-employed? Indeed, the existence of a minimum wage in exchange for work, the prohibition of discrimination on grounds of gender, race, religion, the right to work with safety measures that protect workers, coverage for occupational contingencies, are issues that the market itself does not ensure, while they are desired by citizens (and also understood as rights inherent to the human condition or human rights). Therefore, it seems unreasonable to exclude these social values and rights simply on the grounds of not being a dependent worker according to a specific regulatory concept of what a worker is deemed to be.

Finally, there is the imbalance of bargaining power or, in other words, the lack of real free will to accept certain working conditions. In this case, just as factory workers could not freely negotiate their contractual terms and working conditions, given the difference in power vis-à-vis the capitalist (factory owner), today many self-employed workers are unable to negotiate their working conditions. In most cases, when individual service providers are subcontracted, the conditions are pre-established by the main company without any real negotiation. This implies that the self-employed can only accept or refuse to work.[37] The refusal option is only strictly possible on paper given that the self-employed live off their labour.

In general, all personal work that is not carried out by a genuine business owner involves an imbalance of bargaining power, market failures and the need to uphold certain social values and rights. These circumstances justify the application of labour law to these contractual relationships.

Legal dependence was not originally (and is not now) the reason for the emergence of a large mass of workers in need of labour law protection. Instead, at that time (as now) it was the non-ownership of the required means of production. The fact that they needed the tangible and intangible assets of a third party (the employer) to produce was what made them vulnerable and put them in a weak bargaining position (imbalance of bargaining power). It is precisely the fact that they did not own the consolidated organisational structure that meant that they had to follow the orders of the employer, work long hours, and accept wages below the survival threshold. In other words, hierarchy and the existence of mandatory instructions from the employer (legal dependence) is an indication of unequal bargaining power, but not the only one.

The fact that there is currently an imbalance of bargaining power without direct instructions does not mean workers are not vulnerable, given that this is only one of the consequences of being dependent on a company structure that is not their own. Confusing the consequence (legal dependence) with the fact causing the vulnerability (the lack of a company structure and bargaining power of their own) is what has caused labour law to cease to apply to many workers who need it.

[37] A Robert Hillman and Jeffrey Rachlinski, 'Standard-Form Contracting in the Electronic Age' (2002) *Cornell Law Faculty Publications* 1062.

Legal dependence as a compulsory criterion for the application of labour law prevents it from serving its purpose. Subordination should not be exclusively equated with legal dependence on (or control by) the employer. Instead, the scope of application of labour law should be interpreted in purposive terms,[38] i.e., meaning it can achieve its objectives of protecting those who need it and regulating the labour market in the pursuit of efficiency. To this end, labour rules should be applied to all those who provide services on a personal basis, regardless of the level of control over the worker, as opposed to those who provide services through *the ownership of a consolidated organisational structure* (making them a genuine business owner). This interpretation ensures that labour regulations are targeted at all workers in need of protection.

[38] Davidov, *A Purposive Approach to Labour Law*.

11

'Consolidated Organisational Structure' as a Criterion for Applying Labour Law

'Personal Work'

So far it has been shown that for labour law to serve its purpose it needs to apply to all workers who provide economically subordinate services. However, terms such as 'lack of bargaining power' and 'economic subordination' are too vague, on their own, to clearly identify the boundaries of labour law. They are intangible concepts that cannot be directly verified in actual reality. Therefore, to capture the essence of economic subordination so that it can be of use to a judge or to a legal practitioner, who must decide whether to apply labour law to a specific service provision, a series of material requirements (which can be verified in reality) must be drawn up so as to identify when there is economic subordination and when there is not.

The various proposals that have been put forward to extend the scope of application of labour law include personal service provision. This proposal consists of applying labour law (not the employment contract) to all work carried out personally.[1] This would imply that it would not matter whether the service beneficiary had a formal contract with a company, since if the work was actually carried out by the owner of the company in an (utterly) personal manner, labour law would apply to that relationship. Furthermore, in order to determine the application of labour law, the occasional or habitual nature of providing a service to a specific beneficiary would also be irrelevant. The fact that the worker, during the service provision, takes risks would be irrelevant and, of course, whether there were instructions or control by the beneficiary would not be a valid criterion for application either. Hence, the only way to exclude the provision of services would be to carry it out, either with someone who has their own workers who actually carried out the activity, or for the service provision to be capital-intensive and, therefore, it is understood that the beneficiary does not hire personal services, but that it is

[1] M Freedland and N Countouris *The Legal Construction of Personal Work Relations* (Oxford, Oxford University Press, 2011).

the capital (the technology, machinery, infrastructures owned by the contracted company) that is acquired in this contract.

However, this proposal does not advocate equating the rights and duties of all 'people who work' with the rights and duties of the employment contract, but instead suggests that differentiations should be made over mandatory content according to the needs of each legal relationship. In short, these authors propose an extension of the personal scope of labour law through the establishment of what could be called a list of special employment relationships. These would include dependent employment relationships, as well as those that are not dependent.[2] The authors thus establish, as a guideline, a list of personal employment services that should come under labour law, such as the liberal professions, the self-employed, external consultants, and business agents.[3]

This proposal is very appealing for many reasons. Firstly, it responds to a clear and easily identifiable concept. As there is a single criterion, personal provision of services, the argument over whether labour law applies or not is straightforward. Secondly, by applying labour law to all persons in employment, the protection of people who provide services is ensured.

However, it also has some notable drawbacks. The first and most obvious is that in many of the cases covered by this proposed scope of application there would be no economic subordination. For example, in the case of a hairdressing salon open to the public where the owner of the salon worked for the market, using their own premises, their own brand and obtaining customers themselves, e.g., through word of mouth, with their own advertising, this would be a personal service provision (hairdressing) but not economically subordinated to anyone. In the same way, lawyers working individually (getting their own clients, using their own brand and directly offering services to the market) and other liberal professionals would be included, as they do personal work. It would not be very clear who should ensure their labour rights. Obviously, the authors of this proposal are aware of this problem and, for this reason, they argue that the concept of 'personal work' would not apply to *all* the rights and duties contained in the employment contract (e.g., who would be liable for protection in terms of occupational health and safety for the personal worker who works without economic subordination? who would pay the severance pay when working for end consumers?).

However, despite this, the concept of 'personal work' is relatively useful for securing most labour rights. Thus, for example, one could apply the same social security rights (risk coverage) to all personal workers. Social security contributions, at the same rate as paid by an employer) could be compulsorily included in

[2] The authors give as an example that certain legal transactions, where there is short-term personal service provision, should not be entitled to compensation for unfair dismissal since this only makes sense when there is continuity in the service provision, Freedland and Countouris *The Legal Construction of Personal Work Relations* 317.

[3] Freedland and Countouris (n 2) 285.

the price of the service (hairdressing, legal services) paid by the final consumer. Furthermore, in terms of the minimum wage, it would be relatively easy to apply a legal minimum fee per hour actually worked, as happens with employees. This would enable liberal professionals operating in the market to compete with each other on any price above this minimum. In terms of unionisation and collective bargaining, it would also be conceivable to allow workers without economic subordination to join trade unions and have sectoral collective bargaining apply to them, e.g., minimum hourly wages negotiated by unions for salaried employees.

However, given the difficulty in applying some of the labour rights (e.g., maximum working hours, right to work–life balance, occupational health and safety, severance pay), these authors argue that a specific regulation should be designed for these individuals who carry out personal work and cannot be included in the employment contract, which is adapted to their specific characteristics.

This implies that, within labour law, which would encompass all personal work, it would be necessary to draw a distinction between workers with an employment contract and other legal arrangements which would have to be adapted to the needs of each 'profession' or way of working in the market. This would mean, firstly, that the concept of employee could remain as restrictive as it is now (requiring legal and economic subordination) and, secondly, that although it would be simple and straightforward to determine who is covered by labour law, it would still be difficult to specify which legal status would apply. In other words, it would be necessary to organise different types of personal workers into different applicable legal systems (and labour rights).

In this sense, this book has argued that good labour market regulation (preventing or reducing social dumping) implies that the entire labour force should be subject to the same regulation (or at least similar in the main areas). Moreover, a classification based on 'professions' with different labour rights could end up further dividing the working class, creating inequality and undermining the legitimacy of labour law.

'Not Being a Genuine Business Owner'

One of the proposals that comes closest to capturing the material essence of economic subordination is to include within the employment contract (and labour law) all those who perform services without being a genuine business owner, i.e., without having a consolidated organisational structure of their own.

One of the biggest drawbacks of the current defining criterion of the employment contract is that it excludes many workers who provide services without being a genuine business owner, given that their main activity is merely limited to providing labour. As suggested by Deakin in 2004 'dissolve entirely the traditional boundary between employees and the self-employed, leaving only independent entrepreneurs (those with business assets and the opportunity to capture residual profits) outside employment law'.[4]

As labour history has shown us, with the rise of capitalism, artisans and farm workers, who were originally truly independent, lost the two main elements they needed to be competitive in the market. Firstly, the marketing of their products and services and secondly, the technological means *required* to produce efficiently. Therefore, only those who have the necessary elements to produce and distribute directly in the market can be considered as genuine business owners so as to exclude them from labour regulations.

As discussed below, the characterisation of workers as 'those who provide services without being genuine business owners' also means that labour law can be modernised through interpretation[5] without the need for legislative change, although legislative change may be desirable.[6]

In fact, given that the purpose of labour regulations has historically been (and continues to be today) the protection of subordinate work, the way to determine who is subordinate and who is not, in accordance with the economic-productive model at any given time, depends on the interpretative work carried out by the courts. The employment status indicators known to date and applied by the courts are nothing more than the visible embodiment of subordination. In other words, when labour law was created, the subordinate worker had certain working hours, received certain orders and was supervised by the employer, therefore these manifestations of subordination were taken into account. However, there is no 'jusnaturalistic' concept of a worker. What is a worker and what is a self-employed worker is simply a doctrinal and jurisprudential construction based on the material reality of the moment in which it is created. Thus, given the changes that have taken place in business models and the effects they have had, nowadays, subordination is manifested in and determined by other elements, and the courts are entitled to consider these new ways of worker subordination in order to make a distinction between what is a worker and what is a genuine business owner.

In addition, the 'genuine business owner' criterion, as a way of classifying workers, also has the advantage of fitting in with the exceptions in competition law for access to collective bargaining. Accordingly, European law, which prevents collusive agreements on prices, etc., only applies to undertakings (TFEU, Art 101). This has been construed by the CJEU as meaning that workers are excluded from this prohibition and can therefore benefit from collective bargaining (*Albany* case).[7] On the other hand, the CJEU has expanded the concept of undertaking, including a

[4] S Deakin, *Renewing Labour Market Institutions* (Budapest, Central European University, 2004) 14.

[5] G Davidov, *A Purposive Approach to Labour Law* (Oxford, Oxford Monographs on Labour Law, 2016).

[6] A Todolí-Signes, 'El ámbito subjetivo de aplicación del Estatuto de los Trabajadores ante las nuevas formas de trabajo: la nueva ley de California (AB5)' (2020) 66 *Trabajo y Derecho*.

[7] *Albany International BV v Stichting Bedrijfspensioenfonds Textielindustrie* C-67/96, ECLI:EU:C:1999:430 [1999] ECR I-05751.

large part of workers (specifically self-employed workers), which materially prevents them from having access to collective bargaining (*FNV Kunsten* case).[8] However, the CJEU itself, when interpreting competition rules, recognises that bogus self-employed persons should be considered as employees so they can be excluded from competition rules. It is therefore clear that, in both cases, the dividing line between labour law and competition law must be the same: where a genuine business owner begins, a worker ends. What seems to make less sense is the existence of intermediate figures such as dependent workers, Italian para-employees or self-employed persons who only provide labour who, in the end, are not genuine business owners and yet still do not come under labour law.[9]

This is the line of interpretation defended in this book. Finally, the interpretation proposed here, whereby anyone who provides services without being a genuine business owner should be understood as a worker, serves both to apply labour rights to these individuals and to remain within the exclusion of competition rules.

From this point onwards, we will analyse what is a genuine business owner for the purpose of recognising the non-application of labour law only for this group of people.

To this end, it must be assumed that compliance with the mere formalities of registration as a business owner are irrelevant for the application of labour law (e.g., incorporation as a trading company or formally as a self-employed person, etc.). A genuine business owner has a *consolidated organisational structure* with which it provides services that are the purpose of a contract. In this sense, when a service provision contract is drawn up with a company that provides services and has a consolidated organisational structure to carry them out, this is understood as a commercial contract. Otherwise, if the person who provides services only provides labour, we are talking about an employee.

When using this criterion to define the scope of application of labour regulations, the focus shifts from 'how the work is performed' to 'who performs the work'. Thus, it becomes irrelevant how the work is carried out (with or without legal dependence), i.e., whether it is carried out following the instructions of the employer, whether there is supervision and checks by the employer, etc. These are elements that do not exclude the concept of employment. The duration of the contract is not relevant either, i.e., whether it is short or long term, sporadic or regular, for the purposes of applying labour regulations. Nor is it relevant whether the worker has the power to refuse work commissioned by the employer, to decide their working hours and where or how the work is carried out.

[8] *FNV Kunsten Informatie en Media vs Staat der Nederlanden* C-413/2013, ECLI:EU:C:2014:2411 [2014].

[9] Some authors have defended this same idea based on fundamental rights. That is, it is argued that regardless of (or in addition to) the fact that an individual self-employed person cannot be considered a genuine business owner for economic purposes, the reality is that there are fundamental rights to be protected, such as collective bargaining, see N Countouris, V De Stefano and I Lianos, 'The EU, Competition and Workers' Rights' (2021) *Center for Law, Economics and Society. Research Paper Series.*

Thus, in order to agree on whether or not a worker is included in labour law's scope of application, the key factor is whether or not the contracted service provider has a consolidated organisational structure to perform the job. In this way, the employment contract is applied with a negative definition, i.e., all services that are not provided through a production structure owned by the employer (company) would be included in the scope of application. This is where the first difference with the classic interpretation appears, which understands that only dependent and subordinate work is deemed to be employed work, leaving the rest outside its scope of application.

The situation is actually the opposite based on the interpretation proposed here: what is relevant is to define what a company is. If a person does not provide services as a genuine business owner, they will be classed as a worker. In this sense, the decisive factor in the case of an employment contract is proof that the service provider is a genuine company. If this is not the case, the service provider is classed as a worker. A genuine business owner will be deemed to be real when it has the following.

Equity Ownership

The ownership of relevant tangible assets (infrastructure, machinery, buildings, etc.) or intangible assets (brand, data, goodwill, specific software, etc.) belongs to the service provider.

In fact, the main difference between workers and capitalists is that workers are remunerated for their work and capitalists for their investment. Thus, in order to understand that we are dealing with a genuine business owner with a relevant productive structure, there has to be ownership of production assets of significant economic value. This is easily recognisable in industry in terms of who owns the facilities (factory, warehouses, infrastructure, etc.) and the technology (machinery, robots, etc.). The simple identification of a genuine business owner in industry is marked by two features: firstly, the tangible assets are physically recognisable and, additionally, they are usually of significant economic value, which prevents the employer from 'forcing' the worker to own these elements to reduce costs and avoid labour regulations.

Conversely, in the service sector, the material elements tend to be of lower value (a computer, a van, a smartphone), which makes it relatively easy for the labour provider to also provide these work tools. However, this does not mean that the owner of these work tools should be considered a 'capitalist' (remunerated for their investment and not their labour). There is a need, instead, to take into account the ownership of the intangible elements of the business (information, know-how, brand, software, intellectual property, data, patents, goodwill, etc.). These factors are more difficult to identify because they are intangible but, in the twenty-first century, they are at the core of most businesses. Therefore, ownership must be used to distinguish between a real business owner and a worker.

This includes owning the major investment in branding (marketing and advertising) required to enter the market with true economic independence. As has been stated elsewhere,[10] if the service provider does not own the brand that gives them access to the market, they will have little bargaining power and will be subject to the wishes and conditions imposed by the brand owner. This allows the brand owner not only to prevent the service provider from accessing the market by prohibiting them from using the brand, but also to impose their terms and conditions (salary) without any real negotiation.

A good example is the case of health insurance. In the past, many doctors had private, independent practices and, thanks to their social recognition, they obtained patients/clients directly from the market. However, it is becoming increasingly common for these small clinical practices to obtain patients/clients by joining private insurance companies who 'send' patients/clients to them. These insurance providers, although they do not impose timetables or a way of working (technical and legal independence), the reality is that the doctor needs the brand name provided by the insurance company to continue to earn income. Moreover, they cannot set their own fees, as these are dictated by the insurance company. These are likely to be very similar or identical for all doctors in a given area who provide services for the same health insurance company, demonstrating their high level of replaceability in the eyes of the insurance company. Finally, the insurance company which 'sends' the patients to the given doctor can exclude a given medical professional from its lists of 'partners' at any time (dismissal) depriving them of income, for example, if the doctor does not meet the quality standards required by the insurer or in the event of customer complaints. This implies that the doctor is subordinate to the wishes of the main company since they depend on the main company to continue working, although they do not receive instructions on how they must provide their services.

Thus, it does not seem feasible to consider that, even if the doctor owns the clinic, they have the necessary productive structure to provide services. The doctor lacks the production assets required to be regarded as a genuinely *independent* professional because they do not own two essential twenty-first century elements, i.e., the brand name and the clients (which really belong to the insurance company).

Likewise, in the case of a hairdressing salon which is open to the public, in which the person who performs the work also owns the facilities and the necessary equipment, it is difficult to accept that it has a relevant productive structure if it lacks the ownership of the brand under which it works. In other words, if a person needs a brand which they do not own (it is owned by a third party) in order to obtain clients, they cannot be regarded as independent. In effect, these workers are subordinated to the wishes of that brand, which can 'dismiss' them at any time and withdraw its consent for them to continue using that brand.

[10] A Todolí-Signes, 'Judgment Designating Deliveroo "Rider" an Employee and Analysis of its Impact on the "Gig Economy"' (2018) 24(4) *Transfer* 487.

Specifically, it is precisely this brand ownership[11] that theory has deemed to be hardest for companies to manipulate when trying to disengage an employment link. Any strategy that requires companies to fight against their own brands is unlikely to be successful in the long term.[12] In fact, advertising Uber as a transport service makes it difficult to consider it as a simple technology company. Thus, any individual service provider that carries out an activity which is related to a company's brand must be considered as an employee.[13]

As I have argued on other occasions, in the twenty-first century, brand ownership is one of the most important factors in differentiating between an employee and a self-employed person.[14] Thus, an individual worker who does not operate under their own brand (a brand that the market recognises as belonging to this worker), but does so under the umbrella of an external brand, is subordinated to the wishes and instructions of that brand. They can be dismissed, as they lack their own bargaining power because they are easily replaceable (as they are not recognised by the market) and are not the owner of that intangible means of production.

Along the same lines, the Spanish Supreme Court has also ruled that an individual worker is an employee if the main company decides how they should introduce themselves to customers; if they decide which customers they should see, if they set the price of the service, if they advertise the service, etc.[15]

This criterion has the advantage of being difficult to manipulate, since if a company needs customers, it must show the market what its services are (through advertising, a brand name, etc.) regardless of what it claims in the courts. This approach prevents the economically more valuable part of the business (the brand) from being separated from the salaried employees. Thus, the labour obligations are attributed to the party who has the power to meet them, i.e., the brand owner.

In short, this criterion means that those who materially provide the services 'sold' to the public must be regarded as employees of the company that markets them.

[11] A Deknatel and L Hoff-Downing, 'ABC on the Books and in the Courts: An Analysis of Recent Independent Contractor and Misclassification Statutes' (2015) *Penn Law Legal Scholarship Repository* 67.

[12] K Cunningham-Parmeter, 'Gig-Dependence: Finding the Real Independent Contractors of Platform Work' (2019) 39(3) *Northern Illinois University Law Review* 379–427. There is a certain consensus in accepting the 'chameleon-like' capacity of companies to change their structure and adapt to each of the new jurisprudential requirements to date, see A Álvarez Montero, 'Yacimientos de falsos autónomos más allá de las plataformas digitales: ramificaciones de un arraigado problema' (2018) *Revista de Trabajo y Seguridad Social, CEF 113*, 124.

[13] Cunningham-Parmeter, 'Gig-Dependence: Finding the Real Independent Contractors of Platform Work' 414.

[14] A Todolí-Signes, 'The End of the Subordinate Worker? Collaborative Economy, On-Demand Economy, Gig Economy, and the Crowdworkers' Need for Protection' (2017) 33(2) *International Journal of Comparative Labour Law and Industrial Relations* 241–268 *(IJCLLIR)*.

[15] Spanish Supreme Court Ruling 16 November 2017 (rec 2806/2015).

In addition, a series of factors beyond the ownership of tangible and intangible assets must also be taken into account to ensure the existence of a productive structure that is independent from the main company's structure. Thus, for example, a worker whose income comes mainly from a single 'client' cannot be considered to have a business that is truly independent of that client. Specifically, the New Jersey State Supreme Court Judgment in *Hargrove, et al. vs Sleep's LLC* of 14 January 2015, ruled that if, at the time the relationship with that client ends, the service provider goes out of business (or closes down), it cannot be considered to be truly independent, meaning that this factor alone makes them a salaried employee.

In a similar vein, the existence of this independent structure must precede the existence of the commercial contract with the main company (Dynamex).[16] In other words, if the worker was unemployed or was in another business before starting the relationship with the main company and 'created' their business structure as a necessary precondition for starting the commercial contractual relationship with the main company, it is not appropriate to speak of an 'independent business structure'. It is argued that an economically independent structure cannot exist if it was created as a precondition for entering into a contract with a particular company (or following instructions from that company) or when the structure created cannot remain active after the contract is terminated. It seems logical to assume that if the employee is economically dependent on a specific client for their existence or survival, there is no real independence, as required by this principle.

Non-ownership in the Market and of the Benefits of Labour

Real management and decision-making in key parts of the business related to the market (price, search and choice of customers, direct contact with end consumers, amount of business) is led by the service provider.

This implies that genuine business owners offer their services directly to the market, find their own customers, determine the price of their product or service and have real potential for business growth. This characteristic of genuine business owners is closely related to the previous one regarding real independent management of the business. The difference is that, while in the previous case the assumption is that the lack of the necessary production assets leads to the worker's lack of real independence, here it must be shown directly that the service provider is free to make real business management decisions independently. These decisions do not only refer to being free to choose the timetable or the way the work is done without employer supervision. It refers to the core of business management

[16] Judgment of 30 April 2018, No S222-732, handed down by the Supreme Court of California (*Dynamex Operations West, Inc v The Superior Court of Los Angeles County*).

in the twenty-first century. In other words, making decisions about the price of services, the company's business strategy (there must be a real business strategy for the company that differs from that of the main employer to be considered a real company), the freedom to choose the type of services offered and what customers, as well as a direct relationship with them.

In this sense, the simple imposition of a general contract that the service provider must accept is tantamount to a clear manifestation of economic subordination and an indication that there is no real freedom for the service provider.

Another argument put forward to understand that we are dealing with a subordinate worker is the lack of business opportunities. Workers who provide services by contributing purely work or labour without any business development cannot be classed as business owners.[17] Moreover, a genuine business owner must be able to grow their business beyond working longer hours to receive higher pay. When there is a link between the remuneration paid and the number of hours spent providing services, they are unlikely to be a genuine business owner.[18]

In fact, a genuine business owner is someone who must provide services in an activity where there is professional development, obtaining their own clients through good service provision, which enables them to grow as a company. It is not rational to describe someone as an independent business owner if they only offer their labour and have no (potential) chance to obtain the benefits inherent to an employer.

Accordingly, it is understood that a self-employed worker must provide experience, training and skills and a productive structure that the company itself does not possess so it must therefore rely on an independent third party. Thus, if the service provider performs tasks that are simply part of the ordinary activities of the contracting company, they cannot be considered as a genuine independent business owner. The California Supreme Court, in the aforementioned *Dynamex* judgment, explained this using two examples: first, a worker who sews clothes at home for a clothing manufacturer is an employee (no matter how much legal independence or 'formal freedom' they have), given that the contracting company engages in the business of manufacturing and selling clothes. Likewise, a bakery which sells bread and cakes will not be able to consider the cake decorator as a genuine business owner, since this job or profession can be regarded as the usual work of a company engaged in this business. Conversely, the hiring of a plumber or electrician in businesses that require one-off repairs yet do not engage in the plumbing or electrical business will be considered 'outside the ordinary course of business' – the performance of occasional or one-off work which does not form part of the range of products or services offered by that business to the market.

[17] B Rogers, 'Employment as a Legal Concept' (2015) *Legal Studies Research Papers Series*.

[18] *Uber BV and others (Appellants) v Aslam and others (Respondents)* [2021] UKSC 5 On appeal from: [2018] EWCA Civ 2748; In Spain, Supreme Court Ruling 16 October 2017, *Ofilingua* case.

The Real Provision of the Commissioned Service is Carried Out by Workers Hired by the Employer

In other words, the employer benefits from the work performed by others, not the party who actually performs the work. If the work entrusted by the client, by means of the service provision contract, is carried out directly by the 'owner' of the company, we would be dealing with a worker (an employment contract), given that they are actually providing labour.

This factor can be used to identify a genuine business owner when the activity does not require significant production assets. Thus, for example, the contract between an office company and a cleaning person can hardly be considered as a commercial contract. In fact, if the person who cleans the offices is hired directly, they must be given an employment contract. However, the office company may hire a cleaning company to provide these services, though this would require the cleaning company to take someone on, through an employment contract, to carry out the service. In other words, there is nothing to prevent companies from using a commercial contract to provide a service; what is required in this concept is that the person who actually does the job has an employment contract. Thus, it is perfectly feasible for a cleaning company to offer its services on the market, as long as the person who performs the services is actually employed and is covered by labour regulations.

In short, this classification criterion (consolidated organisational structure) consists of identifying the difference between a genuine business owner and one who only provides labour.[19] In the twenty-first century, this means focusing on factors that are relevant to the technological, productive and organisational set-up of companies today. In this sense, the main criteria to detect a bogus self-employed person are: ii) the non-ownership of capital or technology assets; ii) the non-ownership of the fruits of one's labour and the non-ownership of the market; iii) the hiring of sufficient workers to carry out one's business activities. In this context, the lack of legal dependency or the lack of independence in terms of risk should not be considered as determining factors. They are the result of the ease and expediency for those who have bargaining power to impose risk-taking on those who lack bargaining power. In this way, the lack of risk-sharing should be considered a consequence of the employment contract and not a prerequisite.

[19] Basically, all of this is similar to what has been discussed above on 'the new employment status indicators', given that, in the end, these new indicators only serve to point out the importance in the twenty-first century of production assets that are different (now mainly intangible) to those that were important in the twentieth century (machinery, factories). On the lack of ownership of these new significant production assets as what really subordinates the worker, see Todolí-Signes, 'Judgment Designating Deliveroo "Rider" an Employee and Analysis of its Impact on the "Gig Economy"'.

12

Conclusions. Myths about Labour Regulations and the Economy

Over the last 40 years, labour law has been losing ground in complying with its three main functions. This book has analysed the main reasons behind this decline in the use of labour market regulations: (i) the creation of an upper working class that nowadays does not require state intervention to ensure the economic security it obtains through alternative incomes; (ii) the emergence of other priority interests over and above the 'social agenda' when it comes to voting; and (iii) the weakening of trade unions and the disconnect between trade unions and political parties.

In turn, from an economic theory perspective, there are two main arguments used to justify a non-interventionist approach to the labour market: (a) first, it is claimed that labour law regulations can lead to unemployment; and (b) second, it is contended that legislative intervention leads to inefficiencies in the labour market. This book has sought to argue that both claims are misguided in most cases. They correspond instead to myths about the functioning of the labour market that are insufficiently supported by empirical evidence. In fact, empirical studies point to the opposite situation in many cases: labour market intervention and labour rights improve efficiency, productivity and can help job creation.

Labour lawyers often bandy about the expression 'labour reforms neither create nor destroy jobs'. The purpose of this statement is none other than to try to disconnect job destruction, or job creation, from labour regulations.

At an ideological and political moment in time in which the prevailing narrative is that labour law destroys jobs, it seems logical to argue that there is no causality between labour regulations and employment rates to defend the continuity of labour regulations.

Thus, this expression, commonly used by progressive academics, is most often used as a defence mechanism to prevent labour market deregulation. It is thus reasoned that the labour market should not be deregulated because this will have no effect on employment rates in a country. This is tantamount to asserting that labour regulations have a neutral effect on the economy. It is also true that, in many cases, this discourse on labour law and the economy does not aim to suggest that labour regulations have no effect on the economy, but rather to point out that employment rates in a country depend on factors other than labour regulations to a much greater extent. Indeed, the demand for labour depends mainly on the amount of demand for existing products and services in that market, on the efficiency of the firms located in that country, on the amount of existing investment, and so on.

However, as argued in this book, the reality is that all these factors are in turn conditioned by labour market regulation. Minimum wages and effective collective bargaining can improve a country's purchasing power (demand). Reducing temporary employment improves incentives for training and new work methods, and boosts efficiency. Ending competition via labour costs encourages business innovation, and so on. Therefore, this book concludes that the positive impact that labour regulations can have on employment rates in a country and also on the efficiency of firms, which will ultimately lead to higher employment rates, should not be underestimated.

Thus, this book rejects this supposedly neutral approach (understood as the lack of real power to have a negative or positive effect on the economy) towards labour regulations with respect to the economy. On the contrary, the conclusion is that they have a positive effect. To support this conclusion, this book firstly dismantles the myth of 'non-intervention' and secondly justifies the need for labour law for reasons of economic efficiency, wealth redistribution, meritocracy and equality.

There is no such thing as deregulation. The labour market is always regulated. When we speak of 'labour market deregulation' we are referring to the removal of a specific labour market regulation that takes into account its special features (e.g., people are not 'melons', the difference in bargaining power between the employer and workers) and fall within the scope of civil regulation. In this way, defending 'deregulation of the labour market' implies that there is no difference between the provision of services by an individual or by a genuine business owner. However, the reality is quite different. In this sense, labour law recognises the differences that exist between the inter-company service market and service provision by individuals (without being a genuine business owner) and regulates them according to this reality.

In fact, there is no evidence that market deregulation can be sustained from non-interventionist market positions given that, as demonstrated in this book, the State permanently intervenes for the benefit of the economy itself (levels of money supply, interest rates and exchange rates decided by the central bank, degree of public spending decided by governments, etc.). These interventions have a huge impact on employment rates in a country and in no case is it argued that they should cease (on pain of returning to a medieval-type economy).

Thus, when one defends labour deregulation, but does not do the same for state intervention in the level of the money supply decided by the central bank of the day, the choice is not for 'non-intervention' in the economy, but rather for a specific type of intervention: that is, one that benefits the owners of capital (in the short term) over the owners of labour. Indeed, as argued in this book, labour law does not protect the worker. Instead, it rebalances what civil law (and economic policy) throws out of balance in favour of the owner of capital. Thus, the dichotomy between 'too much regulation' or 'too little regulation' is a fallacy since there is always regulation. The problem is the type of regulation: what it does, how it does it and what its effects are.

Labour market 'deregulation' harms the economy. It seems obvious to argue that ignoring the specificities of the labour market is poor regulatory policy. To establish efficient regulation, one must first admit that the labour market does not function in the same way as the market for goods or services provided by other parties. As the Declaration concerning the aims and objectives of the International Labour Organisation, commonly known as the 'Declaration of Philadelphia', stated on 10 March 1944: *labour is not a commodity*. However, this should not only be seen as a moral principle whereby it does not seem ethically correct to treat people as commodities, but also as an economic principle. Indeed, the economic principles of commodity markets (or of the provision of services between genuine business owners) cannot be applied to the labour market and, consequently, a generalist regulation is not valid either when dealing with the sale of labour power.

As a matter of fact, the historical perspective shows that the law of supply and demand does *not* explain the functioning of the labour market. The 1970s saw multiple periods of low wages and high unemployment demonstrating that wage reductions do not imply, at least not always, an increase in the number of employed workers. There are many possible explanations for this phenomenon. The most obvious is that low wages reduce purchasing power, which prevents employers from being able to sell their products. In fact, no matter how cheap labour is, if employers have no one to buy their products, they will have little incentive to produce.

Similarly, a monopolistic or highly concentrated firm position in the labour market may result in the employer being able to keep workers' wages low without creating employment. This is because the firm can use its market power to force workers to work for low wages, but this does not lead to an increase in existing employment in the economy. Even without a monopsonist position, the bargaining weakness of workers (in the absence of collective bargaining) can lead to low wages while unemployment persists.

In short, the law of supply and demand holds that reducing the price of something increases its demand. Applying this theory to the labour market, lower wages increase employment. However, historical data series show that the reality of the labour market is the opposite. High unemployment implies that workers have very low bargaining power (fear of unemployment and dismissal), which means that they cannot negotiate for better wages and other working conditions, resulting in an economy with high unemployment and low wages. For this reason, removing labour safeguards does not lead to higher levels of employment; on the contrary, countries with very high unemployment levels require higher levels of labour market regulation.

As a result, workers in countries with higher unemployment have less bargaining power, which means that companies can abuse their bargaining power leading to low wages, poorer working conditions and resulting in market inefficiencies (low worker training, low level of technological and organisational innovation, low purchasing power, etc.). Labour rights break this vicious circle by enabling efficiency gains.

It should be remembered that 'flexibility' and 'deregulation' are merely euphemisms for an increase in the unilateral power of the employer (civil law regulation), meaning that the employer can take the lion's share of the income generated by workers, enabling them to behave in the market as if they were monopsonists. In other words, they maintain low wages despite high unemployment in the country.

Even from a neo-classical perspective and accepting that the law of supply and demand applies to the labour market without adaptations, the economic literature holds that markets suffer from failures that must be addressed by regulation. The lack of perfect information, transaction costs, collective order problems, the need for collaboration and trust, the inelasticity of labour supply and negative externalities prevent the labour market from functioning properly, so regulations are needed to improve its performance. Thus, another of the myths about economics and labour law must be rejected: deregulation as a way to improve efficiency.

As the Nobel Prize-winning economist John Kenneth Galbraith rightly pointed out, when the state exercises control over the environment, no matter how badly it does so, it will always be better than if there was no regulation at all. To illustrate this example, the economist described the planning of city expansions that took place at the end of the nineteenth and beginning of the twentieth centuries. In this case, Galbraith admitted that the broad avenues planned and developed by Washington DC's municipal architects left room for improvement, but also noted that the result was certainly much better than if everyone had been able to build where they wanted without any planning or public control as in other parts of the city (and in other cities).[1]

The myth of the invisible hand that 'solves' everything has been refuted on many occasions. Accordingly, there are many examples in which the labour market requires legislative intervention to solve market failures and improve efficiency: (i) insufficient level of insurance in labour contingencies arising from imperfect information (economic myopia) that justifies compulsory social security; (ii) reduced cooperation and increased conflict arising from employers' opportunistic exercise of power that requires limits to curb it; (iii) low levels of cooperation and specific training when workers are not guaranteed job stability which justifies the preference for permanent contracts; (iv) the inability of civil law and liability for damages to reduce accidents at work which requires specific occupational health and safety regulations; (v) incentives for employers to externalise the costs of training their workers by laying off older workers and hiring young, trained workers,

[1] JK Galbraith, *The New Industrial State* (Boston, Houghton Mifflin, 1967) 360.

etc; and (vi) transaction costs make it necessary to standardise the rules applicable to all workers by means of collective rather than purely individual solutions.

Thus, even though labour regulations can be improved (and very much improved in some cases), this is not a reason to eliminate them (i.e., to replace them with general civil regulations). On the contrary, what is relevant is to publicly evaluate the effects of a specific regulation to find out if it is working well and to replace it with a different one if it is not.

Labour regulations improve the economy. The fact is that labour regulations should not merely be an intervention to reduce market failures. Quite the opposite, good regulation can improve efficiency, boost innovation, improve investment in human capital and training, encourage competition on product quality rather than labour costs, and facilitate an increase in the size of firms so that they can take advantage of the economies of scale resulting from their investments. This book has analysed multiple empirical studies that show how labour regulation improves productive efficiency. Thus, for example, minimum wages and collective bargaining encourage technological and organisational innovation in firms, improving productivity, as well as investment in human capital and training. In fact, when the lack of regulation leads to zero wages, firms have little incentive to invest in technology and train human capital since it is relatively cheaper to hire more labour to obtain the level of output they require. In other words, labour market 'deregulation' leads to poor levels of training and technological investment.

In the same way, without specific regulation, companies will pass on the inefficiencies of the business to the worker, thereby discouraging companies from becoming more efficient (better organisation, better working methods). In general, this would not be a problem for the economy if companies were not the only ones to have the capital to technologically improve production processes, provide training, and innovate in terms of methods, etc. In other words, if companies do not take up the challenge of reducing inefficiencies, and have no incentive to improve, the economy will not become more efficient.

In turn, industry collective bargaining agreements and standardised protection would enable companies to compete on the quality of their products and services rather than on low labour costs (which discourage training, investment in technology and efficiency). In fact, if certain companies are allowed to compete on labour costs and monopolise a large part of the market share thanks to these 'comparative advantages', the remaining companies will have little incentive to invest in technological and productive improvements given that their investment efforts will not be rewarded with a better market share because this is monopolised by inefficient companies who can undercut prices due to the poor working conditions of their employees.

Finally, this book concludes that there is no trade-off between economic efficiency and labour regulations. On the contrary, the empirical studies analysed show that the two go hand in hand: solid economic growth can only be achieved through good labour regulation.

Another of the myths that this book debunks is the dichotomy between economic efficiency and equality. Neo-liberal proponents argue that if everyone is treated equally, there will be no incentive to work hard, thus productivity and economic growth will suffer. For this reason, it is claimed that these regulations should be dropped or, at least, the principles of equality should be limited to only the most egregious cases of discrimination (e.g., gender, nationality, religion, age, etc.).

However, this book argues that there is no trade-off between efficiency and equality. What actually harms efficiency is treating those who are equal differently without sufficient justification. To reach this conclusion, first of all, the theories of meritocracy were analysed. Indeed, the meritocratic ideal requires that what a worker receives in wages, or whether a worker is hired or fired, depends solely on merit: i.e., that economic operators are rewarded according to their contribution and effort is a maxim of the market. In fact, economists argue that without a balanced distribution between what one contributes and what one receives ('merit'), incentives to work hard and cooperate will quickly disappear (and with them, productivity and economic growth).

Thus, differences decided by the employer based on historical stereotypes, which have nothing to do with what one contributes and 'deserves', will lead to reductions in the level of effort and incentives to cooperate. Thus, regulations prohibiting discrimination are justified to ensure productive efficiency and collaboration.

Moreover, while it is true that differences in treatment based on historical stereotypes may be those that cause the highest levels of unfairness (and thus the worst efficiency outcomes), the reality is that any kind of difference in treatment that is not 'deserved' is likely to cause disaffection at work and bring productive inefficiencies. For this reason, it is argued that regulation should only allow for differences in treatment based on merit. This should imply that decisions based on criteria irrelevant to merit should be prohibited. Thus, this would include differences (including non-hiring and dismissal) based on gender, race, religion and non-employment grounds, but also those based on the type of contract (temporary or permanent, part-time or full-time), whether one works for a temporary agency, a contract or for a different company within the same corporate group.

In turn, it is claimed that merit does allow for differences in treatment based on objective criteria related to service provision. Thus, this book does not argue that all workers should be treated equally, but advocates differences based on objective, justified, proportionate and work-related grounds. In short, for reasons of efficiency and commitment to a merit-based functioning of the economy, the principle of equality should not only apply to public administrations and regulations, but also to private individuals, and specifically to the employment contract.

In short, the relationship between labour law and economic policy currently seems to be plagued by prejudices that do not stand up to empirical scrutiny. There are a series of myths created to reduce social support for workers' rights which cast doubt on every existing labour regulation and paralyse regulatory innovation in the field of social rights. Any proposal for new regulation made by academics or political parties is attacked for causing market inefficiency. This attack is not accompanied by data or empirical evidence that refutes the usefulness of regulation, but instead by myths and prejudices.

This book argues that this situation has been condoned by the defenders of labour regulations because they refuse to engage in the economic debate. Many labour authors prefer not to try to deny the negative effects of labour law on the economy, preferring instead simply to defend the neutrality or irrelevance of labour regulations in the economy. Instead, the staunchest defences are played out on the battlefield of values. Thus, labour literature has historically advocated the need for regulation based on social values, the moral imperatives to help the unprotected, and human rights. However, these enthusiastic defences do not seem to have achieved their goal in a world where the economy seems to be at the centre of everything. The prevailing pro-market ideology has succeeded in convincing people of the economy's ability to improve the situation of all concerned. If the economy is doing well, everything will get better. Therefore, in the imagination, social values are only achieved if there is economic growth. It is probably for this reason that arguments used to defend labour regulation focusing solely on social values and which are not linked to its effects on the economy have not been convincing.

In this context, labour regulations need a narrative adapted to the new political and ideological circumstances if they are to achieve their objective. They need to modernise their philosophical rationale to include the priorities of today's society. This does not mean abandoning justifications based on social values or the protection of the weaker contracting party, but it does mean no longer ignoring, or downplaying, the social importance of other justifications. Labour law proposals should be justified not only by social values, where the labour lawyer feels comfortable, but also, where possible, on economic grounds. Otherwise, ignoring economic effects will leave this flank open to attack with prejudices and myths that can easily be refuted.

Thus, it is concluded that the efficiency factor, as an argument for the social legitimacy of labour regulations, should not be monopolised by those who support the deregulation of labour markets when, on many occasions, the opposite is true: the search for efficiency requires strong labour regulation.

However, economic growth alone is not enough to halt the rise of nationalism, division and social conflict that is flooding back into our societies. It seems increasingly clear that the 'hands-off' policies of recent years have generated an unprecedented increase in social inequality and disaffection with the political and economic system in developed countries, putting both in jeopardy if they continue along the same road. The *laissez-faire* system has proved incapable of providing opportunities for all segments of the population. Instead, growth has slowed, and the benefits of the economy have been distributed in a way that does not correspond to the efforts made to generate them.

It cannot be a coincidence that the golden years of capitalism (the years with the highest level of economic growth) have coincided with the years when labour protection was at its strongest. Achieving high levels of economic equality and job security for all layers of society brings better economic development. In particular, only a merit-based, value-based distribution of the income generated can guarantee the involvement of economic agents in the actual creation of value. If employers are allowed to use their superior bargaining power to reap higher earnings than they deserve at the expense of workers, this will not only generate inequality, uprooting and social instability, it will also fuel demotivation and discourage efforts to produce value. At a company level, collective bargaining, the minimum wage and other well-known labour regulations are the only things that can bring about the desired results.

Recent trends show how, in the coming years, digital transformation, teleworking, automation and the development of artificial intelligence will extend the detrimental effects of unregulated labour markets even further. These will become global (globalisation of service provision through digital platforms), and the bargaining power of the workforce will shrink as technology replaces more and more human tasks. This means that workers who were traditionally able to protect themselves, without the need for legislative intervention, i.e., highly skilled professionals (doctors, engineers, computer scientists, architects, lawyers, etc.) will be dragged into this globalisation of services with a consequent loss of bargaining power vis-à-vis the owners of the technology (digital platforms).

This opens up new opportunities for labour law. First, it is a way to rebalance the bargaining power that globalisation and technological progress have thrown off balance in favour of capital owners. Second, in the coming years, these technological changes will lead to the emergence of more and more individuals who will require labour protection.

In this sense, this book concludes that, in order to prevent rent-seeking behaviour (obtaining more than one deserves as a result of a superior bargaining position) which generates inequality, disaffection and inefficiency in the market, labour regulations should always be applied when there is a relationship of economic subordination of the personal service provider. To this end, a restrictive concept of workers, based on the existence of legal dependence, should be discarded in order to apply labour law to all those who sell their labour power. In other words, to all those who provide services without being a genuine business owner.

In fact, the adaptation of the concept of worker to the economic-entrepreneurial reality of the twenty-first century should be seen as a challenge for labour law, but also as a great opportunity. As has been argued in this book, one of the historical reasons for the success of labour law as a source of efficiency, redistribution and equality was precisely that the 'upper' part of the working class found itself in need of regulation in order to enjoy economic security ('living like the bourgeoisie while being wage earners'). In this sense, the globalisation of work (teleworking), digital platforms and algorithmic management could once again provoke an unusual interest in labour law by individuals who currently believe that they no longer need it. The first step towards satisfying these needs for protection is to disassociate labour law from a restrictive scope of application that excludes a large number of workers.

BIBLIOGRAPHY

Abbott, R, and Bogenschneider, BN, 'Should Robots Pay Taxes? Tax Policy in the Age of Automation' (2018) 12 *Harvard Law and Policy Review* 145.

Abdih, Y, and Danninger, S, 'What Explains the Decline of the US Labor Share of Income? An Analysis of State and Industry Level Data' (Washington DC, 2017) *IMF Working Paper* (WP/17/167).

Able, J, and Fitzroy, FR, 'Cooperation and Productivity: Some Evidence from the West German Experience' (1980) 14 (2) *Economic Analysis and Workers Management* 163–80.

Acemoglu, D, and Autor, D, 'Skills, Tasks and Technologies: Implications for Employment & Earnings' (2011) 4 *Handbook of Labor Economics* 1043–171.

Acemoglu, D, and Restrepo, P, 'Artificial Intelligence, Automation and Work' *The Economics of Artificial Intelligence: An Agenda* (Chicago, University of Chicago Press, 2018) 197–236.

Acemoglu, D, and Restrepo, P, 'Artificial Intelligence, Automation and Work' (2018) 24196, *NEBER Working Paper.*

Acemoglu, D, and Restrepo, P, 'Robots and Jobs: Evidence from US Labour Markets' (2017) 23285, *NBER Working Paper.*

Acemoglu, D, and Restrepo, P, 'Secular Stagnation? The Effect of Aging on Economic Growth in the Age of Automation, American Economic Growth in the Age of Automation' (2017) 107(5) *American Economic Review Papers and Proceedings* 174–79.

Acemoglu, D, and Restrepo, P, 'The Race Between Man and Machine: Implications of Technology for Growth, Factor Shares, and Employment' (2018) 208(6), *American Economic Review* 1489–542.

Adams, JS, 'Inequity in Social Exchange', in LR Berkowitz (ed) *Advances in Experimental Social Psychology (Vol. 2)* (New York, Academic Press, 1965) 267–99.

Adams, RJ, 'From Statutory Right to Human Right: The Evolution and Current Status of Collective Bargaining' (2018) 12 *Just Labour: A Canadian Journal of Work and Society* 137–55.

Addison, JT and Hirsch, BT, 'The Economic Effects of Employment Regulation: What Are The Limits?', in Kaufman (ed), *Government Regulation of the Employment Relationship* (1997).

Alba Ramírez, A, 'Capital humano y competitividad en la economía española: una perspectiva internacional' (1993) 56 *Papeles de economía española* 131–43.

Albrecht, J, 'Search Theory: The 2010 Nobel Memorial Prize in Economic Sciences' (2011) 113(2) *The Scandinavian Journal of Economics* 237–59.

Alchian, A, and Allen, W, *University Economics* 3rd edn (Belmont CA, Wadsworth, 1972).

Aloisi, A, 'Commoditized Workers. The Rising of On-Demand Work, Case Study Research on a Set of Online Platforms and Apps" (2016) 37(3) *Comparative Labor Law & Policy Journal* 653.

Alston, P, *Labour Rights as Human Rights* (Oxford, Oxford University Press, 2005).

Álvarez Montero, A, 'Yacimientos de falsos autónomos más allá de las plataformas digitales: ramificaciones de un arraigado problema' (2018) *Revista de Trabajo y Seguridad Social, CEF* 113–32.

Álvarez, I, et al, 'Missing Links in the Inclusive Growth Debate: Functional Income Distribution and Labor Market Institutions' (2011) 160(3) *International Labour Review* 337–62.

Arthurs, H, 'Labour Law After Labour', in Davidov, G, and Languille, B, (eds), *The Idea of Labour Law* (Oxford, Oxford University Press, 2011) 22.

Arthurs, H, 'What Immortal Hand or Eye? Who will Redraw the Boundaries?', in G Davidov and B Languille (eds), *Boundaries and Frontiers of Labour Law* (Oxford, Hart Publishing, 2006) 376.

Arup, C, Gahan, P, Howe, JB, Johnstone, RS, Mitchell R, and O'Donnell, A, *Labour Law and Labour Market Regulation: Essays on the Construction, Constitution and Regulation of Labour Markets and Work Relationships* (New South Wales, Federation Press, 2006).

Askenazy, P, 'Working Time Regulation in France from 1996 to 2012' (2013) 37 (2) *Cambridge Journal of Economics* 336–47.

Atkinson, J, 'Human Rights as Foundations for Labour Law' in *Philosophical Foundations of Labour Law*, (Oxford, Oxford University Press, 2018) 133.

Autor, D, 'Work of the Past, Work of the Future' (2019) 25588, *NBER Working Paper.*

Autor, D, 'Why Are There Still So Many Jobs? The History and Future of Workplace Automation' (2015) 29(3) *Journal of Economic Perspectives* 3.

Autor, D, Manning, A, and Christopher, LS, 'The Contribution of the Minimum Wage to US Wage Inequality over Three Decades: A Reassessment' (2016) 8(1) *American Economic Journal: Applied Economics* 58–99.

Autor, D et al, 'The Skill Content of Recent Technological Change: An Empirical Exploration' (2017) 118 (4) *Quarterly Journal of Economics* 1279–333.

Autor, D, et al, 'Does Employment Protection Reduce Productivity? Evidence from US States' (2007) 117 (521) *The Economic Journal* F189–F217.

Azar, JA, Marinescu, M, Steinbaum, M, and Taska, B, 'Concentration in US Labor Markets: Evidence from Online Vacancy Data' (2018) 24396, *NBER Working Paper.*

Baker, D, *Rigged: How Globalization and the Rules of the Modern Economy Were Structured to Make the Rich Richer* (Washington DC, Center for Economic and Policy Research, 2016).

Baldwin, JR, 'Were Small Producers the Engines of Growth in the Canadian Manufacturing Sector in the 1980s' (1998) 10 *Small Business Economics* 349–64.

Baldwin, JR, and Gu, W, 'Plant Turnover and Productivity Growth in Canadian Manufacturing' (2006) 15(3) *Industrial and Corporate Change*, 417–65.

Baldwin, JR, Jarmin, RS, and Tang, J, 'The Trend to Smaller Producers in Manufacturing: A Canada/U.S. Comparison' (2002) Statistics Canada, Analytical Studies – Economic Analysis, Series 1F0027MIE No 003, US Census Bureau Center for Economic Studies Paper No CES-WP- 02-06.

Banerjee, A, and Chiplunkar, G, 'How Important are Matching Fictions in the Labor Market? Experimental and Non-experimental Evidence from a Large Indian Firm' (2018), *Working Paper.* Available at: https://ssrn.com/abstract=4441896 or http://dx.doi.org/10.2139/ssrn.4441896.

Banerjee, A, and Duflo, E, *Good Economics for Hard Times* (New York, Random House, 2019).

Banerjee, A, et al, 'Me and Everyone Else: Do People Think like Economists?' (2019) *MIMEO, Massachusetts Institute of Technology.*

Barker, JR, 'Tightening the Iron Cage: Concretive Control in Self-managing Teams' (1993) 38 *Administrative Science Quarterly* 408.

Basu, P, 'Understanding Labour Market Frictions: An Asset Pricing Approach' (2009) 61(4) *Bulletin of Economics Research* 305.

BBVA, 'La participación del trabajo en la renta nacional'. Available at: www.bbva.com/es/la-participacion-del-trabajo-en-la-renta-nacional.

Becker, GS, *The Economics of Discrimination*, 2nd edn (Chicago, University of Chicago Press, 1971).

Belcher, DS, *Sistemas de retribución y administración de salarios* (Bilbao, Ediciones Deusto, 1978) 21.

Belman, D, and Belzer, M, 'The Regulation of Labor Markets: Balancing the Benefits and Costs of Competition', in Kaufman (ed), *Government Regulation of the Employment Relationship* (1997) 188.

Benmelch, E, Bergman, NK, and Kim, H, 'Strong Employers and Weak Employees: How Does Employer Concentration Affect Wages?' (2018) 24307, *NBER Working Paper.*

Berger, D, Herkenhoff, K, and Mongey, S, 'Labour Market Power' (2019) 25719, *NBER Working Paper.*

Bessen, JE, 'How Computer Automation Affects Occupations: Technology, Jobs and Skills' (2016) *Boston University School of Law, Law and Economics Working Paper* 15.

Blair, RD, and JL Harrison, JL, *Monopsony in Law and Economics* (Cambridge, Cambridge University Press, 2010) 81.

Blau, FD, and Kahn, LM, 'Institutions and Laws in the Labor Market, in Ashenfelter and Card', *Handbook of Labour Economics* (Elsvier, North-Holland, 1999).

Böhm, MJ, 'The Price of Polarization: Estimating Task Prices under Routine-Biased Technical Change' (2017) 11220 *IZA (Institute for the Study of Labor) Discussion Paper Series.*

Boltanski, L, and Chiapello, E, *The New Spirit of Capitalism*, (London, Verso, 2005) 39, 536, 538.
Borrajo Dacruz, E, *Introducción al Derecho del Trabajo*, 5th edn, (Madrid, Tecnos, 1988).
Breza, E, Kaur, S, and Shamdasani, Y, 'The Morale Effects of Pay Inequality' (2018) 133(2) *Quarterly Journal of Economics* 611–63.
Brown, C, 'Minimum Wage Laws: Are They Overrated?' (1988) 2(3) *Journal of Economic Perspective* 133–45.
Brown, W, *In The Ruins Of Neoliberalism. The Rise of Antidemocratic Politics in the West* (New York, Columbia University Press, 2019).
Brown, W, Deakin, S, Nash, D, and Oxenbridge, S, 'The Employment Contract: From Collective Procedures to Individual Rights' (2000) 38, *British Journal of Industrial Relations* 611.
Brynjolfsson, E, and McAfee, A, *The Second Machine Age: Work, Progress, and Prosperity in a Time of Brilliant Technologies* (New York, WW Norton & Company, 2014).
Bull, C, 'Business Cycle and Wage Determination in the United States' in Haig, R, (ed) *Incentives, Cooperation, and Risk Sharing: Economic and Psychological Perspectives on Employment Contracts* (New Jersey, Roman & Littlefield, 1987).
Bulow, JI, Summers, LH, 'A Theory of Dual Labor Markets with Application to Industrial Policy, Discrimination and Keynesian Unemployment' (1986) 4(3) *Journal of Labor Economics* 376–414.
Cable, J, and FitzRoy, F, *Cooperation and Productivity: Some Evidence from West German Experience* (Coventry, University of Warwick, 1979).
Cabrelli D, and Zahn, R, 'Civil Republican Political Theory and Labour Law', in *Philosophical Foundations of Labour Law* (Oxford, Oxford University Press, 2018) 107.
Cantwell Smith, B, *The Promise of Artificial Intelligence: Reckoning and Judgment* (Cambridge MA, The MIT Press, 2019).
Card D, and Krueger, A, *Myth and Measurement: The New Economics of the Minimum Wage* (New Jersey, Princeton University Press, 1995).
Card D, et al., 'Firms and Labor Market Inequality: Evidence and Some Theory' (2016) 22850 *NBER* Working Paper, 17.
CEDEFOP, 'People, machines, robots and skills' (2017) 9121 *Briefing note.*
CEDEFOP, *Insights into Skill Shortages and Skill Mismatch: Learning from CEDEFOP's European Skills and Jobs Survey* (Luxembourg, 2018).
Cherry, M, 'Working for (Virtually) Minimum Wage: Applying the Fair Labor Standards Act in Cyberspace' (2009) 60 (5) *Alabama Law Review* 1077–110.
Chletsos, M, and Giotis, GP, 'The Employment Effect of Minimum Wage Using 77 International Studies Since 1992: A Meta-Analysis' (2015) Paper 61321, *MPRA University of Munich.*
Clark, JB, 'The Possibility of a Scientific Law of Wages' (1889) 4 *Publications of the American Economic Association* 39.
Click, RL, and Duening, TN, *Business Process Outsourcing: The Competitive Advantage* (Chichester, Wiley, 2004).
Coase, RH, 'The Nature of the Firm' (1937) 16(4) *Económica, New Series* 386–405.
Coase, RH, 'The Problem of Social Cost' (1960) 3 *Journal of Law and Economics* 1.
Cohen, GA, 'Where the Action Is: On the Site of Distributive Justice' (1997) 26 *Philosophy and Public Affairs* 3–30.
Collins, H, 'Justification and Techniques of Legal Regulation of the Employment Relations', in H Collins, P Davies and R Rideout (eds), *Legal Regulation of the Employment Relation* (Alphen aan den Rijn, Kluwer International, 2000) 7–11.
Collins, H, 'Justification and Techniques of Legal Regulation of the Employment Relation' (2000) 3 *WG Hart Legal Workshop Series* 19.
Collins, H, 'Regulating the Employment Relationship for Competitiveness' (2001) 30 *Industrial Law Journal* 17.
Collins, H, 'Theories of Rights as Justifications for Labour Law', in Collins (ed) *The Idea of Labour Law* (Oxford, Oxford University Press, 2011) 145.

Collins, H, GL Lester, and V Mantouvalou, 'Introduction: Does Labour Law Need Philosophical Foundations?', in *Philosophical Foundations of Labour Law* (Oxford, Oxford University Press, 2018) 3.
Commons, JR, *Labor and Administration* (New York, McGraw-Hill, 1923) 411.
Coon, JS, 'Collective Bargaining and Productivity' (1929) 19(3) *The American Economic Review* 419–27.
Costa Morata, PC, *Por el decrecimiento, Libros de economía y empresa* 1 (2010) 24–27.
Countouris, N, and De Stefano, V, 'New forms of employment' (2019) *Syndicat European Trade Union.*
Countouris, N, and De Stefano, V, and Lianos, I, 'The EU, Competition and Workers' Rights' (2021) *Center for Law, Economics and Society. Research Paper Series.*
Cowen, T, *Average is Over* (New York, Plume, 2013).
Cruz Villalón, 'El debate en torno a la adaptación o superación de la subordinación como elemento referencial del Derecho del Trabajo ante las nuevas formas de trabajo. Un debate global desde la perspectiva española' (2020) 6 (2) *Labour & Law Issues* 32.
CSI, *Invertir en protección social y su impacto en el crecimiento económico* (CSI, 2021).
Cunningham-Parmeter, K, 'Gig-Dependence: Finding the Real Independent Contractors of Platform Work' (2019) 39 (3) *Northern Illinois University Law Review* 379–427.
DA Webber, DA 'Firm Market Power and the Earnings Distribution' (2011) CES-WP *US Census Bureau Center for Economic Studies* 11. Available at: www.dx.doi.org/10.2139/ssrn.1969785.
Dauth, W, Findeisen, S, Südekum, J, and Wössner, N, 'German Robots – The Impact of Industrial Robots on Workers' (2017) 30 *IAB Discussion Paper* 5.
Davidov, G, *Distributive Justice and Labour Law. Philosophical Foundations of Labour Law* (Oxford, Oxford University Press, 2018) 143.
Davidov, G, *A Purposive Approach to Labour Law* (Oxford, Oxford Monographs on Labour Law, 2016).
Davies, P, and Freedland, M, *Towards a Flexible Labour Market: Labour Legislation and Regulation since the 1990s* (Oxford, Oxford University Press, 2007).
Davies, P, and Freedland, M, *Kahn-Freund's Labour and the Law* (London, Stevens, 1983).
De Stefano, V, 'Non-Standard Work and Limits on Freedom of Association: A Human Rights-Based Approach' (2017) 46(2) *Industrial Law Journal* 185–207.
De Stefano, V, 'The Rise of the "Just-In-Time Workforce", On-Demand Work, Crowdwork and Labour Protection in the Gig-Economy' (2016) 37(3) *Comparative Labour Law and Policy Journal* 471.
Deakin, S, *Renewing Labour Market Institutions* (Budapest, Central European University, 2004).
Deakin, S, 'The Contribution of Labour Law to Economic and Human Development', in Davidov, G, and Languille, B, (eds), *The Idea of Labour Law* (Oxford, Oxford University Press, 2011) 165.
Deakin, S, 'The Evolution of the Employment Relationship' in P Auer and B Gazier (eds), *The Future of Work, Employment and Social Protection: The Dynamics of Change and the Protection of Workers* (Geneva, International Institute for Labour Studies, 2002).
Deakin, S, 'The Evolution of the Contract of Employment 1900–1950: The Influence of the Welfare State', in N Whiteside and R Salais (eds), *Governance, Industry and Labour Markets in Britain and France, The Modernising State in the Mid-Twentieth Century* (London, Routledge, 1998) 212–30.
Deakin, S, and Wilkinson, F, *The Law of the Labour Market: Industrialization, Employment, and Legal Evolution* (Oxford, Oxford University Press, 2005) 290–303.
Deakin, S, and Wilkinson, F, 'Justifications and Techniques of Legal Regulation of the Employment Relation', in H Collins, P Davies and R Rideout (eds), *Legal Regulation of the Employment Relation* (London, Collins, 2001).
Deakin S and Wilkinson, F, 'Labour Law, Social Security and Economic Inequality' (1991) 15(2) *Cambridge Journal of Economics* 125–48.
Deknatel, A, and Hoff-Downing, L, 'ABC on the Books and in the Courts: An Analysis of Recent Independent Contractor and Misclassification Statutes' (2015) *Penn Law Legal Scholarship Repository.*
Denice, P, and Rosenfeld, J, 'Unions and Non-union Pay in the United States, 1977–2015' (2018) 5 *Sociological Science* 541.
Dhawan, R, 'Firm size and Productivity Differential: Theory and Evidence from a Panel of US Firms' (2001) 44 *Journal of Economic Behavior and Organization* 169.

Diaz, M, and Sánchez, R, 'Film Size and Productivity in Spain: A Stochastic Frontier Analysis. Small Business Economics' (2008) 30(3) *Small Business Economics* 315.

Dinardo, J, Nicole, MF, and Lemieux, T, 'Labor Market Institutions and the Distribution of Wages, 1973–1992: A Semiparametric Approach' (1996) 64 (5) *Econometrica.*

Dockés, E, (ed), *Proposition de Code du Travail* (Dallorz, 2017).

Dos Santos, T, 'The Concept of Social Classes' (1970) 34(2) *Science & Society* 166.

Dow, GK, 'The New Institutional Economics and Employment Regulation', in Kaufman (ed), *Government Regulation of the Employment Relationship* (1997) 64.

Drago, R, and Turnbull, GK, 'On the Incidence of Profit Sharing' (1996) 31 *Journal of Economic Behavior & Organization* 129–38.

Dube, A, J Jacobs, S Naidu and S Suri, 'Monopsony in Online Labour Markets' (2018) 24416, *NBER Working Paper.*

Dukes, R, 'Constitutionalizing Employment Relations: Sinzheimer, Kahn-Freund and the Role of Labour Law' (2008) 35 *Journal of Law and Society* 341–63.

Dukes, R, 'Hugo Sinzheimer and the Constitutional Function of Labour Law' in Davidov, G, and Languille, B, (eds), *The Idea of Labour Law* (Oxford, Oxford University Press, 2011).

Edsforth, R, *The New Deal: America's Response to the Great Depression* (Oxford, Blackwell Publishers, 2000).

Engellandt, A, and Riphahn, RT, 'Evidence on Incentive Effects of Subjective Performance Evaluations' (2011) *IRL Review* 241–57.

Epstein, G, and Burke, J, *Threat Effects and the Internationalization of Production* (University of Massachusetts Amherst, PERI Working Paper Series no 15, 2001).

Estevao, M, and Sá, F, 'The 35-hour Workweek in France: Straightjacket or Welfare Improvement?' (2008) 23(55), *Economic Policy* 422.

Estrin, S, and Wadhwani, S, 'Profit-sharing' in Sapford, D, and Zafiris, T, (eds), *Current Issues In Labor Economics* (New York, Macmillan, 1990).

EU-OSHA, 'Second European Survey of Enterprises on New and Emerging Risks (ESENER-2). Overview Report: Managing Safety and Health at Work' (2013). Available at: www.osha.europa.eu/en/tools-and-publications/publications/second-european-survey-enterprises-new-and-emerging-risks-esener.

EUROFOUND 'Self-employed or not self-employed? Working conditions of economically dependent workers' (Dublin, 2013) *Background Paper.*

European Commission, *Consultation Document. Second phase consultation of Social Partners under Article 154 TFEU on a possible action addressing the challenges related to fair minimum wages* (Brussels, European Commission, 2020).

European Commission, *European Semester Thematic Factsheets on Public Procurement* (Brussels, European Commission, 2017).

European Commission, *PEPPER II Report – Promotion of Employee Participation in Profits and Enterprise Results in the Member States of the European Community* (Brussels, European Commission, 2017).

European Commission, *Promotion of Participation by Employed Persons in Profits and Enterprise Results II* (Brussels, European Commission, 1996).

Eurostat, 'Average number of usual weekly hours of work in main job, by sex, professional status, full-time/part-time and occupation (hours)' (2019). Available at: www.ec.europa.eu/eurostat/web/products-datasets/-/LFSA_EWHUIS

Ewing, KD, Hendy, J, and Jones, C, *Rolling Out the Manifesto for Labour Law* (London, Institute of Employment Rights, 2018) 36.

Ewing, KD, Hendy, J, and Jones, C, *A Manifesto for Labour Law: Towards a Comprehensive Revision of Workers' Rights* (London, Institute of Employment Rights, 2016) 35.

Fehr, E, and Schmidt, KM, 'Adding a Stick to the Carrot? The Interaction of Bonuses and Fines' (2007) 97 (2) *American Economic Review* 177–81.

Fernandez Avilés, JA, 'NTIC y riesgos psicosociales en el trabajo: estado de situación y propuestas de mejora' (2017) 2 *Diritto della Sicurezza sul Lavoro* 69–101.
Fine, S, *Laissez Faire and the General Welfare State: A Study of Conflict in American Thought, 1865–1901* (University of Michigan Press, 1956).
Firpo, S, Fortin, NM, and Lemieux, T, 'Occupational Tasks and Changes in the Wage Structure' (2011) 5542 *IZA (Institute for the Study of Labor) Discussion Paper Series.*
Ford, M, *Architects of Intelligence: The Truth about AI from the People Building It* (Birmingham, UK, Packt Publishing, 2018).
Ford, M, *The Rise of the Robots* (New York, Basic Books, 2016).
Fox, A, *Beyond Contract: Trust, Power, and Work Relations* (London, Allen & Unwin, 1974).
Freedland, C, Jacqueson, C, and Countouris, N, *Public Employment Services and European Law* (Oxford, Oxford University Press, 2007).
Freedland, M and Countouris, N, *The Legal Construction of Personal Work Relations* (Oxford, Oxford University Press, 2011).
Freeman, RB and Lazear, EP, 'An Economic Analysis of Work Councils' in J Rogers, and W Streeck (eds), *Works Councils: Consultation, Representation, and Cooperation in Industrial Relations* (Chicago IL, University of Chicago Press, 1995) 27–50.
Freeman, RB and Medoff, JL, *What Do Unions Do?* (New York, Basic Books, 1984).
Frey, C, and Osborne, M, 'The Future of Employment: How Susceptible are Jobs to Computerisation?' (2017) 114 *Technological Forecasting and Social Change* 254.
Fudge, J, 'Labour as a "Fictive Commodity"' in Davidov, G, and Languille, B, (eds), *The Idea of Labour Law* (Oxford, Oxford University Press, 2011) 120–35.
Fudge, J, 'The New Discourse of Labour Rights: From Social to Fundamental Right?' (2007) 29 *Comparative Labor Law and Policy Journal* 29–66.
Galbraith, JK, *The New Industrial State* (Boston, Houghton Mifflin, 1967) 360.
Garland, H, 'The Effects of Piece-Rate Underpayment and Overpayment on Job Performance: A Test of Equity Theory With A New Introduction Procedure' (1973) 3 *Journal of Applied Social Psychology* 325–34.
Gil, JL, 'Concepto de trabajo decente' (2012) 15 *Relaciones Laborales: Revista Crítica de Teoría y Práctica* 77.
Ginès, A, and Fabrellas, I, 'El tiempo de trabajo en plataformas: ausencia de jornada mínima, gamificación e inseguridad algorítimica' (2021) 2(1) *Labos* 19–42.
Gordon, DM, Edwards, R, and Reich, M, *Segmented Work, Divided Workers* (Cambridge, Cambridge University Press, 1982).
Guielen, AC, Kerkhofs, MJ, and Van Outs, JC, 'How Performance-related Pay Affects Productivity and Employment' (2010) 23 *Journal of Population Economics* 291–301.
Hamilton, JT, Brown, C, and Medoff, J, *Employers Large and Small* (Cambridge MA, Harvard University Press, 1990).
Hardin, G, 'The Tragedy of the Commons' (1968) 162 (3859) *New Series* 1243–48.
Hayek, F, *Law, Legislation and Liberty* (London, Routledge, 1980).
Heneman, RL, and Werner, JM, *Merit Pay; Linking Pay to Performance in a Changing World*, 2nd edn (Greenwich, Connecticut, Information Age Publishing, 2005) 34.
Hepple, B, 'Factors Influencing the Making and Transformation of Labour Law in Europe', in Davidov, G, and Langille, B, (ed), *The Idea of Labour Law* (Oxford, Oxford University Press, 2011).
Hepple, B, *Labour Laws and Global Trade* (Oxford, Hart Publishing, 2005).
Hepple, B, (ed), *The Making of Labour Law in Europe: A Comparison of Nine Countries up to 1945* (Oxford, Hart Publishing, 2010) 32.
Hepple, B, and Veneziani, B, 'Introduction' in Hepple, B, and Veneziani, B, (eds), *The Transformation of Labour Law in Europe* (Oxford, Hart Publishing, 2009).
Hernández-Bejarano, M, 'Empleo garantizado y sus posibles yacimientos: atención a la dependencia como propuesta' (2020) 38 *Trabajo: Revista Iberoamericana de Relaciones Laborales* 101.

Higgs, H, *The Physiocrats: Six Lectures on the French Economists of the 18th Century* (London, Macmillan and Co, 1897) 27–49.

Hilbert, M, 'The End Justifies the Definition: The Manifold Outlooks on the Digital Divide and Their Practical Usefulness for Policy-Making' (2011) 35(8) *Telecommunications Policy* 715.

Hillman, Robert, A, and Rachlinski, Jeffrey, J, 'Standard-Form Contracting in the Electronic Age' (2002) *Cornell Law Faculty Publications* 1062.

Hirsch, BT, 'What Do Unions Do for Economic Performance?' (2004) 25 *Journal of Labor Research* 193–237.

Hirsch, B, Schank, T, and Schnabel, C, 'Differences in Labour Supply to Monopsonistic Firms and the Gender Pay Gap: An Empirical Analysis Using Linked Employer-Employee Data from Germany' (2010) 28 (2) *Journal of Labor Economics* 291–330.

Horton, JJ, and Chilton, LB, 'The Labor Economics of Paid Crowdsourcing' (2010) *Proceedings of the 11th ACM conference on Electronic Commerce.*

Howe, J, 'The Broad Idea of Labour Law: Industrial Policy, Labour Market Regulation, and Decent Work', in Davidov, G, and Languille, B (eds), *The Idea of Labour Law* (Oxford, Oxford University Press, 2011) 309.

Howell, D, ('Theory-Driven Facts and the Growth in Earnings Inequality' (1999) 31(1) *Review of Radical Political Economics* 54–86.

Huertas Arriba, E, and Larraza Kintana, MC, 'Tecnologías de la información e innovación organizativa en la empresa española' (2010) 340 *Economía industrial* 57.

Hyde, A, 'What is Labour Law', in G Davidov and B Langille (eds), *Boundaries and Frontiers of Labour Law* (Oxford, Hart Publishing, 2006).

ILO, OECD, IMF and World Bank, *Boosting Jobs and living standards in G20 countries*. Available at: www.oit.org/wcmsp5/groups/public/---dgreports/---dcomm/documents/publication/wcms_183705.pdf.

IMF, *Guidance Note for Surveillance under Article IV Consultations* (Washington DC, 2015).

International Labour Organization, *Monitor on the World of Work.* Tenth edn *Multiple Crises Threaten the Global Labour Market Recovery* (Geneva, 2022).

International Labour Organization, *Global Wage Report 2012/2013* (Geneva, 2013) 48–49, graph 36.

International Labour Organization *Employment Relationship Recommendation* (Geneva, 2006).

Jaumotte, F, and Osorio Buitron, C, 'Inequality and Labor Market Institutions' (July 2015) *IMF Staff Discussion Note.*

Jobert, B, and Théret, B, 'France: la consécration républicaine du néo-libéralisme', in Jobert, B, (ed), *Le tournant néo-liberal en Europe* (Paris, Le Harmattan, 1994).

JP Morgan Chase Institute, *Uber drivers are earning 53% less than they did in 2013* (2018). Available at: www.bigthink.com/technology-innovation/uber-drivers-earning-less.

Kahn-Freund, O, *Labour Law and Politics in the Weinmar Republic* (Oxford, Blackwell, 1981) 75.

Katz, HC 'Industry Studies of Wage Inequality: Symposium Introduction' (2001) 54 *Industrial and Labor Relations Review.*

Kaufman, BE, 'Labour's Inequality of Bargaining Power: Changes Over Time and Implications for Public Policy' (1989) 10 (3) *Journal of Labor Research* 285–98.

Kaufman, BE, 'The Old Institutionalists', in Kaufman (ed), *Government Regulation of the Employment Relationship* (Madison WN, Industrial Relations Research Association, 1997) 16.

Kaufmann, C, *Globalisation and Labour Rights. The Conflict Between Core Labour Rights and International Economic Law* (London, Bloomsbury, 2007).

Kehrig, M, and Vincent, N, 'Growing Productivity Without Growing Wages: The Micro-Level Anatomy of the Aggregate Labor Share Decline' (2017) 244 *Economic Research Initiatives at Duke (ERID).* Working Paper available at SSRN: www.ssrn.com/abstract=2943059.

Kelley and Harrison, 'Unions, Technology and Labor Management Cooperation', in Lawrence Mishel and Paula Voos (eds), *Unions and Economic Competitiveness* (New York, ME Sharpe, 1991).

Keynes, JM, 'Economic Possibilities for our Grandchildren' in *Essays in Persuasion* (New York, Harcourt Brace, 1932) 358–73.

Kochar, A, 'An Empirical Investigation of Rationing Constraints in Rural Credit Markets in India? (1997) 53 *Journal of Development Economics* 339–71.

Kok, W, (Dir) *Facing the Challenge. The Lisbon Strategy for Growth and Employment* (Luxembourg, EU, November 2004).

Kronman, A, 'Contract Law and Distributive Justice' (1980) 89 *Yale Law Journal* 472.

Kruse, DL, 'Profit Sharing and Productivity: Microeconomic Evidence from the United States' (1992) 102 *Economic Journal* 24–36.

Laezar, EP, 'Performance Pay and Productivity' (2000) 90(5) *American Economic Review* 1346–1461.

Landes DS, *The Unbound Prometheus. Technological Change and Industrial Development in Western Europe from 1750 to the Present* (New York, Cambridge University Press, 1969).

Languille, B, 'Labour Law's Theory of Justice', in in Davidov, G, and Languille, B (eds), *The Idea of Labour Law* (Oxford, Oxford University Press) 105–10.

Laskin, B, *A Selection of Cases and Materials on Labour Law* (Toronto, University of Toronto Press, 1947).

Lavine, DI, and Richard, JP, 'Work Organization, Employment Security and Macroeconomic Stability' (1995) 24 (3) *Journal of Economic Behavior and Organization* 251–71.

Lavine, DI, and Tyson, L, 'Participation, Productivity, and the Firm's Environment', in AS Blinder (ed), *Paying for Productivity: A Look at the Evidence* (Washington DC, The Brookings Institute, 1991) 183–237.

Lee, DS, 'Wage Inequality in the United States during the 1980s: Rising Dispersion or Falling Minimum Wage?' (1999) 114(3) *Quarterly Journal of Economics* 977–1023.

Lee, FC, and Tang, J, 'Multifactor Productivity Disparity between Canadian and U.S. Manufacturing Films' (2001) 15 *Journal of Productivity Analysis* 115–28.

Lehrer, S, *Origins of Protective Labor Legislation for Women, 1905–1925* (University of NY Press, 1987).

Leung, D, Meh, C, and Terajima, Y, 'Firm Size and Productivity' (2008) *Bank of Canada Working Paper 45*.

Levin-Waldman, OM, 'How Inequality Undermines Democracy' (10 December 2016) *E-International Relations*. Available at: www.e-ir.info/2016/12/10/how-inequality-undermines-democracy/.

López Terrada, E, and Sala Franco, T (dir. tes.), *La descentralización de la estructura de la negociación colectiva y sus posibilidades de articulación* (1999).

Lundvall, K and Battesse, GE, 'Firm Size, Age and Efficiency: Evidence from Keynan Manufacturing Firms' (2000) 36(3) *Journal of Development Studies* 146–63.

Lyon-Caen, G, *Le droit du travail non salarié* (Sirey, Paris, 1900) 7–9.

Malthus, TR, *An Essay on the Principle of Population* (1798), critical edition by P James, (Cambridge, Cambridge University Press, 1989).

Manning, A, 'The Elusive Employment Effect of the Minimum Wage' (2021) 35(1) *Journal of Economic Perspectives* 3–27.

Manning, A, *Monopsony in Motion: Imperfect Competition in Labor Markets* (New Jersey, Princeton University Press, 2003) 15–16.

Marginson, P, 'Power and Efficiency in the Firm: Understanding the Employment Relationship' in C Pitelis (ed), *Transaction Costs, Markets and Hierarchies* (Oxford, Blackwell, 1993).

Marshall, A, *Principles of Economics*, 8th edn (London, Macmillan, 1947).

Mazzucato, M, *Mission Economy* (London, Penguin Books, 2021).

Mazzucato, M, *The Value of Everything: Making and Taking in the Global Economy*, (London, Allen Lane, 2018).

Mazzucato, M, *The Entrepreneurial State: Debunking Public vs Private Sector* (London, Penguin Books, 2017).

Mcgregor, J, 'Some Swedish Workers are Getting Microchips Implanted in their Hands' (2017) *The Washington Post*.

Méda, D, 'The French Experience' in A Coote, and J Franklin, *Time On Our Side: Why We All Need a Shorter Working Week* (New Economics Foundation, 2013).

Mercader Uguina, JR, 'Nuevos escenarios para el Estatuto de los Trabajadores del siglo XXI: digitalización y cambio tecnológico' (2020) 63 *Trabajo y Derecho: Nueva Revista de Actualidad y Relaciones Laborales*.

Messenger, JC, and Ghosheh, N, (dir), *Offshoring and Working Conditions in Remote Work* (Geneva, ILO, 2010).
Miller, D, Principles *of Social Justice* (Cambridge, MA, Harvard University Press, 1999) 151–55.
Montgomery, D, *The Fall of The House of Labour: The Workplace, The State and the American Labor Activism, 1865–1925* (New York, Cambridge University Press, 1987).
Montoya Melgar, A, *Ideología y lenguaje en las leyes laborales de España (1873–1978)*, 1st edn (Madrid, Civitas, 1992).
Morales Ortega, JM, 'Trabajo garantizado: luces y sombras sobre su régimen jurídico' (2020) 38 *Trabajo: Revista Iberoamericana de Relaciones Laborales* 51.
Morissette, R, 'Canadian Jobs and Firm Size: Do Smaller Firms Pay Less?' (1993) 26 *Canadian Journal of Economics* 159.
Mundlak, G, 'Corporatist and Pluralist Labor Laws', in *Fading Corporatism*, (New York, Cornell University Press, 2007).
Mundlak, G, 'The Right to Work: Linking Human Rights and Employment Policy' (2007) 146 (3–4) *International Labour Review* 189–215.
Mundlak, G, 'Human Rights and the Employment Relationship: A Look Through the Prism of Juridification' in Daniel Friedmann and Daphne Barak-Erez, (eds) *Human Rights in Private Law* (Oxford, Hart Publishing, 2001) 297–330.
Mundlak, G, 'The Third Function of Labour Law: Distributing Labour Market Opportunities among Workers', in Davidov, G, and Languille, B (eds), *The Idea of Labour Law* (Oxford, Oxford University Press, 2011) 318–28.
Murphy, L, 'Institutions and the Demands of Justice' (1999) 27(4) *Philosophy and Public Affairs* 251–91.
Naidu, S, Posner, EA, and Weyl, G, 'Antitrust Remedies for Labor Market Power' (2018) 132 *Harvard Law Review* 536–601. Available at: https://harvardlawreview.org/wp-content/uploads/2018/12/536-601.
Nalbatian, HR, *Incentives, Cooperation, and Risk Sharing: Economic and Psychological Perspectives on Employment Contracts* (New Jersey, Roman & Littlefield, 1987).
Nickell, SJ, and Andrews, M, 'Unions, Real Wages and Employment in Britain 1951–79' (1983) 35 *Oxford Economic Papers* 183.
Nickle, J, *Making Sense of Human Rights*, 2nd edn (Oxford, Blackwell, 2002).
OECD, *Competition in Labour Markets* (Paris, OECD, 2020).
OECD, 'Decoupling of Wages from Productivity: What Implications for Public Policy?' (2018) 20(2) *OECD Economic Outlook* 51.
OECD, *Employment Outlook* (Paris, OECD, 2018).
OECD, 'Collective Bargaining in a Changing World of Work' in *OECD Employment Outlook 2017* (Paris, OECD Publishing, 2017).
OECD, *Jobs Study* (Paris, OECD, 1994).
Okun, AM, *Equality and Efficiency: The Big Tradeoff*, (Washington DC, Brookings Institute, 1975).
Ostry, JD, Berg, A, and Tsangarides, CG, 'Redistribution, Inequality and Growth' (2014) *IMF Staff Discussion Notes*.
Paarsch, HJ, and Shearer, B, 'Piece Rates, Fixed Wages and Incentive Effects: Statistical Evidence from Payroll Records' (2000) 41(1) *International Economic Review* 59–92.
Pérez Amorós, F, 'El trabajador como sujeto del Derecho del Trabajo Español' (1982) 133 *Revista de Política Social* 87.
Pérez García, F, et al, *Cambios tecnológicos, trabajo y actividad empresarial: el impacto socioeconómico de la economía digital* (XXI CES Research Award, 2019).
Pérez Zapata et al, 'Digitalización, intensificación del trabajo y salud de los trabajadores españoles', (2019) 5 *Congreso Interuniversitario OIT sobre el futuro del trabajo*, electronic version. Available at: www.ccoo.es/24c0e370fa4b4d1f3682b1780854af9c000001.pdf.
Pesole, A et al, 'Platform Workers in Europe Evidence from the COLLEEM Survey' (Brussels, Publications Office of the European Union, 2018).
Philippon, T, *The Great Reversal* (Cambridge MA, The Belknap Press of Harvard University Press, 2019) 281.

Philips, AW, 'The Relation Between Unemployment and the Rate of Change of Money Wage Rates in the United Kingdom' (1958) 25 (100) *Economica* 283–99.
Piketty, T, *Capital in the Twenty-First Century* (Cambridge MA, The Belknap Press, 2017).
Piketty, T, *Capital and Ideology* (Cambridge MA, The Belknap Press, 2020).
Polyani, K, *The Great Transformation* (New York, Reinhold, 1944).
Porter, M, *Competitive Strategy: Techniques for Analyzing Industries and Competitors* (New York: Free Press, 1980).
Prosser, T, 'Regulation and Social Society' (2006) 33(3) *Journal of Law and Society* 364.
Rand, A, *Atlas Shrugged*, (New York, Random House, 1957).
Rawls, J, *Political Liberalism* (Oxford, Oxford University Press, 1972).
Rawls, J, *A Theory of Justice* (Cambridge, MA, Harvard University Press, 1971).
Reich, M, Jacobs, K, Bernhardt, A, and Perry. I, 'The Proposed Minimum Wage Law for Los Angeles: Economic Impacts and Policy Options' (March 2015) *UC Berkeley ILRE.*
Ricardo, D, *On the Principles of Political Economy and Taxation (1817)* (Cambridge, Cambridge University Press, 1951).
Robins, PK, 'A Comparison of the Labour Supply Findings from Four Negative Income Tax Experiments' (1985) 20(4) *Journal of Human Resources* 567.
Roderik, D, 'Normalizing Industrial Policy' (2008) Working Paper 3 *World Bank Commission on Growth and Development.* Available at: www.openknowledge.worldbank.org/handle/10986/28009.
Rodriguez Piñero, M, 'La dependencia y la extensión del ámbito del Derecho del Trabajo' (1996) 71 *Revista de Política Social* 147–68.
Rodríguez-Piñero Royo, M, and Todolí-Signes, A, *Trabajo a Distancia y Teletrabajo: análisis del marco normativo vigente* (Cizur Menor, Aranzadi, 2021).
Rodríguez-Piñero Royo, M, and Todolí-Signes, A, *Vigilancia y control en el Derecho del trabajo digital* (Cizur Menor, Aranzadi, 2020).
Rogers, B, 'Employment as a Legal Concept' (2015) 33 *Temple Legal Studies Research Papers Series.*
Rubin, PH, 'The Theory of the Firm and the Structure of the Franchise Contract' (1978) 21(1) *The Journal of Law and Economics* 223.
Ruesga Benito, S, (Dir), *Instrumentos de flexibilidad interna en la negociación colectiva* (Ministerio de Empleo y Seguridad Social, 2012) 49.
Ruesga Benito, S, 'Reforma laboral, salarios y productividad en España' (2005) 55(2) *Comercio Exterior*, 174, 176 and 178.
Davis, S and Von Wachter, T, 'Recession and the Costs of Job Loss' *Brooking Papers on Economic Activity* (Washington DC, Brookings Institute, 2011).
Saadi Sedik, T, and Xu, R, 'A Vicious Cycle: How Pandemics Lead to Economic Despair and Social Unrest' (Washington DC, 2020) 216, *IMF Working Paper.*
Sala Franco, T, and López Gandía, J, 'El Derecho del Trabajo', in I Montesinos Albiol et al *Derecho del Trabajo. Tomo I. Fuentes y relaciones colectivas*, 3rd edn (Valencia, Tirant lo Blanch, 2001).
Sanguineti Raymond, W, 'La tutela sustancial del derecho de huelga en las estructuras empresariales complejas' (2016) 74 *Revista de Derecho Social* 11.
Satpathy, LD, Chatterjee, B, and Mahakud, J, 'Firm characteristics and total factor productivity: Evidence from Indian manufacturing firms" (2017) 11(1) *The journal of applied economic research* 77.
Schwab, K, *The fourth industrial revolution* (Geneva, World Economic Forum, 2016).
Sciarra, S, 'National and European Public Policy: The Goals of Labour Law', in Davidov, G, and Languille, B, (ed), *Boundaries and Frontiers of Labour Law* (Oxford, Hart Publishing, 2006) 258.
Sen, A, 'Trabajo y derechos' (2000) 119 (2) *Revista Internacional Del Trabajo* 129–140.
Skidelsky, L, 'How to achieve shorter working hours' (2013) *Progressive Economy Forum*, www.progressiveeconomyforum.com/wp-content/uploads/2019/08/PEF_Skidelsky_How_to_achieve_shorter_working_hours.pdf.
Smith, A, *La riqueza de las naciones* (1776).
Smith, A, *The Wealth of Nations: An Inquiry into the Nature and Causes*, 1st edn 1776 (Eireann Press, 2023).

Smith, CW, *Digital corporate citizenship: the business response to the digital divide* (Indianapolis, The Center on Philanthropy at Indiana University, 2002).

Snodgrass D, and Biggs, T, *Industrialization and small firms patterns and policies* (San Francisco, International Center for Economic Growth, 1995).

Sokolova, A, and Sorensen T, 'Monopsony in Labor Markets: A Meta-Analysis' (2018) Discussion Paper Series 11966 *IZA Institute of Labor Economics* available at www.ftp.iza.org/dp11966.pdf.

Solow, R, *The Labour Market as a Social Institution* (Blackwell, 1990) 50 and 76.

Spector, H, 'Philosophical Foundations of Labour Law' (2006) 33 *Florida State University Law Review* 1133.

Sprage, R, 'Worker (Mis)Classification in the Sharing Economy: Square Pegs Trying to fit in Round Holes' (2015) 31 *A.B.A. Journal of Labor & Employment Law*, University of Wyoming, 16.

Steinfeld, R, *The invention of free labor: The employment relation in English and American and Culture* (1991).

Steinfeld, R, *The invention of free labor: The employment relation in English and American and Culture*, 1991.

Stiglitz, JE, *The Price of Inequality* (New York, W.W. Norton, 2012).

Stone, K, 'The legacy of industrial pluralism: the tension between individual employment rights and the new deal collective bargaining system' (1992) 59 *The University of Chicago Law Review* 575.

Stone, K, 'The Origin of Job Structures in the Steel Industry', in D Gordon, M Reich. and R Edwards, *Labour Market Segmentation* (1975).

Stone, K, *From Widgets to Digits: Employment Regulation for the Changing Workplace* (Cambridge University Press, 2004).

Stone, K, The Origin of Job Structures in the Steel Industry, in Gordon, D., Reich M. and Edwards, R., *Labour Market Segmentation*, 1975.

Suárez, B, 'The 'Gig' Economy and its Impact on Social Security: The Spanish example' (2017) 19 (4) *European Journal of Social Security* 293–312, 307.

Sullivan, D, and Von Wachter, T, 'Job Displacement and Mortality: An Analysis Using Administrative Data' (2009) 124 (3) *Quarterly Journal of Economics* 1265–1306.

Sundararajan, A, *The Sharing economy, The End of Employment and the Rise of Crowd-Based Capitalism* (MIT Press, 2016) 85.

Supiot, A, et al, *Beyond Employment. Changes in Work and the Future of Labour Law in Europe*, (Oxford, 2001).

Tegmark, M, *Life 3.0: Being Human in the Age of Artificial Intelligence* (London, Allen Lane, 2017) 121.

Teodoro, R, et al, 'The Motivations and Experiences of the On-Demand Mobile Workforce' (New York, 2014), *Conference on Computer Supported Cooperative Work and Social Computing (CSCW 2014)* 5.

Tobin, J, 'Neoclassical Theory in America: J.B. Clark and Fisher' (1985) 75(6) *American Economic Review* 28.

Todolí-Signes, A, 'El ámbito subjetivo de aplicación del Estatuto de los Trabajadores ante las nuevas formas de trabajo: la nueva ley de California (AB5)' (2020) *Trabajo y Derecho* 66.

Todolí-Signes, A, 'El principio de igualdad y las dobles escalas salariales' 2015 (383) *CEF* 47.

Todolí-Signes, A, 'Falsos autónomos en contrato de Agencia: Análisis a el acta de la Inspección de Trabajo de CEPSA (I)' (2020) *Argumentos en Derecho Laboral*. Available at: www.adriantodoli.com/2020/03/11/falsos-autonomos-en-contrato-de-agencia-analisis-a-el-acta-de-la-inspeccion-de-trabajo-de-cepsa-i/.

Todolí-Signes, A, 'Judgment Designating Deliveroo "Rider" An Employee and Analysis of its Impact on the "Gig Economy"' (2018) 24(4) *Transfer* 487–90.

Todolí-Signes, A, 'The End of the Subordinate Worker? Collaborative Economy, On-Demand Economy, Gig Economy, and the Crowdworkers' Need for Protection' (2017) 33(2) *International Journal of Comparative Labour Law and Industrial Relations* 241–68.

Todolí-Signes, A, 'The Evaluation of Workers by Customers as a Method of Control and Monitoring in Firms: Digital Reputation and the European Union's General Data Protection Regulation' (2020) 160 (1) *International Labour Review* 65.

Todolí-Signes, A, 'The "Gig Economy": Employee, Self-Employed or the Need for a Special Employment Regulation?' (2017) 23(2) *Transfer: European Review of Labour and Research* 193–205.

Todolí-Signes, A, *El bonus salarial* (Valencia, Tirant lo Blanch, 2017).

Todolí-Signes, A, *Salario y productividad* (Valencia, Tirant lo Blanch, 2017).

Todolí-Signes, A, *El trabajo en plataformas digitales en la Comunidad Valenciana* (Cátedra de Economía Colaborativa, Universitat de Valencia, 2019).

Trottman, M, 'AFL-CIO Poll Shows Union Households Boosted Brown' (22 January 2010) *The Wall Street Journal.*

US Congress, Joint Economic Committee, *1976 Joint Economic Report, Senate Report No. 94-690, Congress 2nd Session* (Washington DC, Government Printing Office, 1976) 100.

Valdés Dal-Ré, F, 'Flexiseguridad y mercado de trabajo' (2010) 9 *Relaciones Laborales* 129.

Valdés Dal-Ré F, 'Descentralización productiva y desorganización del derecho del trabajo' (2001) *Revista Universitaria de Ciencias del Trabajo* 45.

Van Ark, B, and Monnikhof, E, 'Size Distribution of Output and Employment: A Data Set for Manufacturing Industries in Five OECD Countries, 1960–1990' (1996) 166 *OECD Economics Department Working Paper.*

Van Biesebroeck, J, 'Firm Size Matters: Growth and Productivity Growth in African Manufacturing' (2005) 53 *Economic Development and Cultural Change* 546.

Veneziani, B, 'The Evolution of Employment Relationship', in Hepple, B (ed) *The Making of Labour Law in Europe* (Washington DC, Mansell, 1986).

Visser J and Checchi, D 'Inequality and the Labour Market: Unions' in Wiemer S, Nolan B and Smeeding TM (eds) *The Oxford Handbook of Economic Inequality* (Oxford, Oxford University Press, 2011).

Vivarelli, M, 'Innovation, Employment and Skills in Advanced and Developing Countries: A Survey of Economic Literature' (2014) 48(1) *Journal of Economic Issues* 123.

Webb, S, and Webb, B, *The History of Trade Unionism (Revised Edition Extended to 1920)* (London, Longmans, Green and Co, 1894), reprinted 2021.

Weil, D, 'Implementing Employment Regulation: Insights on the Determinants of Regulatory Performance', in Kaufman (ed), *Government Regulation of the Employment Relationship* (1997) 430.

Weil, D, *The Fissured Workplace, Why Work Became So Bad for So Many and What Can Be Done to Improve It* (Cambridge, MA, Harvard University Press, 2014).

Weiss, M, 'Re-inventing Labour Law?', in Davidov, G, and Languille, B (eds), *The Idea of Labour Law* (Oxford, Oxford University Press, 2011) 47.

Weitzman, ML, 'Profit Sharing as Macroeconomic Policy' (1985) 75 *American Economic Review* 41–45.

Weitzman, ML, 'Some Macroeconomic Implications of Alternative Compensation Systems' (1983) 93 *Economic Journal* 763–83.

Weitzman, ML, *The Share Economy* (Cambridge MA, Harvard University Press, 1984).

Weitzman, ML, and Kruse, F, 'Profit Sharing and Productivity', in Blinder AS (ed) *Paying for Productivity: A Look at the Evidence* (Washington, DC, The Brookings Institute, 1990).

Western, B, and Rosenfeld, J, 'Unions, Norms, and the Rise in US Wage Inequality' (2011) 76(4) *American Sociological Review* 513–37.

Williamson, J, 'What Washington Means by Policy Reform', in Frieden, J, Pastor, M, and Tomz, M, *Modern Political Economy and Latin America* (Washington DC, Institute for International Economics, 1990).

Williamson, O, *The Economic Institutions of Capitalism* (New York, Free Press, 1985).

Williamson, O, Wachter, M, and Harris, J, 'Understanding the Employment Relation. The Economics of Idiosyncratic Exchange' (1967) 6 *Bell Journal of Economics and Management Science* 250.

Williamson, OE, 'Hierarchical Control and Optimum Firm Size' (1967) 75 *Journal of Political Economy* 123.

INDEX

www.ingramcontent.com/pod-product-compliance
Ingram Content Group UK Ltd.
Pitfield, Milton Keynes, MK11 3LW, UK
UKHW021907150926
475560UK00003B/226

9 781509 973880